Sam Stern's STUDENT COOKBOOK

with Susan Stern

WALKER BOOKS

CONTENTS

Students and good food don't usually go together but I want to change all that. This book's packed with cracking recipes to suit your tastes, your student lifestyle, health and budget.

Leaving home is a key moment when it comes to eating. You can go the fast food route and feel like crap a lot of the time or take the independent alternative which this book is designed to help out with. OK, it might seem that cooking your own stuff's a hassle but once you're into it, you'll find it's worth it. For a start, cooking from scratch is cheaper. Ready meals, takeaways, pre-prepared stuff taste pretty average and empty the bank account pretty damned quickly. Cooking for yourself means getting hold of good fresh ingredients and turning them into great meals while saving a load for your beer and shoe money.

Keeping fit is a great motivation. If you're into sport, training, or just want to feel good about the way you look, cooking's key to sorting energy and performance. Tailor your menu to your physical needs and you can trust that what you're eating is fit for purpose – e.g. carbs for energy (eat pasta), protein for muscle (get pork or tofu). Same goes for exams, work, etc. Eating the right stuff (iron, protein, omega 3s, vitamins) gives you the focus you need but hey, do it in style with some great home-cooked tastes and maximize the pleasure.

Cook for your mates every chance you get. They'll be indebted. You'll be a magnet. Whether it's a late breakfast or a full-on dinner, make every meal a top social occasion and good

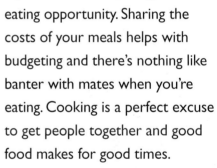

eating opportunity. Sharing the costs of your meals helps with budgeting and there's nothing like banter with mates when you're eating. Cooking is a perfect excuse to get people together and good food makes for good times.

Cooking as a process is well pleasurable. Slap on the music and get everyone helping out. Or use it as therapy if you've been working or partying hard and need some solitary chilling and relaxing (the chopping, blitzing and whizzing does it).

Most important though is the flavour factor. All the recipes in this book taste great (even if I say so myself). So whether you're a first-time cook or more experienced you've got some awesome eating to look forward to. Student food means brilliant home cooking.

THE STRATEGY

Savvy planning and smart shopping's the key to good cooking on a budget. So save yourself cash, time and grief by getting a strategy. Here're my top tips – ways to make the most of every meal without emptying your bank account…

THINK ABOUT WHERE TO SHOP

✳ Supermarket prices vary wildly. Check out comparison websites for latest updates.

✳ Consider internet shopping. You can weigh up price options calmly, save time, not get tempted by impulse buys, avoid lugging stuff about. Split the delivery costs with mates. One van trip saves energy.

✳ Check out the SU minibus – it may take trips to supermarkets.

✳ If you care about fair trade, organic foods, check out local health food/community/veggie shops. Check which supermarkets have the best range.

✳ Try buying food from ethnic shops. Split large bags of rice etc. with mates but store it properly (dry goods in jars/airtight boxes).

✳ Check out farmers'/local markets for cheaper fresh food. Seasonal food is always better.

✳ Hunt down your local butcher, baker, deli, fishmonger, etc. to get single items – e.g. one chop, one good croissant instead of a supermarket pack. Get too much and you're likely to waste it – chucking cash away and sapping the planet.

MAKE A PLAN

✳ Write a list. Don't turn up at the supermarket without one – and try to stick to it.

✳ Base your list on a strategy. Plan what to eat at least a couple of days at a time and you can factor in big money-saving strategies.

✳ Key top tip – plan food that will last for more than the one meal. A roast chicken costs more than a fillet but can make four other meals (risotto, salad, sarnie, soup). A curry or tart lasts for days. Saves major cash, time, waste, effort.

✳ Check individual recipes so you won't forget key ingredients.

✳ Check the cupboard/fridge so you don't overstock.

✳ Build your basic needs into a mantra – i.e. eggs, butter, milk/soy, juice, garlic…

✳ Split the costs for shared meals like roast dinners – everyone's a winner.

✳ Consider sharing all food bills.

✳ Plan to use leftovers.

SAVVY SHOPPING

✳ Shop when your money's in.

✳ Don't shop when you're hungry – you'll spend more…

✳ Do it at the end of the day when supermarkets reduce some prices. Same at fruit and veg markets.

✳ Supermarket own brands can be better value than named brands – e.g. pastas, rice, beans, pulses, etc.

✳ Don't get ripped-off by pretty packaging/health/ethical promises – take time to read the labels.

✳ Always buy food with the longest

sell-by dates – less goes to waste.

✳ Buy up bargains when you see them – get great discounts on olive oil, multi-pack tins of tuna, beans, etc.

✳ Check out the freezer section. Find good value frozen fish bits (great for pies), veg and berries (nutritionally brilliant and really convenient).

✳ Get savvy about special offers. Ignore "buy 1 get 1 free" or "3 for 2" offers if it's fresh food you know you can't eat by the use-by date. Snap up the real bargains that you can store/afford/freeze/eat now.

✳ Do you really need it – e.g. Mexican blackberries? Local stuff may be cheaper, use less airmiles.

GET IT FOR FREE

✳ Work in a food shop. Get discounts, even free food.

✳ Go beach fishing. Cook it there or take it home.

✳ Grow it – check out allotments, landlord's garden, pots. Grow tomatoes and herbs from seed on windowsills (well cheap), potatoes in old tyres by the doorstep.

BEFORE YOU START TO COOK

✳ Get organized. Check you've got all the ingredients in. Sort timings, equipment. Read the recipe right through.

✳ Cooking for mates? Check ahead that no one has allergies, dislikes, diets, veggie/vegan needs, etc.

SAVE ENERGY – AND CASH

✳ Use a pan that covers the hob. If it's smaller the spare heat's useless.

Don't use a huge pan to cook small quantities.

✳ Speed the pan boiling process – get water from a boiling kettle.

✳ Cover pans with a lid. Food cooks faster, water boils more quickly.

✳ Food cooks faster chopped into small bits, e.g. potatoes for boiling/ roasting.

✳ To cook frozen peas – boil kettle. Pour over peas. Defrost 1 minute. Drain. More boiling water. Leave 2 minutes. Cooked. Sorted.

✳ Get a steamer. Cooks simultaneously on different levels, saves energy, nutrients.

✳ Oven cooking? Make more than one meal at a time to maximize energy.

✳ Don't keep opening the door while cooking – heat escapes, food can spoil.

✳ Ovens retain heat. Slow cooking? Turn off 20 minutes before finish time (not for baking).

MAKING THE MOST OF YOUR FOOD

✳ Make meals-in-one (soups, stir-fries, one pan meals) when money's tight.

✳ Grate cheese for salads/sarnies. Don't slice it. Grating boosts flavour so you'll need less.

✳ Slap breadcrumbs/lentils into meat sauces in place of some of the meat.

✳ Dried beans/peas are much cheaper than tinned. Soak overnight in masses of water. Boil rapidly for at least 10 minutes then simmer till tender (see packet).

✳ Made too many noodles? Slap

extra into dressing for next day's salad.

✳ Recycle cooked pasta. Bake it up with meat or veg sauces, top with cheese. Stick it into frittatas and omelettes, dress it for salads.

✳ Crisp up day-old bread. Flash under a cold tap. Re-heat 5 mins in hot oven.

✳ Slice slightly stale bread. Wrap. Freeze. Toast straight from frozen.

✳ Use stale bread for bruschetta. Or make into breadcrumbs for coating food.

✳ Fruit looking sad? Don't chuck it. Cook it in a pud, cake, or blitz for a smoothie/sauce for yogurt.

✳ Don't store bananas in the fruit bowl. Their gases make other fruit rot faster.

✳ Middle-aged veg make great soup or get them into sauces.

✳ Store salad leaves and bean sprouts in sealed bags at the bottom of the fridge.

✳ Wrap cheese in greaseproof paper and keep in a storage box in the fridge.

✳ Love your freezer. Keep frozen peas, berries, store extra stock, sauces, pizza bases, fish, moussaka, curries, fruit and meat pies, soups.

✳ When the money's in and you've got time, make more than you need. Freeze it for lean times.

✳ Save jars for own jams, dressings, mayo, etc.

✳ Get creative. Have a skint fridge night once a week. Turn left-over stuff into something awesome (OK, a great omelette).

✳ Taste your food as you go along so you can adjust it till you like it – develop your palate.

THE EQUIPMENT

You don't need a lot to get going. Get value brands from supermarkets. Hunt down old-style hardware stores, Asian shops (woks, balti dishes, utensils), charity shops (plates etc). Borrow from home … kettle and toaster taken for granted.

ESSENTIALS
Can-opener
Saucepan
Frying pan
Mixing bowl
Bread knife
Small sharp knife
Teaspoon & tablespoon
Measuring jug
Baking tray
Sieve (doubles as colander)
Spatula
Grater
Potato peeler
Wooden spoon
Balloon whisk
Plastic chopping board
Simple compact kitchen scales
Ovenproof dish
Cling film/foil
Plastic storage boxes

NEXT LEAGUE
Wok
Different size mixing bowls
Different size pans
Griddle pan
Larger board for chopping/rolling out
Colander
Fish slice
Crêpe/omelette pan

Big casserole dish
Roasting tin
Muffin tin
Yorkshire pudding tin
Loose-bottomed flan tin
Loose-bottomed cake tin
Potato masher/ricer
Slotted spoon (for frying/stir-fry)
Garlic press
Lemon squeezer
Kebab skewers (metal)
Ramekins
Scissors
Rolling pin
Cooling rack
Pestle & mortar
Greaseproof paper

Cocktail sticks (for cocktails & cake testing)

Handheld electric stick blender (star item)

THE STORECUPBOARD

Stock yourself up and you're up and running. Don't rush out and get it in one. Build as you work through the recipes – maybe get mates to chip in. Use as a checklist before you go shopping.

Cans, bottles & jars

Beans: baked, kidney, haricot, cannellini, butter
Chickpeas
Sweetcorn
Tomatoes: chopped, plum
Tomato puree
Tuna, salmon, sardines, anchovies
Capers
Olives
Jalapeño peppers
Oils: good olive (cooking), extra virgin (salads), groundnut (curries), sesame (stir-fries), sunflower (frying/baking)
Vinegars: Chinese rice, red/white wine, cider, balsamic
Chinese cooking wine
Mustard: English, Dijon
Mayonnaise
Tomato ketchup
HP sauce
Worcestershire sauce
Sweet chilli sauce
Thai fish sauce
Teriyaki sauce
Hoisin sauce
Oyster sauce
Soy sauce
Harissa paste

Curry paste
Chilli jam
Redcurrant/cranberry jelly
Branston pickle
Marmite/Vegemite
Maple syrup
Golden syrup
Black treacle
Squeezy honey
Jam

Dry stuff

Tea & coffee
Cocoa
Drinking chocolate
Marigold Swiss vegetable bouillon
Knorr chicken stock cubes
Mustard powder
Dried yeast
Rices: basmati, jasmine, risotto, brown
Couscous
Bulgar wheat
Polenta
Lentils: green, brown, Puy, red
Dried pastas
Noodles: egg, rice

Dried chickpeas, beans
Flour: plain, bread, self-raising, gram
Cornflour
Baking powder
Bicarbonate of soda
Sugar: granulated, caster, soft brown, icing
Creamed coconut
Raisins, sultanas, currants
Dates, apricots
Pinenuts
Seeds, nuts
Porridge oats

Spices & flavourings

Sea salt (Maldon)
Fine salt
Black peppercorns
Natural vanilla extract
Chinese 5 spice
Ground cinnamon
Turmeric
Cumin
Garam masala
Curry powder
Cardamom pods
Ground coriander
Nutmeg
Whole cloves
Mixed spice
Fennel seeds
Dried chilli flakes
Chilli powder
Cayenne pepper

Paprika (plain, smoked, sweet)
Ground ginger
Dried oregano, thyme
Tubes of lemon grass/ginger/garlic/coriander (if no fresh)

Dairy

Semi-skimmed milk
Butter/soy spread
Eggs
Cheese: Cheddar/Gruyère/Feta/Halloumi/Parmesan

Freezables

Frozen green/other veg
Frozen berries
Frozen fish portions
Bread

Really useful

Lemons, limes
Fresh garlic, ginger
Shallots, onions
Fresh herbs for flavourings

THE BASIC TECHNIQUES

THE JARGON

SIFT Give flour/other dry ingredients a good shake through a sieve to aerate, mix, smooth and lighten.

RUB IN Incorporate flour and fat by rubbing lightly between fingertips till mix looks like fine breadcrumbs – hold hands high over bowl to aerate.

CREAM Mix soft butter and sugar to a light airy cream by beating with a wooden spoon using brisk wrist action.

FOLD IN Incorporate ingredients like flour, melted chocolate, whisked egg whites into any mix by using a large metal spoon and gentle figure-of-8 scooping movements.

BEAT Blend ingredients together using a wooden spoon/balloon whisk/fork and v. strong wrist action (use for eggs, batters, cakes, sauces, etc).

BLITZ Blend or fragment food with hand blender/processor/blender (use for soups, smoothies, dips, breadcrumbs).

SIMMER Cook food or liquid at just below boiling point (it sounds and looks calm, bubbles sometimes, and cooks steadily without burning/toughening).

SEASON Add salt and pepper to boost flavour. Also use lemon/lime juice, spices, garlic, onions, wine, fresh and dried herbs for healthy enhancers.

MARINATE Sit a raw food in an appropriate mix (e.g. Asian or barbecue sauces; oil, herb, lemon juice and garlic combo; or a spicy herby rub). Leave a few minutes, overnight, or even a few days to flavour/tenderize.

REST Leave roast meat to relax in a warm place at least 10 mins after cooking to restore juices and tenderize. Leave steaks/chops for just a few minutes.

CHOP Cut food into different sizes as specified in recipe using a small sharp knife on a flat surface. Dice – small or tiny regular cubes. Finely chop – very small bits. Slice – cut across. Roughly chop – go freestyle. Bite size – bite-size bits. Shred – cut veg across in thin ribbons or tear meat with two forks.

THE HOW TO

SEPARATE EGGS
Tap egg sharply on side of bowl to crack the middle. Hold over bowl and open it with both thumbs, tilting to one side so yolk ends up in one half of shell. Let white spill into bowl. Tip yolk/rest of white into empty half of shell, spilling more white. Repeat. Tip separated yolk into second bowl.

WHISK EGGS UP
Check whites are totally yolk-free (or they won't work) and utensils, hands, bowls are grease-free. Whisk in a large bowl with balloon or electric hand-whisk. Whisk slowly at first, then faster for soft peaks. Continue for stiff peaks. Don't overbeat – loses air.

CHOP AN ONION
Top and tail onion with small sharp knife on board. Peel off brown then papery skin. Sit it upright. Hold firmly. Cut down into thin slices, stopping 1 cm before the base to hold it together. Gripping firmly, turn it onto its side. Slice down and though. It falls into small dice.

STOP BUTTER BURNING
Add a little oil to the pan with the butter. Modify temp.

STOP ONIONS BURNING
Add a tiny pinch of salt to onions in the pan. Modify temp.

MELT CHOCOLATE
Break bits into heatproof bowl. Sit it into open top of a pan of barely simmering water. Check base isn't touching water and liquid/steam can't get into chocolate. Let it melt slowly without stirring. Remove bowl from pan. Stir choc and use in recipe.

ROLL OUT PASTRY AND GET IT INTO A TIN
Sit ball of pastry on lightly floured surface next to greased tin to judge size required to cover base and sides. Roll pastry out lightly using floured rolling pin. Turn a few times until you get the size, shape and thickness required. Lift it into the tin – for larger bits, roll pin underneath and lift across. Fit into corners/sides and mould. Trim. Keep any spare for repairs if pastry shrinks in cooking. Mould into cracks. Cook a further 3–4 min.

KNEAD PIZZA/ BREAD DOUGH
Roll dough into a ball on floured board/surface. Press down and away with heel of your hand. Fold dough back over. Turn. Repeat for 8–10 minutes, roughing up and stretching it till smooth/elastic.

MAKE DRY BREADCRUMBS
Leave bread out for hours, uncovered, until completely dried out. Blitz, grate or bash to small/fine crumbs.

COOK A ROAST
Weigh joint. Calculate cooking time – see below. For beef/lamb, pierce with a knife to check for doneness – juices should run pink. (Give more or less time for well-done/ rare.) For pork/chicken, juices must run clear. Always rest meat. Use the time to make gravy.

HOW TO MAKE THE MOST OF THE RECIPES

Follow the signs:

 FEEDS 1 how many it feeds

 £ how much it costs (approx.) per person:

£ skint/saving
££ average
£££ flush/celebration

 V vegetarian meal

 V OPTION vegetarian option to a meat meal

EXPRESS fast to cook

Measuring: don't stress about getting ingredients exact unless baking/pastry making.

Seasoning: use it to boost not mask flavours.

Plating up: make everything look great.

Teaming: experiment with different menu combos.

Panicking: don't. If something goes wrong start again.

Enjoying: every time you make a dish it'll look and taste a bit different.

ROASTING TIMES

MEAT TYPE	FIRST BLAST	REMAINING TIME
Beef	20 minutes at 220°C/425°F/gas 7	13 minutes per 500g/1lb at 180°C/350°F/gas 4
Lamb	20 minutes at 220°C/425°F/gas 7	13 minutes per 500g/1lb at 180°C/350°F/gas 4
Pork	20 minutes at 220°C/425°F/gas 7	25 minutes per 500g/1lb at 180°C/350°F/gas 4
Chicken	20 minutes at 190°C/425°F/gas 7	20 minutes per 500g/1lb at 190°C/375°F/gas 5

SNACKS
& LIGHT BITES

Capture the world in your kitchen with global snacking plates, sandwiches, toasts, treats, drinks, all day breakfast bowls. Cooking real food is cool and saves money.

MEZE

Simple but beautiful. Hummus is cheap as chips, well tasty and easy to make. Team it up with mellow baked garlic and gorgeous griddled veg for this outstanding sharing plate. Keep a good olive oil in, for dipping.

FEEDS 4 | **£** | **V** | **EXPRESS**

1 x 400g/14oz can chickpeas
2 cloves garlic, crushed
Juice of 1 large lemon
1 tbsp tahini (sesame paste)
Salt
2 tbsps good olive oil
2 tbsps water/chickpea liquid

Topping
Extra olive oil
Sprinkle paprika (optional)
Fresh coriander (optional)
Pine nuts (optional)

Hummus

1. Drain chickpeas through a sieve into a bowl. Save liquid.

2. Tip chickpeas into a processor or bowl (to mash or handblend).

3. Add garlic, lemon juice, tahini, salt.

4. Heat oil and 2 tbsps water/chickpea water in a pan. (Don't boil.) Add to chickpeas. Blitz hummus or mash it with a fork. Add more water for smoother texture.

5. Adjust taste with lemon, salt. Tip into bowl. Drizzle more olive oil. Scatter with paprika, coriander, pine nuts. Eat warm or chill it.

YOU CAN
* add cumin, chilli, ground coriander
* blitz in caramelized onions
* top with chickpeas
* stuff hummus into a hollowed-out pepper for a box-to-go with bread/pitta/veg sticks
* cheat: mash drained chickpeas with a bit of soy sauce, parsley, olive oil

Bread & Oil

Tear bread. Dip into oil. Eat. Enjoy with olives or pickles.

YOU CAN
* buy oil when on offer
* team with tomatoes, cheeses and deli meats

Good bread (white/brown/
   focaccia/ciabatta)
Good olive oil

Griddled Vegetables

1. Heat a griddle pan till very hot.

2. Brush vegetables with a little olive oil.

3. Slap onto griddle (don't overcrowd it).

4. Turn veg as soon as they colour/soften. Remove whenever they look done.

5. Season with salt, pepper, lemon juice. Eat hot or cold.

Choice of:
1 aubergine, sliced
1 courgette, sliced
1 red pepper, de-seeded,
   quartered
1 Portobello mushroom,
   whole or sliced
Butternut squash, sliced
Olive oil
Salt and pepper
Lemon juice (optional)

Baked Garlic

1. Preheat oven to 200°C/400°F/gas 6.

2. Slice top off each head.

3. Sit on baking trays. Drizzle with a little olive oil and a scattering of sea salt.

4. Roast 20–30 minutes till tender.

5. Plate. Spread paste onto bread or crackers.

1 whole head of garlic
Olive oil
Sea salt

15

FALAFEL

Take a break from going out. Set up this healthy little plate of nutty-tasting falafel. Soak your chickpeas ahead. Bang on the old TV and get in there.

175g/6oz dried chickpeas
1 small onion (approx 50g/
   2oz), very finely chopped
2–3 fat cloves garlic, crushed
1½ tsps ground cumin
1 tsp ground coriander
½ tsp salt
1 tsp chilli powder, or 1 small
   chopped de-seeded chilli
2 tbsps fresh coriander
1–2 tbsps fresh parsley or mint,
   finely chopped and dried
Black pepper
1½ tbsps warm water
¾ tsp baking powder
Sunflower or vegetable oil, for
   frying

15cm/6in bit of cucumber
   (skin on)
175g/6oz creamy natural
   yogurt – Greek's best, or
   make own (pg 46)
1–2 cloves garlic, crushed
Bit of sea salt
Sprinkle dried or fresh mint
   (optional)

Falafel with Red Onion and Tomato Salad

1. Soak dried chickpeas in double depth of water for minimum 12 hours. Drain. Dry very well.

2. Blitz in processor with onion, garlic, spices, herbs, seasoning. Remove to bowl.

3. Mix water, baking powder in cup. Stir into falafel mix.

4. Roll firmly into balls. Chill for at least 30 minutes.

5. Tip 5cm/2in oil into frying pan/wok. When hot enough to crisp a breadcrumb, fry a few falafels at a time, turning, till golden brown, cooked through. Sit on kitchen paper.

YOU CAN
* use bit of beaten egg to bind falafel if tricky
* eat festival-style in pittas-to-go
* eat in wraps with salad, relish, or slap in a lunch box
* grow your own herbs to keep costs down

Tzatziki

1. Grate cucumber into a bowl.

2. Tip onto a tea towel or kitchen paper. Blot excess moisture out.

3. Tip back into bowl. Add yogurt, garlic, bit of salt to taste. Chill. Sprinkle with mint.

Baba Ganoush

1. Heat oven to 200°C/400°F/gas 6.
2. Bake aubergine for 20–30 minutes till black and soft.
3. Slice open. Spoon flesh out. Blitz with other ingredients. Taste. Adjust seasoning. Chill.

FEEDS
4

£

V

1 large aubergine
1½ tbsps olive oil
1 clove garlic
1 small onion
Juice of ½ large lemon
Salt
Bit of parsley

TEX-MEX

Chilli up with cool Tex-Mex dishes. Chill out with soothing guacamole.
Good party food. Tasty crowd-pleasers. Single out for delicious dinners.
Make own tortillas (pg 266).

FEEDS 4 · **£** · **V** · **EXPRESS**

2 ripe avocados, halved,
   stones out
2 shallots or 1 small red or
   white onion
1 clove garlic
Juice of 2 limes/1 lemon
Cayenne pepper
Salt and black pepper
1 tbsp fresh coriander

Guacamole

1. Scoop flesh out of avocado down to skin using spoon.
2. Tip into processor (or a bowl to use with handblender).
3. Add shallot/onion, garlic, juice, cayenne, salt, pepper, coriander. Process or blend till smooth.
4. No machine? Finely chop onion/shallot, garlic. Mash into avocado with other ingredients.
5. Spoon into a bowl. Sit avocado stone in mix before serving (delays browning/oxidation).

YOU CAN
* chop or blitz in some de-seeded red chilli

FEEDS 4 · **£** · **V** · **EXPRESS**

4 ripe tomatoes
2 shallots or 1 small onion
1 small red or green chilli
2 tbsps fresh coriander,
   chopped
Juice of 1 lime
Pinch of caster sugar
Salt and black pepper

Fresh Red Salsa

1. Finely chop tomatoes and shallots or onion.
2. Slit chilli in half with a knife and fork. Scoop out seeds without touching chilli. Finely chop flesh.
3. Mix tomatoes, chilli, shallots, coriander with lime, sugar, seasoning.

Tostadas

1. **Beans:** fry onion, garlic gently in oil for 5 minutes or till soft.
2. Add beans, spice, herb, sugar. Continue cooking on a low heat till mushy. Crush with a spoon. Add vinegar. Remove. Leave rough or mash till smooth.
3. **Tostadas:** heat oil in pan. Quickly fry tortillas till crisp each side.
4. Stack with beans and toppings. Or serve toppings at the table.

YOU CAN
* serve in a soft wrap instead of stacking
* buy re-fried bean mix
* make quesadillas. Warm tortilla in dry pan. Sprinkle grated Mozzarella/Cheddar on half. Fold over. Press edge down. Cook 1 minute per side. Cut into wedges. Add sliced raw chilli if you like it.

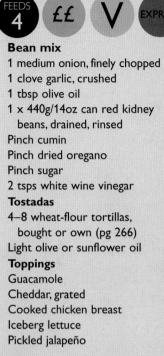

FEEDS 4 | **££** | **V** | **EXPRESS**

Bean mix
1 medium onion, finely chopped
1 clove garlic, crushed
1 tbsp olive oil
1 x 440g/14oz can red kidney beans, drained, rinsed
Pinch cumin
Pinch dried oregano
Pinch sugar
2 tsps white wine vinegar

Tostadas
4–8 wheat-flour tortillas, bought or own (pg 266)
Light olive or sunflower oil

Toppings
Guacamole
Cheddar, grated
Cooked chicken breast
Iceberg lettuce
Pickled jalapeño

Fajitas

1. Slice chosen chicken/beef into 1cm/½in strips. Or cube tofu. Or thickly slice mushrooms.
2. Chuck in a bowl to marinate with lime juice, sugar, oregano, spices, garlic for at least 30 minutes. Drain well.
3. Heat tortillas in oven or frying pan. Keep warm.
4. Heat oil in large pan or preheated wok. Fry steak/tofu/mushrooms for 2 minutes, or chicken for 5. Add onions, chilli, pepper. Stir-fry for 3–4 minutes till cooked.
5. Divide mix between tortillas. Add optional extras: salsa, sour cream, guacamole, Cheddar. Roll over.

FEEDS 4 | **££** | **V OPTION**

Choose from:
2 large chicken breasts
2 rump steaks
2 packs tofu
4 Portobello mushrooms

Marinade
Juice of 2 limes
1 tbsp caster sugar
1 tbsp dried oregano
Pinch cinnamon/cumin
Pinch cayenne
Clove garlic, crushed

Stir-fry
2 tbsps sunflower oil
1 small red onion, thinly sliced
1 small red chilli, de-seeded, finely chopped
2 peppers (red/yellow), de-seeded, cut in thin strips
8 tortillas/wraps

19

INDIAN

Five-star restaurant-style bhajis look and taste amazing. Serve with these combos or cook them up as part of a curry-night banquet. The dhal's a classic, by the way, and the cheapest way I know of boosting protein. Sort your own chapattis (pg 196).

MAKES 12

Bhajis
450g/1lb onions, halved, very
   thinly sliced, crescent-moon
   style
1 tsp salt
1 tsp cumin
1 tsp ground coriander
1 tsp turmeric
2 green chillies, de-seeded,
   very finely chopped
Fresh coriander, chopped
60g/2½ oz gram flour (from
   Indian/health food stores)
½ tsp baking powder
Sunflower/groundnut oil

Raita
Few tbsps plain yogurt (pg 46)
Length of cucumber, peeled,
   diced
1 clove garlic, crushed
   (optional)

1 SERVING

1 mango, peeled, diced
Bit of red onion, diced
½ small red chilli, de-seeded,
   chopped
1 tbsp lime juice
½ tsp caster sugar
Fresh coriander
Salt and pepper

Onion Bhajis with Raita

1. Sprinkle onion slices with salt in colander or sieve. Leave 30 minutes to draw out moisture.
2. Rinse under running water. Squeeze. Dry very well in tea towel. Transfer to bowl.
3. Separately, mix cumin, ground coriander, turmeric, chillies, fresh coriander, gram flour, baking powder. Mix in with onions.
4. Shape into bhajis. Squeeze well into 12 spiky balls.
5. Heat 8cm/3in oil in wok, deep saucepan or frying pan. When hot enough to crisp a breadcrumb, fry 4 bhajis at a time, carefully turning till cooked, browned and golden. Drain on kitchen roll.
6. To make raita, tip yogurt into a bowl and mix with cucumber and garlic.

Mango chutney

1. Chuck the lot in a bowl. Taste for seasoning.
2. Leave 1 hour or eat now.

YOU CAN
✱ team this with griddled fresh tuna
✱ cheat. Use Sharwoods.

Curry-Night Dahl

1. Heat oil in a saucepan. Cook onions, salt, garlic very gently for 5–10 minutes till soft, not coloured. Add ginger, cumin, chilli, turmeric, optional asafoetida (helps digestion). Cook for 1–2 minutes.

2. Add lentils, cinnamon, optional curry leaves and water.

3. Simmer 10 minutes. Add tomato purée, tamarind. Cook 20 minutes or till lentils soften, adding lemon juice, chutney to season. Enjoy as is or blitz half for a creamier mixture. Garnish with fresh coriander.

YOU CAN

✳ cook ahead. Leave to eat next day when flavour's developed. Keeps a few days. Freezes well.

✳ team with veg/meat curries

✳ throw in diced potato/carrot/green beans for a fuller meal deal

✳ top with hard-boiled eggs. Eat with chapattis.

2 tbsps light olive/groundnut/ sunflower oil
1 large onion, finely chopped
Pinch salt
4 cloves garlic, crushed
Little grated fresh ginger
1 tsp cumin powder
½ tsp chilli/cayenne
½ tsp turmeric
Pinch asafoetida (optional)
225g/8oz red lentils
1 stick cinnamon (optional)
3–4 curry leaves (optional)
850ml/1½ pints water
3 tsps tomato purée
2 tsps tamarind paste
Juice of ½–1 lemon
Bit of mango chutney
Chopped fresh coriander

21

TAPAS NIGHT

Whenever I get the chance I get stuck into these. I'm addicted to strong Spanish flavours so this is my favourite snacking plate. Team with chorizo, ham and cheese or a tasty bean, chorizo and tomato ragu (pg 180). Get into these and suddenly you're on holiday.

12 fresh dates, stoned
4 rindless bacon rashers
Pepper sauce/Tabasco sauce
(optional)

Hot Dates & Bacon

1. Preheat grill on max. Cut each bacon rasher into three.

2. Wrap a short length of bacon around each date. Fix each in place with metal skewer/wooden skewer pre-soaked for 20 minutes. Or thread them all onto one or two long skewers.

3. Grill, turning till dates are hot and bacon crispy. Add optional sauce.

YOU CAN
✱ use lengths of banana instead of dates

100ml/4oz olive oil
3 big onions, thinly sliced
3–4 big old potatoes, peeled,
   sliced to thickness of
   £1 coin
8 eggs
Salt and black pepper

Spanish Omelette

1. Heat oil in large frying pan. Add onions. Cook for 5–10 minutes over gentle heat till soft, not browned.

2. Add potatoes. Leave on gentle heat, stirring occasionally to cook evenly (approx 20 minutes).

3. When potatoes are just tender and still holding their shape, spoon the contents into a sieve over a bowl to drain off the oil.

4. Crack eggs into a bowl. Beat with a fork and add seasoning.

5. Return 2 tbsps of the drained oil to the pan. Heat. Add potato/onion mix. Pour egg over the lot. Cook slowly till just set. Finish under grill for a few seconds. Eat warm or cold.

2 slices good-quality bread
Extra virgin olive oil
1 clove garlic, cut in two
1 ripe tomato, cut in two
Sea salt

Tomato Garlic Toasts

1. Make toast. Drizzle with a bit of oil. Rub garlic over each slice.

2. Rub and squeeze ripe tomato over each piece. Sprinkle with salt.

YOU CAN
✱ eat for breakfast/when tomatoes are ripest

Patatas Bravas

1. Make tomato sauce (pg 83), adding chillies and paprika at step 1.
2. Parboil then fry potatoes until crispy (pg 214).
3. Sieve the spicy tomato sauce. Reheat it.
4. Quickly fry whole chilli.
5. Pour sauce over hot potatoes. Top with chilli. Eat with garlic mayo.

YOU CAN

* recycle cold boiled spuds this way. Next meal sorted…

FEEDS 4–6 £ V

1 x tomato sauce (pg 83) plus 1–2 chopped red chillies and ½ tsp paprika
1 x Frying Pan Crunchy Potatoes (pg 214)
1 whole red chilli (optional)

23

Flatbread

110g/4oz strong white bread
  flour
Good pinch salt
¼ tsp dried fast-action yeast
100ml/3½fl oz warm water
1 tbsp olive oil
(or use bought, or tortilla wrap)

Filling

250g/9oz best minced lamb
  (or mince own in processor)
Olive oil
1 small onion, finely chopped
1 clove garlic, crushed
2 good pinches cinnamon
¾ tsp mixed spice
Handful of pine nuts
Salt and black pepper

Salad

Red onion, finely chopped
Tomatoes, diced/sliced
Fresh coriander, torn
Hummus (pg 14, or bought)

Moroccan-Style Lamb & Homemade Flatbread

A little bit of meat goes a long way wrapped in your own flatbread (cheap, fast and easy – do it). Team with healthy spreads and salads. Spicy, crunchy, pretty gorgeous.

1. Dough: sift flour, salt into large bowl. In cup, mix yeast, water. Tip into flour bit by bit and mix with fork/fingers for a rough dough ball. Work oil in with your hand. Knead dough till smooth (pg 11) on lightly floured surface for 5 minutes. Rest in covered bowl for 15–30 minutes.

2. Filling: fry lamb in very hot pan without oil. Turn quickly to brown. Drain in a sieve. Wipe pan. Fry onion in a little oil on low heat for 5 minutes. Add garlic, cinnamon, spice. Cook 2 minutes. Add meat, seasoning, pine nuts. Stir 1 minute. Remove from heat.

3. Flatbread: cut dough into 4 balls. Cover. Roll one into very thin circle with rolling pin/wine bottle. Heat oil-free pan.

4. Cook bread for 1 minute till faint brown spots appear. Turn. Repeat. Don't overcook. Remove. Cover. Make the other three.

5. Fill: spread warm flatbreads with hummus. Top with meat filling, salad. Roll and eat.

YOU CAN
∗ whack a fried egg onto the meat before flat-wrapping it
∗ eat flatbread with koftas (pg 158), lamb kebabs (pg 159) and griddled vegetables (pg 15)
∗ mix garlic and yogurt to spread instead of hummus

Chinatown Char Sui Buns

Bun dough (stage 1)
3 tbsps caster sugar
250ml/9fl oz warm water
1 x 7g sachet dried yeast
400g/14oz plain flour
2 tbsps sunflower oil

Bun dough (stage 2)
1½ tsps baking powder
Greaseproof paper for steaming

Filling
250g/9oz cooked Char Sui
   Pork (pg 135)
1 tsp groundnut oil, for frying
1 tsp sesame oil
2 tbsps oyster sauce
3 tsps caster sugar
2 tsps soy sauce
3 tsps rice wine
Dash of rice wine vinegar

Lovely authentic Chinese snacks. The amazing contrast between sweet dough and gorgeous meat does it for me. Check out an essay or whatever while they're on the rise.

1. Dough: stir sugar into warm (not hot) water to dissolve. Add yeast. Stir. Cover with tea towel. Leave for 10 minutes, till frothy.
2. Sift flour into bowl. Add liquid yeast and oil. Beat in. Draw to a soft dough with your fingers. If dry, add a little water. Sticky? Add more flour.
3. Knead dough by hand on a board or using a machine (pg 11) till elastic. Roll into a ball. Place in large bowl lightly greased with oil. Cover with a cloth. Leave 3 hours to rise. Cook the pork (pg 135).
4. Sit raised dough back on board. Knead for 2 minutes. Use now, or cover with clingfilm and chill in fridge till needed.
5. Filling: cut cooked pork into small dice. Heat groundnut oil in wok. Add pork, sesame oil, oyster sauce, sugar, soy sauce, rice wine, wine vinegar. Cook and turn for 1 minute. Set aside.
6. Buns: sit dough on a board. Flatten it. Spoon baking powder into centre. Pull the dough up and over it. Knead it for 3–4 minutes. Divide into 12. **To stuff:** flatten into circles. Pull edges to thin them a bit. Put 2 tsps filling into each one. Pull 2 sides of dough up. Nip together. Pull last 2 up till filling's covered. Nip well to seal.
7. Heat steamer (bamboo or other). Sit each bun on own bit of greaseproof paper. Steam for 10–15 minutes, till cooked though. Test. A skewer should come out hot.

YOU CAN
* eat as is or dunk into sweet chilli sauce or own dipping sauce (pg 193)
* slice plain or sauced char sui onto rice or noodles
* scoop up char sui with lettuce leaves or roll in steamed cabbage and dip in sauce
* improvise steamer with sieve and lidded saucepan

PILE ON THE PÂTÉ

Make it at the weekend. Snack on it through the week. Pâtés are cheap, neat and pretty damn tasty. Standard toasting bread makes retro melba toast, aka crispbread.

MAKES 1 DISH £

400g/14oz chicken livers
1 heaped tbsp butter
3 fat shallots or 1 small onion, finely chopped
3 cloves garlic, crushed
3 rashers bacon, chopped
Big slug of Jack Daniels, brandy or apple juice
Thyme or oregano (fresh or dried)
Salt and black pepper
175g/6oz Philadelphia cream cheese
Juice ½ lemon
2–3 tbsps melted butter

My-Style Chicken Liver Pâté

1. Roughly chop livers. Cut away any fatty/wacky bits.

2. Melt butter gently in frying pan. Cook shallots/onion, garlic for 5–10 minutes without browning.

3. Add chopped bacon. Cook, turning, for 4 minutes.

4. Increase heat. Add livers. Cook and turn till browned outside but still pinkish inside.

5. Add JD or other liquid to sizzle for 2 minutes. Add herbs, pepper, little salt (bacon can be salty).

6. Tip in processor. Add cheese, lemon juice. Blitz till smooth. Taste. Adjust seasoning/lemon.

7. Spoon into a bowl. Allow to cool for 5 minutes. Cover top with gently melted butter. Best eaten 1 day on. Keeps for a week.

YOU CAN

✷ make mushroom pâté. Very gently fry 2 shallots/1 small onion, 2 crushed cloves garlic, in 1 tbsp butter for 5 minutes. Add 200g/7oz brown/flat mushrooms, roughly chopped. Fry gently for 10 minutes. Season with salt, pepper, thyme, 2 tbsps wine/cider. Cook 5 minutes. Cool. Blitz with 100g/3½oz cream cheese, 50g/2oz sour cream/crème fraîche.

MAKES 1 DISH £ EXPRESS

1 x 180g/6oz tin tuna, drained
1 x 200g/7oz pack Philadelphia cream cheese
Juice 1 large lemon
3 anchovy fillets, drained
1 tsp capers, drained
Small pinch salt
Black pepper

Speedy Tuna Pâté

1. Tip all ingredients into a processor or a bowl to use with handblender.

2. Blitz till smooth. Taste mix. Adjust seasoning. No blender? Mash everything together.

3. Chill. Store 2/3 days under clingfilm.

YOU CAN
* make sardine pâté: blitz in 1 drained can instead of the tuna
* try using smoked trout/mackerel for a taste change

Sundried Tomato & Bean Pâté

1. Drain beans into sieve or colander over bowl.
2. Transfer to processor, or to plastic jug/bowl to use with handblender. Add garlic, 1 tbsp oil, honey, vinegar. Blitz to a thick paste.
3. Add more oil, 2 tbsps water or liquid from beans. Blitz till mix is light and fluffy.

1 x 400g/14oz can butterbeans
2 cloves garlic, peeled
1–2 tbsps olive oil
½–1 tsp runny honey
½ tsp wine vinegar/balsamic vinegar
1 tbsp sundried tomato purée
Bit of fresh coriander/basil (optional)
Salt and black pepper

4. Spoon into bowl. Stir in purée, seasoning, optional herbs. Taste. Adjust seasoning. Chill 30 minutes.

YOU CAN
* use as a dip with veg sticks
* eat with toast/melba toast or in sandwiches
* stuff into hollowed cherry tomatoes for lunch box
* mash well if no blender

Crispbreads (Melba Toast)

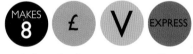

4 slices fresh toast, crusts off

1. Cut sideways through toasts with a sharp knife, separating each toast into two thin slices.
2. Dry under medium grill, white side up, till light brown – or bake at 150°C/300°F/gas 2 for 10 minutes, till crisp.
3. Allow to cool. Stores in airtight container for ages.

HOT DOGS

The great American dream in a bread roll. Chilli Dogs bite. Jammy Dogs are sweet (see veggie option). Own Dogs behave and the Ketchup Dogs are classic.

FEEDS
4   ££

450g/1lb best minced steak
1 good glug olive oil
1 medium onion, finely chopped
1 clove garlic, crushed
1 tsp chilli powder
4 tbsps tomato ketchup
2 tsps mustard
Black pepper and salt
Pinch dried oregano (optional)
4 shakes Worcestershire sauce
4 sausages
4 rolls
Shredded iceberg lettuce
Grated Cheddar

US-Style Chilli Dogs

1. Fry meat in very hot pan (no oil). Stir to brown quickly. Tip into sieve. Leave there.

2. Wipe pan clean. Add oil. Reduce heat. Gently fry onion, garlic, chilli powder for 5 minutes. Stir in meat, ketchup, mustard, seasoning, optional herb, Worcestershire sauce. Cook for 10 mins. Taste. Adjust. Add a few drops of water if sticking, but the chilli should be dryish.

3. Meantime, fry sausages slowly in pan, under grill, or bake in the oven (pg 131). Turn to brown evenly and cook through.

4. Slice and toast rolls on griddle or pan if you want. Fill with sausage, lettuce. Top with chilli mix and Cheddar.

YOU CAN
✳ make Sloppy Joes. Reheat chilli mix with a little water/stock/tomato sauce. Slop into warm bread rolls or over baked potatoes.

Jammy Dogs for 2

2 best or veggie sausages
2 tbsps orange marmalade or apricot jam
I splash wine/cider/wine vinegar
2 rolls or 4 slices bread
Green leaves (optional)
Mustard

1. Fry, grill or bake sausages in oven at 200°C/400°F/gas 6 (see pg 131).
2. Heat marmalade or jam gently in a small pan with a splash of wine/cider/vinegar to thin it. Taste for balance.
3. Split rolls or cut bread. Spread one bit with mustard, one with marmalade/jam mix. Add whole/halved sausages, optional green leaves.

Ketchup Dogs for 4

1 tbsp honey
1 tbsp tomato ketchup
2 tsp English mustard
4 best sausages

1. Melt honey in pan. Add ketchup and mustard. Stir.
2. Tip mix over sausages in dish. Turn. Leave to marinate.
3. Preheat oven to 200°C/400°F/gas 6.
4. Line roasting tin with foil. Lay bangers on there. Bake for 20–30 minutes, brushing with marinade once or twice. Eat in warm split rolls with greenery.

YOU CAN
✱ sit bangers on rack over foil
✱ roll up in wraps. Team with chilli jam, chutney, relish and salad.

Own Dogs for 3

225g/8oz pork mince
1 small onion, finely chopped
2 tbsps fresh breadcrumbs (pg 11)
½ tsp dried sage/thyme
Salt and black pepper
Little egg/milk to bind

1. Mix everything with a fork. Shape into sausages.
2. Chill for 30 minutes. Fry in hot oil, turning, for 10–12 minutes.

YOU CAN
✱ customize. Add crushed garlic, grated ginger and/or apple. Or finely chopped chilli. Or lemon rind. Or smoked paprika, ketchup and chilli flakes for chorizo dogs.

BAKED POTATOES

Skint Topped Spuds

1 baking potato (good floury
old varieties include Maris
Piper, King Edward)
Olive oil (optional)
Butter
Salt and pepper

Tricks of the trade for a perfect baked potato? Buy good spuds – organic if possible. Maris Pipers, King Edwards work as they're old and floury. Note: try baking sweet potatoes. They're faster, even more nutritious, packed with fibre and you don't need to butter them.

1. Heat oven to 200°C/400°F/gas 6. Scrub spuds. Prick with fork, or stick metal skewers through. Rub skins with oil and salt for crisp skin. Wrap in foil, oil-free, for soft skin. Bake for 1 hour or till tender.
2. Cut, punch or squeeze open. Mash in butter (soy spread if vegan) and seasoning. Add toppings.

YOU CAN
* top with baked beans, tuna mayo, cheese and guacamole, hummus, coleslaw, cottage cheese, fresh fruit, nuts with raisins, apple, celery in dressing, Bolognese sauce, tzatziki, cheese rarebit, cauliflower cheese
* save skins. Brush with butter. Season. Add bit of cheese. Bake at 200°C/400°F/gas 6 for 10 minutes. Fill with any above or dip in guacamole/salsa etc.
* re-use cold baked spuds. Chop roughly. Bake in hot oven drizzled with olive oil, sliced garlic, herbs till crunchy. Great with ham/bacon/chutney/salad.

Hot baked potatoes
Butter
Salt and pepper
Dijon/English mustard
Ham/own gammon (optional)
Cheese, grated (Cheddar/
Gruyère)
Low-fat crème fraîche

Stuffed Baked Spuds

Take it to the next level. Smash your spuds with tasty extras then bake again. Note: freeze for whenever you need them…

1. Cut freshly baked potatoes in half.
2. Scoop insides into bowl. Mash with butter, salt, pepper, mustard, ham/gammon, half the cheese and crème fraîche (veggies skip ham).
3. Pile back in shells. Top with cheese/crème fraîche. Bake for 10 minutes or till bubbling.

Spuds & Veggie/Vegan Chilli

Ridiculously cheap if you think about what you're getting out of it. Great carbs, protein, range of vitamins. Plus it's tasty and filling. Pretty much a student classic. Suits vegans.

1. **Spuds:** heat oven to 200°C/400°F/gas 6. Prepare spuds to your taste (crisp or soft finish) as Skint Topped Spuds (opposite). Cook 1 hour or till tender.

2. **Chilli:** heat oil in large pan. Fry onions, garlic very gently till soft. Add peppers. Cook for 5–8 minutes till softening.

3. Add chillies, cumin, cayenne/chilli powder, paprika, sugar, tomatoes, beans, tomato purée, coriander, water. Bring to boil, stirring.

4. Reduce heat. Cover. Simmer gently for 20 minutes. Taste. Season.

5. Remove spuds from oven. Punch or cut to open. Mash with bit of butter. Team with the chilli, cheese, sour cream.

FEEDS 4 · ££ · V

4 baking potatoes
Olive oil
Sea salt

Veggie/vegan chilli
2 tbsps olive or vegetable oil
1 large onion, finely chopped
2 cloves garlic, crushed
1 red and 1 yellow pepper, de-seeded, cored, chopped
1–2 red chillies, de-seeded, finely chopped, or ½ tsp chilli flakes
1½ tsps ground cumin
½ tsp cayenne or chilli powder
1 tsp paprika
1 tsp sugar
1 x 400g/14oz can chopped tomatoes
1 x 400g/14oz can kidney beans, drained, rinsed
2 tbsps tomato purée
2 tbsps fresh coriander (optional)
125ml/4fl oz water
Salt and pepper
Bit of butter/soy margarine

Extras
Handful grated Cheddar/vegan cheese/cottage cheese
Sour cream/soy cream

YOU CAN

✳ cook spuds in microwave, then crisp 30 minutes in oven

✳ stuff chilli in a wrap to griddle (see BLT Wrap, pg 34) or eat on rice bowl

✳ top with meat chilli (pg 141)

33

HOT SARNIES, TOASTIES AND WRAPS

Save cash, packaging and up the health and taste factor by
sorting your own gorgeous hot stuff anytime.

Cheap & Cheerful Chip Sarnie

1–2 fresh spuds, peeled (or use cold boiled spuds or roasties)
Olive oil
2 slices any bread
Salt
Malt vinegar
Ketchup or brown sauce

1. Cut uncooked spuds into big wedges and boil 10 minutes. Drain well.
2. Fry in a small pan in a bit of oil, turning, for 10–15 minutes or till well browned. Drain on kitchen paper.
3. Pile into bread with ketchup or sauce, salt, a spinkle of vinegar.

YOU CAN

✱ forget the sarnie. Eat as bread and butter and chips. Poach/fry an egg with it (pg 60).

✱ stuff chips into warm pitta with hummus, grated carrot, tomatoes, onion, grated Cheddar

Classic Late-Night Clubbing

3 slices bread
3 slices back/streaky/veggie bacon
Bit of olive oil
1 large egg
Lettuce/rocket/spinach (optional)
1 tomato, thinly sliced

1. Toast bread. Grill (or fry) bacon till crisp. Sit it on kitchen paper.
2. Heat oil in small pan. Crack egg on hard surface. Hold between both hands. Stick thumbs into crack. Pull shell apart over pan so the egg slips in neatly.
3. Cook for 1–2 minutes, flicking fat over yolk to set it.
4. Layer toast, leaves, bacon, tomato. Then toast, leaves, bacon, egg, toast. Pass the ketchup.

YOU CAN

✱ club with cream cheese, salmon, watercress, tomato

✱ use Mozzarella, Parma ham, olives, tomato

✱ try left-over roast chicken (pg 156), mayo, tomato, ham

BLT Wrap

2 rashers bacon
1 tortilla wrap, homemade (pg 266) or bought
Mayo
Mango chutney
Grated Cheddar
Iceberg/little gem lettuce
1 tomato

1. Grill/fry bacon till crisp. Sit it on kitchen paper.
2. Heat griddle or frying pan.
3. Prep tortilla. Warm it. Spread it with mayo, chutney. Top with bacon, Cheddar, lettuce, tomato.
4. Roll tortilla, fixing with toothpick.
5. Wrap in foil or cook naked. Place, seam side down, on hot griddle. Heat 1–2 minutes per side

till hot through.

YOU CAN

✱ fill wrap with chilli (pg 141) or veggie chilli (pg 33)

✱ foil-wrap. Take along to beach and barbie it.

Speedy Pizza Bread

Baguette or ciabatta, sliced open
Clove garlic, cut in half
Olive oil
2 tbsps passata or own tomato sauce (pg 83)
Pinch dried oregano (optional)
Gruyère/Cheddar, sliced/grated

1. Preheat oven to 230°C/450°F/gas 8.
2. Rub garlic over bread. Drizzle with a little olive oil. Bake on tray for 5 minutes.
3. Make a mix of passata/tomato sauce, crushed garlic, oregano. Spread over hot bread. Top with cheese. Cook 5 minutes or till bubbling.

YOU CAN

✱ layer drained anchovy fillets, sliced chorizo, pepperoni, ham, olives on topping

✱ make tuna melt. Mix 1–2 tbsps drained tuna into tomato sauce or mix 4 tbsps tuna with chopped red onion, lemon juice. Cover with cheese. Cook as above.

Juicy Mushroom Sarnie

2 slices bread
Mustard
Little olive oil
A few mushrooms, roughly
   chopped
Crushed garlic or purée
Soy sauce

1. Spread mustard on one slice of bread.
2. Fry mushrooms quickly in a little oil with crushed garlic/garlic purée. Add 4 drops soy sauce. Pile onto bread. Sandwich it.

YOU CAN
∗ eat mushrooms on hot buttered toast. Works well with field/chestnut mushrooms.

∗ for vegans, add a bit of tamari and a scattering of sesame seeds/furikake – no butter

Cajun Chicken wrap for 2

1 chicken breast, in strips or
   bite-size bits
1 clove garlic, crushed
½–1 tsp Cajun seasoning, bought
   or own mix (use: ½ tbsp
   crushed black and white
   peppercorns, 1 tsp dried sage,
   2 tsps dried oregano and
   thyme, 1 tbsp paprika, 1 tsp
   cayenne, 2 tsps brown sugar)
Bit of oil
Lime/lemon juice
Little salt
Salad and sarnie:
½ tsp Cajun seasoning

Garlic mayo
Fresh coriander (optional)
Tortilla wrap/baguette/roll
Green salad leaves
Red onion
Avocado/guacamole

1. Mix chicken bits/slices with garlic, ½–1 tsp Cajun seasoning, oil, lime or lemon juice. Leave 10 minutes.
2. Fry or griddle chicken in a hot pan for a few minutes till white all through. Salt lightly. Set aside.
3. Mix ½ tsp Cajun seasoning, mayo, optional coriander, more juice. Taste. Adjust.
4. Warm wrap/baguette/roll. Spread with Cajun mayo. Add chicken, salad, onion, optional avocado. Halve it. Eat now or good cold.

Blow-Out Baked Cheeses

Ciabatta/baguette, sliced
Butter
Cut clove garlic
Drizzle white wine
50g/2oz (or more) Gruyère,
  Cheddar, thinly sliced/grated
Salad leaves
Dressing (pg 211)

1. Preheat oven to 230°C/450°F/ gas 8.
2. Rub bread with garlic and butter. Bake on tray for 5 minutes.
3. Drizzle a little white wine. Top with sliced/crumbled/grated cheese. Bake for 5 minutes. Grill till bubbling.
4. Toss salad leaves in dressing. Serve together.

YOU CAN

✳ mark lines on toasted cheese with skewer. Drizzle Worcestershire sauce.

Cheese and Ham French Toasties

My version of Croque Monsieur – makes a filling late night snack or breakfast.
2 slices bread
Butter
Mustard
2 thin slices ham
Cheese, sliced

1. Heat grill/sandwich toaster/ griddle pan.
2. Butter bread. Smear mustard on one slice. Top with ham, cheese, ham again, second bread slice (buttered side in).
3. Grill, turning once, till cooked through and toasted.

YOU CAN

✳ top with poached or fried eggs
✳ replace ham with sliced tomato/mushroom

Grilled Cheese & Salad

1–2 slices white/wholemeal/
  Treacle Bread (pg 266)
Strong hard cheese – Cheddar,
  Lancashire, blue or goat's
Smear mango/apple chutney
Salad
Watercress/spinach
1 pear/nectarine
Chicory (optional)
Dressing (pg 211)

1. Toast one side of bread under grill.
2. Remove. Smear with chutney. Cover completely with sliced/ grated/crumbled cheese. Grill till bubbling.
3. Toss salad leaves in dressing. Serve together.

Black Sheep Rarebit for 2

Slap a bit of good British beer into this one…
25g/1oz butter, softened
110g/4oz strong Cheddar, grated
1 tsp mustard
Shake Worcestershire sauce/
  Henderson's Relish
2 tbsps Black Sheep ale/beer/cider
  or milk
2 slices wholemeal/white/Treacle
  Bread (pg 266)

1. Preheat grill. Mix all topping ingredients.

2. Toast one side of bread. Spread topping on the other.
3. Grill till melted and bubbling.

YOU CAN

✳ top with poached eggs for buck rabbit
✳ add a rasher of crisp smoked bacon
✳ eat with apple chutney
✳ make more mix – keeps for a week in fridge. Handy.
✳ eat with crisp green/tomato/onion salad

3. Spread to cover each toast completely.
4. Grill till golden, bubbly.

YOU CAN
∗ use Cheddar/Lancashire cheese and cider/splash of kirsch/vodka
∗ team with dill pickles/pickled onions/tomato/spinach/onion salad

Ham, Cheese & Egg Toasts
2 large slices crustless bread
2 slices ham
Cheese (Cheddar, Gruyère, Mozzarella), sliced
1 large egg
2 tbsps milk
Olive oil

Salt and pepper
Mustard or chilli jam (optional)
1. Layer ham and cheese between bread slices (spread with mustard or chilli jam if using).
2. Cut sandwich into 4.
3. Beat egg and milk together in a shallow dish.
4. Sit sandwiches in dish, turning. Leave to soak 15–20 minutes.
5. Fry in oil for 4 minutes each side till golden outside, fluffy inside. Eat now.

YOU CAN
∗ add bit of mustard to egg mix

Ski Toasts for 3
Swiss fondue-style cheese on toast – well impressive. Cheaper than skiing.
3 thick slices white/brown bread
1 egg
50ml/2fl oz white wine
175g/6oz Gruyère cheese, grated
Small pinch salt
Small pinch nutmeg (optional)

1. Lightly toast bread under grill, both sides.
2. Beat egg. Mix with remaining ingredients.

COLD SARNIES, WRAPS, ROLLS, PITTAS

Vary breads and spreads for cold quality sandwiches made with trusty ingredients to eat in or take away. Try your own bread (ridiculously easy and tastes amazing). Spread with butter, mayos, dressings, creamy cheese, rub with ripe tomatoes. Treat yourself to sexy bruschetta.

Old English Cucumber or Watercress

4 thin slices white/brown bread
Butter, softened
Cucumber, peeled, thinly sliced, or watercress, chopped
Salt

1. Spread butter thinly on both slices of bread.
2. Arrange cucumber or watercress on one slice. Salt lightly. Sandwich together. Cut into quarters.

YOU CAN

✻ spread with homemade cream cheese (pg 47) or Philadelphia instead of butter
✻ experiment with griddled strips of courgette seasoned with lemon/salt/chopped red chilli
✻ get sliced hard-boiled egg (pg 59) together with watercress and mayo

Spinach, Grape, Chicken Caesar

2 slices wholemeal/granary/white bread
1 heaped tbsp mayo
1 tbsp plain yogurt
1 clove garlic, crushed
Squeeze lemon juice
Salt and black pepper
Parmesan/Cheddar, finely grated

Left-over roast chicken (pg 156)
Few grapes, halved
Spinach or other green leaves

1. Set bread out.
2. Mix mayo, yogurt, garlic, lemon, seasoning, cheese.
3. Add chopped chicken – or leave it in slices.
4. Spread filling over one slice of bread.
5. Top with grapes and spinach. Sandwich it.

YOU CAN

✻ rule out the dairy. Skip cheese, mayo, yogurt. Drizzle chicken with mustardy dressing (pg 211).

✻ add curry paste, mango chutney, chopped dried apricot, lemon juice to mayo for coronation chicken
✻ mix filling. Wrap in a soft tortilla.

Ham, Egg, Mayo, Chilli Jam

2 slices brown/wholegrain/white bread or Treacle Bread (pg 266)
Little chilli jam or sweet chilli sauce
Gammon/ham, bought or own (pg 133), thinly sliced
1 hard-boiled egg (pg 59)
1 tbsp mayo
Black pepper

1. Spread 1 slice of bread with chilli jam/sauce. Lay ham/gammon over it.

2. Mash egg and mayo together with a fork. Season. Spread evenly over ham. Sandwich.

YOU CAN

✱ skip ham. Mix diced tomato into egg mayo. Add spinach/rocket.

✱ try egg mayo, diced tomato, crispy grilled bacon in a crusty baguette – no chilli

✱ team egg mayo with old-style cress or watercress for a health boost

A PLT

4 slices white/wholemeal/malted bread
Crisp lettuce, shredded
Tomato, thinly sliced
Avocado, sliced
Prawn sauce
2 tbsps mayo
Squeeze lemon/lime juice
1 clove garlic, crushed
1 tsp ketchup
Handful prawns

1. Divide lettuce, tomato, avocado between 2 slices of bread.
2. Mix sauce ingredients, adding prawns last.
3. Pile onto salad stuff. Sandwich.

YOU CAN

✱ replace prawns with 2 rashers crisp bacon for a BLT. Spread mayo on bread. Layer bacon separately.

Old-Style Ploughman's

2 slices brown/malted/best white bread
Spoonful chutney/Branston pickle
Mayo or a halved ripe tomato
3–4 slices strong Cheddar/ Lancashire cheese

Few rings red onion
3–4 thin slices tomato
1 stick celery, thinly sliced
Spinach leaves/watercress/iceberg or soft lettuce

1. Spread chutney/pickle over one slice of bread. Spead mayo or squeeze a tomato over the other.
2. Stack with fillings. Sandwich.

YOU CAN

✱ team with a pear/apple/orange or fresh fruit salad

✱ sub in hummus/grated carrot/apple

✱ add sliced ham, own gammon

Sam's Special: Cranberry, Grape & Brie (or Chicken)

2 slices bread/foccacia/ciabatta or white roll
Cranberry sauce/relish
Mayo/garlic mayo
6 red or white grapes
Thinly sliced brie or cooked lean chicken
Iceberg lettuce, shredded
Cucumber, thinly sliced
Tomato, thinly sliced

1. Spread one bit of bread with cranberry. Top with brie or chicken.
2. Spread second with mayo, grapes, salad bits. Press together.

24/7 Bruschetta

Slices baguette, ciabatta or brown bread
Cloves garlic, halved
Olive oil
Toppings – choose from:
Tomatoes, salt, basil
Any pâté (pg 28)
Avocado, tomato, black olive
Roasted red pepper, goat's cheese
Parma ham, blue cheese, walnuts, honey
Warm white beans, crushed garlic, drop of balsamic
Hummus, tomato, Cheddar

1. Prep toppings or invent new ones.
2. Slice bread thinly (1cm/⅓in) and cut into 2 or 3 if large.
3. Griddle or grill both sides. Rub with garlic, drizzle oil. Top.

Spanish Press 'n' Wrap Tuna Baguette

1 baguette/bit of ciabatta
Dressing
1 clove garlic, crushed
Little caster sugar
2 tbsps olive oil
1 tbsp wine vinegar
Salt and pepper
Filling
Bit of red onion, sliced
1 tomato, sliced
Strips of red/orange pepper
½ tin tuna, drained, flaked
1 hard-boiled egg, sliced
4 anchovy fillets
Few black olives, pitted

1. Slice bread open like a book.
2. Mix dressing. Sprinkle over cut sides.
3. Mix filling. Lay over one side of bread.
4. Close bread. Wrap tightly in foil/clingfilm. Sit weights on top. Leave for 30 minutes or more. Or press down hard with your hand. Unwrap. Eat. Can be messy…

YOU CAN

* try this method with griddled veg (pg 15) chicken, prawns, roast belly pork, salmon
* press Greek salad (mix feta, olives, cucumber, tomato, onion, dressing)
* press a whole loaf for picnics. Slice top off big crusty loaf. Brush insides with dressing. Stuff. Press and wrap.

Tuna Mayo

2 slices brown/malted/white bread
Bit of cucumber, thinly sliced
Tuna mayo
½ tin tuna, drained
1–2 tbsps mayo
Good squeeze lemon juice
Black pepper and salt
Bit of Dijon or English mustard
Bit of red onion, finely chopped

1. Lay cucumber slices over 1 bread slice.
2. Mix tuna mayo. Spread it over cucumber.
3. Sandwich. Simple.

Cool Egg Wrap (Gluten-Free Option)

1 egg
2 tsps water
Salt and black pepper

1. Beat egg, water, seasoning in bowl.
2. Heat oil-free non-stick frying pan.
3. Add enough egg to cover base. Let it set (not fry) over very low heat.
4. Turn as soon as set. Cook for another few seconds.

5. Remove. Cool. Spread with filling of choice. Roll. Eat whole or halved.

YOU CAN
* add herbs to egg mix
* fill with cream cheese/basil/ham/ tomatoes/hummus/griddled vegetables/ chicken. Dunk into dipping sauce.

Proper Roast Wrap (Pro Wrapping)

1 tortilla wrap per person
Mayo/sour cream/mustard/ horseradish sauce
Cold beef from roast (pg 144)
Iceberg lettuce
Gherkin, sliced
Tomato, sliced

1. Spread mayo/mustard/sour cream/ horseradish over wrap.
2. Fill. Leave 2.5cm/1in round edges.
3. Fold bottom side up over filling.
4. Fold in one side, then the other to parcel.
5. Hold sides in place and fold top bit over.
6. Press wrap gently to seal/flatten. Cut across diagonally. Prop one half on the other.

YOU CAN
* wrap coronation chicken (pg 204)
* mix cold/hot roast pork with mayo, mustard, tomato, apple sauce

Posh Pitta Pockets for 2

½ avocado
Little salt and black pepper
Squeeze lemon juice
2 wholemeal pittas
3–4 tbsps cottage cheese
Slices cucumber
Sliced smoked salmon or prawns

1. Slice or mash the avocado. Season with salt, pepper, lemon.
2. Stuff into pitta with cottage cheese, fish, cucumber.

YOU CAN
* skip the fish. Add a smear of Marmite or mango chutney.

Freestyle Veg in Bread for 2

Any griddled veg (pg 15) or roast peppers (pg 210)
4 slices malted grain/white bread/ pitta/rolls/wraps
Hummus (pg 14) or cream cheese (pg 47) or garlic mayo
Salad leaves
Crumbled feta cheese (optional)

1. Prep griddled veg/roast peppers.
2. Spread bread/roll/warmed pitta/ wrap with hummus, cream cheese or mayo. Add veg, leaves, cheese.

YOU CAN
* team sliced Mozzarella with roast peppers. Eat cold or grill.
* griddle a few asparagus spears

Rollmop on Brown for 2

2 slices Treacle Bread (pg 266), rye or pumpernickel
Dollop of sour cream/yogurt
2 slices crisp apple
2 slices red onion
2 rollmops, drained
Dill pickle, sliced (optional)

1. Smear bread with tiny bit of sour cream.
2. Add apple, onion, rollmop, dollop sour cream, pickle if using.

FEEDS 2–3 | **££** | **V**

4–6 thick slices ciabatta/small crusty loaf/baguette (stale is fine), cubed
1 tbsp olive oil
Handful cherry tomatoes
4–6 regular tomatoes
1 red onion, finely chopped
1 pack feta cheese, crumbled
Fresh herbs (basil/parsley/oregano)
Black olives

Dressing
1 clove garlic
1–2 tbsps red wine vinegar
2 tbsps tomato juice (optional)
6 tbsps olive oil
Salt and black pepper

Flash Cheese Salad Bowl

A smart piece of cooking as there's very little cooking involved. Croûtons provide a sweet crunchy texture (watch they don't burn). Works with salty cheese, leaves and dressing.

1. Preheat oven to 220°C/425°F/gas 7. Toss bread cubes in olive oil. Bake for 5–10 minutes till crunchy. Don't burn! Tip half into salad bowl.

2. Meantime, mix dressing. Taste. Adjust. Pour over bread in salad bowl. Leave 10 minutes. Add rest of bread, salad, dressing. Toss together. Crumble feta in.

YOU CAN
* use 2 pittas, toasted, chopped, instead of ciabatta
* try adding cucumber, roasted peppers (pg 210)
* do it with goat's cheese, Cheddar, Edam, Gouda, Mozzarella

English-Style Cheese Bowl

Top up your calcium and get some daily fruit portions in. A nicely balanced old-school cheese bowl.

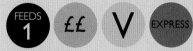

FEEDS 1 | ££ | V | EXPRESS

1. Toss apple/pear in lemon juice. Throw everything into a bowl or arrange neatly on a plate.

2. Top with mayo or a mix of mayo, yogurt, garlic and lemon juice.

YOU CAN

* grate cheese. Arrange salad in layers in box or bowl.
* for low-fat option use cottage cheese. Add chopped orange.
* slap a hard-boiled egg on top, topped with mayo

1 apple or pear, chopped
Lemon juice
1 or 2 or 3 cheeses, cubed
2 sticks celery, sliced
2 tbsps raisins
Few nuts/pine nuts
Few grapes
Few cherry tomatoes
Iceberg lettuce, shredded
Grated carrot (optional)
Mayo or yogurt
Clove garlic, crushed (optional)

FEEDS **2** ££ **V** EXPRESS

1 x 250g/9oz pack halloumi
  cheese
Spinach/rocket/lettuce
1 lime
Dressing (pg 211)
1 red chilli, de-seeded, finely
  chopped
2 pitta breads

Chilli Lime Halloumi

My veggie sister lived on this in her student years. Halloumi can sit in the back of your fridge for ever waiting for you to jazz it up with a bit of chilli and lime. The acid bite cuts across the saltiness. Eat with or in pitta.

1. Cut cheese in thick slices. Throw salad into bowl or prep for pitta.

2. Heat griddle or frying pan. Or line grill pan with foil if grilling.

3. Slap down slices of cheese to fry/grill 1–2 mins per side till golden.

4. Drizzle with lime, dressing, chilli. Chuck onto salad bowl/into pitta with salad.

YOU CAN

✱ marinate chunks of halloumi in lime/garlic/oil. Skewer up with veg. Grill and turn till melting for halloumi skewers.

Champion Cheese Mushrooms

FEEDS 2 · ££ · V

Got a special veggie heading round? Bang out this bad boy. It's a bit of a luxurious one and bloody tasty for a non-meat dish.

1. Toast bread or bake in oven at 170°C/325°F/gas 3 for 10 minutes.

2. Fry onion and garlic gently in 25g/1oz butter in frying pan till soft, not browned. Increase heat. Add wine/cider. Boil rapidly till reduced by half. Stir in cream. Cook till reduced by half again.

3. Melt 25g/1oz butter in a second large pan. Throw in mushrooms with herb, seasoning. Stir over medium heat till juices cook off. Add cream mix.

4. Simmer gently to reheat (2–3 minutes). Preheat grill.

5. Put bread in shallow dish/dishes. Top with mushroom mix then grated cheese. Heat till bubbling.

4 slices baguette/round crusty bread
50g/2oz butter
1 small onion, finely chopped
2 cloves garlic, crushed
175ml/6fl oz white wine/cider
100ml/3½fl oz double cream/crème fraîche
400g/14oz button mushrooms, thinly sliced
Fresh parsley/thyme/tarragon, chopped
Salt and pepper
75–110g/3–4oz grated Cheddar/Gruyère or a mix

YOGURT & BEYOND

Don't get ripped off buying yogurt and cream cheese. Make your own. Tastes better. Mix and match flavourings to suit your own tastes. Sweet...

MAKES 2 PINTS   £   V

1 litre/1¾ pints semi-skimmed
or whole milk
3 tbsps live natural yogurt

Brilliant Own-Style Yogurt

1. **Boil** milk in a deep pan. Remove from heat as it rises.
2. **Tip** into bowl. Leave. Stir in yogurt when milk is lukewarm. Cover with clingfilm. Leave in warm place 6–8 hours or till it thickens. Wrap a towel round the bowl if it's chilly.
3. **Keep** covered in fridge. Eat. Save 3 tbsps for making next batch.

YOU CAN

✱ go Greek: strain yogurt through muslin (see DIY Cream Cheese, to right) till it's as thick as you like it

✱ use in marinades (tenderizes chicken, lamb), curries, smoothies, raita, sauces, mayonnaise

✱ mix with jam, honey, sugar, muesli, fruit or make these yogurt bowls...

Vitamin Boost

1 fresh orange
Natural yogurt
Drizzle of honey
1 or 2 ginger/
  digestive/amaretti
  biscuits, or muesli

1. Peel and chop orange. Retain juice.
2. Mix with yogurt, honey, biscuit or muesli.

Power Boost

1–2 ripe bananas
Natural yogurt
Drizzle of honey
Grated dark chocolate

1. Mash or slice banana.
2. Mix with yogurt and honey.
3. Top with grated chocolate.

Berry Crunch

Natural yogurt
Drizzle of honey
2 tbsps muesli/crunchy
  cereal
Seeds/raisins/dried
  apricots/nuts
Fresh or defrosted
  berries

1. Mix yogurt with honey, cereal, seeds, nuts, dried fruit.
2. Top with fresh berries, more honey.

Choc Crunch for 3

300ml/10fl oz natural
  yogurt
300ml/10fl oz double
  cream
50g/2oz dark
  chocolate, chilled
  and grated
2 tbsps soft brown
  sugar

1. Softly whip yogurt and cream together with a balloon whisk till just holding shape. Mix chocolate in.
2. Spoon into cups/ramekins. Sprinkle sugar over.
3. Chill a few hours or overnight.

DIY Cream Cheese

1. Line sieve/colander with a bit of muslin. Sit it over a bowl.

2. Stir salt into yogurt. Tip into muslin. Leave to drip 6 hours/ overnight. Result: brilliant cream cheese.

MAKES
1 BALL   £   V

1 pint natural yogurt
(own/organic)
1 tsp salt

YOU CAN
* spread on hot toast, top with raspberry jam
* use in puddings
* mash with herbs, seasoning, chilli. Drizzle olive oil.
* eat the French way, drizzled with honey and fresh berries
* spread in sandwiches or eat on salads
* store 1 week in fridge – or in balls in jar covered in olive oil
* get muslin at material shop

ALL-DAY ENERGY BOWLS

A nice little collection of slow-release energy boosters that'll sort you out till your next meal, or great for breakfast.

Swiss Apple Oats

No-cook chic energy bowl. Set it up the night before or chuck it all together and give it five minutes.

1. Tip oats into a bowl. Add apple juice. Stir. Leave for a few hours or overnight, for a soft texture. Mix and leave for 5 minutes if you like more bite.
2. Grate apple into mix (work round core) just before eating. Stir in yogurt, lemon, honey if using.

YOU CAN
* smush in any fresh berries – or slap on top with honey and more yogurt
* miss out the yogurt

FEEDS
1   £   V   EXPRESS

50g/2oz organic oats or other
80ml/3fl oz apple juice/water
½–1 apple, unpeeled
3 tbsps vanilla/honey/plain
  yogurt or own yogurt
  (pg 46)
Squeeze lemon juice (optional)
Runny honey (optional)

House Muesli

Bought muesli's expensive and not always what it's cracked up to be so make your own. Great value and lasts ages.

1. Mix ingredients well. Chuck into jar or airtight container.
2. Eat with milk, soy, yogurt, fruit juice. Top with fresh fruit, chopped banana, yogurt.

YOU CAN
* skip Weetabix. Substitute rye, barley – do health-store recce.
* make muesli smoothie. Blitz ½ pint milk/soy milk, 1 banana, 2 tbsps muesli, drizzle of honey. Add berries if you like.
* drop in some chocolate chips, dried coconut

MAKES
1 JAR   £   V   EXPRESS

8 Weetabix, crushed
250g/8oz All-Bran/bran flakes
250g/8oz oats, flaked/crushed
Seeds – pumpkin, sesame,
  poppy, sunflower
Dried fruit – dates, apricots,
  cranberries, raisins, figs
Nuts – cashews, hazelnuts,
  almonds, Brazils
Fresh wheatgerm
Little organic brown sugar
  (optional)

Porridge

It's old style but eat now. Cheap and non-controversial. Oats keep cholesterol down and tick all the health boxes.

FEEDS 1 | £ | V | EXPRESS

50g/2oz porridge oats
300ml/½pint water or milk/
  water mix
Little salt

1. Sit oats and liquid in small pan.
2. Heat to boil, stirring continuously.
3. Reduce heat. Simmer, stirring for 4 minutes, till thick, smooth and creamy. Don't let it burn.
4. Add salt, stir. Serve.

YOU CAN

* swirl top with brown sugar, syrup, honey, milk or cream
* top with blueberries, raspberries, blackberries
* add spiced apple purée. Peel and chop 2 apples. Cook gently in pan with a little water, sprinkle of sugar and cinnamon. Stir till smooth. Can be stored, covered, in fridge for a week.
* grate in a crisp apple, stir till soft. Add lemon juice, honey/maple syrup.

PER PERSON | ££ | V | EXPRESS

Choice of seasonal fruit:

Orange	Peach
Blueberries	Kiwi
Banana	Apple
Melon	Pear
Grapes	Strawberries

Fruit Salad Energy-Booster

No-brainer. Chop what's in your fruit bowl. Fixes your vitamin needs. Get fruit bargains in local markets.

1. Peel. Chop. Slice. Chuck in a bowl with runaway juices.

YOU CAN
* add apple/orange juice, weak elderflower cordial for instant syrup
* slice up a melon if no time for chopping. Light to eat. Heavy on energy.
* chop rhubarb into short lengths. Simmer in a bit of water and sugar till softened. Great breakfast with yogurt.

SWEET STUFF

Cheeky little sweet snacks to take you back in time… Get the DVDs on.

MAKES
8

£

V

8 good sharp eating apples
(Braeburn/Cox/UK garden),
washed, dried well
450g/1lb granulated sugar
3 heaped tbsps golden syrup
150ml/¼ pint cold water

Toffee Apples

A Halloween classic. Get your trick or treat on with these beauties. Make sure you test drive your apples. You want a crisp eater not a floury-textured one.

1. Stick wooden skewers/lolly sticks into apples.
2. Heat sugar, syrup, water in large deep pan on low heat.
3. Stir with wooden spoon to dissolve sugar.
4. Increase heat to boil mix **without stirring** till syrup's a deep reddish brown liquid caramel (or 170°C/340°F on a sugar thermometer). This can take up to 10 minutes. Remove immediately.
5. Dunk apples in toffee. Swirl to coat evenly. Don't burn yourself. Cool, apple end down, on buttered greaseproof/baking paper.

YOU CAN
* wrap in waxed paper/jam cover sealed with elastic band
* store outside fridge for a few days
* dunk apples on sticks into melted chocolate (pg 11)

Speedy Chocolate Fruit & Nut

Basically melted milk chocolate with a bit of muesli chucked in. Use the best ingredients you can get your hands on – just break a bit off whenever you fancy it.

1. Melt chocolate in bowl over pan of water (pg 11).

2. Remove. Stir in fruit-and-nut muesli.

3. Tip onto greaseproof/baking paper. Leave to set.

YOU CAN

∗ choc-dip fresh fruit. Melt choc. Dip strawberries, cherries, Chinese gooseberries in. Eat immediately or leave to set.

∗ choc-wrap peeled whole satsumas. Melt choc. Dunk to coat. Set. Gorgeous.

∗ freeze halved bananas on sticks. Dunk in melted chocolate. Eat or freeze.

MAKES 1 BAR   ££   V

2 x 100g/4oz bars Divine/organic chocolate, milk or plain

1–2 handfuls House Muesli (pg 48) or quality bought with good grain/nut/fruit/seed/coconut combo

Cinnamon Popcorn

Park a pack of popping corn on the shelf for a delicious, cheap spontaneous snack. Low fat, low cal – without the extras.

1. Cover base of large pan with oil. Cover with corn. Put lid on.

2. Cook corn, shuffling pan as it pops to stop it burning. Hold lid down.

3. Check popped corn for unpopped bits.

4. Stir in sifted sugar, cinnamon, butter. Tip into bowls.

MAKES LOADS   £   V   EXPRESS

Sunflower/groundnut oil
Popping corn
Little sifted icing sugar
Few pinches cinnamon
Little melted butter

Chocolate Hit Popcorn

50g/2oz organic chocolate, broken up
50g/2oz butter
1 tbsp honey
1 quantity cooked popcorn

1. Put chocolate, butter, honey in a bowl. Melt together over pan of water (pg 11).

2. Stir until smooth. Mix into popcorn.

3. Tip onto baking paper. Leave to set.

Sticky Toffee Popcorn

35g/1½oz brown sugar
35g/1½oz butter
1 tablespoon golden syrup
1 quantity cooked popcorn

1. Tip sugar, butter, syrup into pan.

2. Gently heat to melt. Boil for 1–2 minutes.

3. Stir toffee coating into popcorn.

DRINKS

Hot, cold, healthy, happy hour. Brew or mix up the best drinks to go with your food/life. NB: drink loads of water but don't get ripped off by the bottled stuff.

PROPER TEAS, HERB TEAS, HOT & ICED COFFEES AND CHOCOLATES

The Perfect Cuppa

Fresh water
1 heaped tsp top tea leaves or teabag per person
Milk/soy milk
Lemon (optional)
Sugar (optional)

1. Boil kettle of freshly-drawn water (oxygen helps flavour).
2. Pour a bit into teapot to warm it. Swish round. Empty it.
3. Put 1 heaped tsp of leaves/1 teabag in pot for each cup to be made. Fill with just-boiled water. Stir. Put lid on.
4. Leave 3–4 minutes for teas like Assam, English Breakfast. Scented teas (Darjeeling/Earl Grey) want 2–3 minutes.
5. Pour a little milk into each cup. Add tea. Or fill cup with tea and add slice of lemon. Tea in a mug? Add milk later. Sugar if you like.

Jug of Yorkshire Iced Tea

4 Yorkshire Gold teabags or other
2 pints boiling water
Bit of fresh mint
Sugar to taste
Juice 4 large oranges
Juice 1 lemon

Slices apple/orange/cucumber
Ice cubes

1. Drop teabags into pot/heatproof bowl. Add 2 pints boiling water, mint, sugar.
2. Leave 15 minutes. Remove teabags. Chill.
3. Add fruit juice. Tip into jug (or straight into mugs/glasses) with ice, sliced fruit, mint.

Hot Mint Tea for 1–2

Boiling water
4–6 sprigs fresh mint
Sugar to taste

1. Stick mint in pot or mugs.
2. Pour boiling water over.
3. Leave to infuse for 5 minutes.
4. Add sugar.

Hot Ginger Tea – Hangover/Detox/Bad-Cold Special for 1

5cm/2in piece fresh ginger
Juice 1 lemon
Honey to taste or pinch of sugar
Boiling water

1. Peel and chop ginger. Put it in a mug. Cover with boiling water. Leave to infuse for 4 minutes.
2. Add lemon juice, honey or sugar. Sip slowly.

Hot Spicy Apple Tea

3 tbsps concentrated apple juice (from health-food shop)
600ml/1 pint water
1 cinnamon stick

1. Boil apple juice, water, cinnamon in pan. Cover. Simmer on very low heat for 10 minutes.
2. Strain through sieve. Pour into mugs.

YOU CAN
* lemon it up – add a bit of lemon, cloves
* ginger it up – add a bit of peeled ginger

A Proper Cup of Coffee for 1–2

Ground coffee (for jug or cafetière) or grind own beans

1. Boil kettle. Tip water into jug/cafetière to warm it. Swish round. Tip out. Measure coffee in.
2. **Jug:** fill with water just off the boil. Stir. Leave 3–4 minutes covered with teacloth. Pour into cups/mugs through strainer.
3. **Cafetière:** fill three-quarters full with water just off the boil. Stir. Leave for 3–4 minutes. Push plunger down slowly.
4. Drink black or with warm or cold milk. Sweeten with sugar if you like.

YOU CAN

* keep beans/grounds in freezer
* dig used grounds into garden/ allotment to enrich soil and boost veggie growth

Iced Coffee for 2

2 cups strong black coffee
Some vanilla ice-cream, or mix of vanilla and chocolate
Ice cubes
A little cold milk
Pinch of sugar

Tip everything into a blender/jug. Blend or handblend.

Hot Chocolate Treat for 2

110g/4oz 70% cocoa-solids chocolate (I use half dark, half Divine milk)
425ml/15fl oz any milk

1. Melt chocolate in bowl over pan (pg 11).
2. Get milk to boiling point (bubbling) in another.
3. Remove both from heat. Tip a bit of hot milk into melted choc. Stir till smooth. Whisk rest in till frothy.

YOU CAN

* top with marshmallows
* make speedy choc for 1. Mix water with milk. Heat. Add chunks of favourite chocolate. Stir to melt. Froth it.

Chocolate Milk Shake (Power Drink) for 1

A few chunks good dark chocolate
250ml/9fl oz cold milk

2 scoops best chocolate ice-cream, or 1 choc and 1 vanilla

Melt chocolate (pg 11). Tip into blender/jug with milk, ice-cream. Blend or handblend.

YOU CAN

* use 1 tbsp drinking choc in place of the solid stuff
* add 2 tbsps strong black coffee for mocha shake

SPORTS DRINKS, JUICES, SMOOTHIES

Isotonic Sports Drink for 1

DRINK ONE
500ml/18fl oz unsweetened fruit juice
500ml/18fl oz water
⅕ tsp salt

Mix together.

DRINK TWO
50g/2oz sugar/glucose
1 litre/1¾ pints water
⅕ tsp salt

Warm a bit of water. Dissolve salt and sugar/glucose in it. Add rest of water.

Real Lemonade for 2–3

250g/9 oz sugar
500ml/18fl oz water
8–10 lemons
Ice cubes

1. Tip sugar and water into a pan. Boil. Reduce heat. Stir till sugar dissolves.
2. Squeeze juice from lemons.
3. Add to water. Chill till needed.
4. Pour over ice cubes.

YOU CAN

* use oranges and limes
* freeze grapes on baking tray to use as edible ice cubes

Immune-Boost OJ for 1

3–4 oranges, halved
Water
Ice (in summer)

Squeeze halved oranges on citrus press or with hand. Dilute the juice with water. Add optional ice.

YOU CAN
✱ add a bit of vodka/gin, dash of grenadine for OJ cocktail
✱ use straw while drinking, to protect teeth from acid

Carrot, Apple, Ginger Hangover Special for 2

4 carrots
4 apples
2.5cm/1in piece fresh ginger, peeled

Wash and chop fruit. Push through juicer, followed by the ginger. Drink immediately.

OJ Berry Vitamin Boost for 2–3

2 bananas, sliced, frozen
225ml/8oz orange juice
2–3 handfuls strawberries

1. Tip frozen banana slices into blender/tall plastic jug.
2. Add orange juice, strawberries. Blitz in blender or with handblender. Thin with water if needed.

Summerfruit Slushie for 2

1 peach/nectarine
1 banana
Handful strawberries/raspberries

Runny honey
125ml/4fl oz apple/orange juice
Little lemon or lime juice (optional)

1. Slice fruit. Freeze on baking paper on tin.
2. Tip into blender or plastic jug. Blitz with honey and fruit juice. Taste. Add lemon/lime juice.

Brain Boost Smoothie for 1

Handful raspberries
Handful blueberries
1 banana
2 scoops vanilla ice-cream, or 2 tbsps vanilla yogurt
100ml/4fl oz milk

Blitz everything with blender.

Wake-up Smoothie for 1

1–2 bananas
Good handful strawberries
Runny honey
225g/8oz milk/soy milk
Bit of natural or vanilla yogurt (optional)

1. Slice bananas. Chop strawberries if large.
2. Add honey, milk, optional yogurt. Blitz it.

YOU CAN
✱ blitz in 2 tbsps muesli. Add more liquid.

Anyberry Frozen Smoothie for 1

2–3 handfuls any frozen berries
150ml/5fl oz yogurt
Milk/soy milk

Blitz frozen berries, yogurt, milk or soy milk in blender or with handblender till as you like it.

Mango Lassi for 2

1 ripe mango, peeled
100ml/3½fl oz milk
150ml/5oz natural yogurt
2–3 teaspoons runny honey or caster sugar
Pinch of salt
Water if needed

1. Slice mango or chop small.
2. Slap into blender or jug with remaining ingredients. Blitz till smooth.
3. Thin with water if you need to.

YOU CAN
✱ smoothie this up with banana and raspberry

HAPPY HOUR

Sangria

1 bottle good red wine
1 bottle lemonade
Juice 1 fresh orange
1 level tbsp caster sugar
1–2 oranges and lemons,
 sliced/chopped
Shot of vodka or Grand Marnier
 (optional)

1. Tip all liquids into jug.
2. Add sugar, fruit and ice.
3. Serve with wooden spoon for squashing/controlling fruit.
Drink with: tapas (pg 22)

Buck's Fizz

1 bottle, half-bottle or miniature
 champagne, Prosecco or good
sparkling white wine, chilled
Oranges or best orange juice
Ice (optional)

1. Squeeze oranges.
2. Pour juice into the bottom quarter of each glass.
3. Top with champagne/sparkling wine. Or mix in a jug and serve.
Drink with: a special breakfast (Maybe bagels with cream cheese and smoked salmon. Or scrambled/poached eggs. Or pancakes and crisp bacon.)

Bloody Mary for 1

200ml/7fl oz tomato juice
Double shot vodka
3 drops Tabasco sauce
½ tsp Worcestershire sauce
Juice 1 lime or ½ lemon, or 1 tsp
 lime cordial
Pinch celery salt (or salt)
A little black pepper
Ice cubes
Celery stick for stirring
 (optional)

1. Stir or shake everything except ice and celery.
2. Pour mix over ice. Add celery. For a Virgin Mary: up the tomato juice, skip the vodka.
Drink with: Sunday brunch

Pimm's

Lemonade (or mix of lemonade
 and ginger beer)
Pimm's
Ice
Cucumber
Apple
Strawberries
Mint leaves

1. Get a jug. Mix two parts lemonade to one part Pimm's.
2. Add ice, fruit, mint. Stir.
Drink with: cucumber sandwiches (pg 38).

Mulled Wine

1 bottle red wine (Cabernet
 Sauvignon suits)
75–110g/3–4oz sugar or 3 tbsps
 honey
8 cloves
1 orange and 1 lemon
1 cinnamon stick
Pinch ground ginger
Bayleaf (optional)

1. Put sugar, wine into large saucepan/casserole dish.
2. Stick cloves in fruit. Add to liquid with cinnamon, ginger, optional bayleaf.
3. Heat. Simmer gently, stirring to dissolve sugar. Keep hot 15 minutes without boiling.
Drink with: mince pies

EGGS

Eggs and crêpes – the original fast food. Get free range when you can. They're a bit more expensive but taste, cook and are better. Good for you and for the chickens.

FEEDS **1** · £ · V · EXPRESS

Soft-Boiled Eggs with Sprinkles & Dippers

Keep it simple or serve with extras.

1–2 large eggs at room temperature
Salt and black pepper
Sprinkles
Herbs, chopped
Cheese, grated
Black olives, chopped
Cherry tomatoes, chopped
Veg dippers
2–4 lengths asparagus or tenderstem broccoli
Dippers
Toast soldiers
Butter/Marmite/Vegemite

1. Prepare sprinkles if using. Boil asparagus/broccoli dippers for 2 minutes or till just soft. Drain. Keep warm.

2. Boil a small pan of water (enough to cover eggs). Add pinch of salt.

3. Lower eggs in on a spoon. When water re-boils, set timer.

4. Cook approx 4 minutes (soft-boiled), 5 (medium), or 6 (if straight from fridge). Reduce time for small eggs. Make toast.

5. Sit eggs in cups. Slice across with knife, or crack and scoop tops off. Dip asparagus/broccoli/toast soldiers into yolk, and/or sprinkle extras.

Scrambled Eggs

Classic fast food anytime – packed with protein, essential vitamins and minerals.

2 large eggs
Salt and black pepper
Knob of butter

1. Crack eggs into a bowl. Beat well with a fork. Season.

2. Tip butter and eggs into a cold pan. Sit over a very low heat.

3. For creamy eggs: stir constantly with a wooden spoon till done as you like. Get onto plate at once as they keep cooking. **For more textured eggs:** stir, leave a few seconds to shape, stir again, leave again, repeating for a shapely scramble. Eat on toast, muffin, bagel.

YOU CAN

✳ add Tabasco/Worcester sauce at step 2

✳ add 2 tbsps milk at step 1

✳ stir in splash of water and grated Cheddar just as eggs set

✳ make blow-out scramble: at step 3 stir in 1 tsp Dijon mustard, 1–2 tbsps grated Gruyère/Cheddar, dash cream/mayo, fine herbs/chopped spring-onion tops

✳ stir in blow-out extras at step 3: crisp bacon/pancetta, crumbled chorizo sausage, diced and fried tarragon/parsley/basil, chopped smoked salmon, diced

✳ top with cooked asparagus/ tenderstem broccoli, roasted vine tomatoes

Hard-Boiled Eggs

Sort these for breakfasts, picnics, curries, salads.

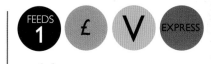

1–2 eggs

1. Heat water to boiling as for soft-boiled. Lower eggs into pan. Set timer for 8 minutes.

2. Remove eggs with spoon. Immediately lower into large bowl of very cold water. When cold, crack the round end to break air pocket.

3. Holding under cold running water, peel shell off neatly.

YOU CAN

✳ get a retro egg-slicer and make '50s-style egg salad with lettuce, tomato, bread and butter (ham if you like)

✳ stuff eggs: cut in half, spoon out yolk, mash yolks with mayo and seasoning, stuff or pipe back into halved whites. Can also add a little curry powder, bit of mashed tuna.

FEEDS 1 · £ · V · EXPRESS

Pinch salt
1 large egg
Buttered toast
Salt and black pepper

Poached Egg Heroes

A top meal 24/7. Trim the edge with scissors if you like.

1. Two-thirds fill a small saucepan/frying pan with water. Add salt. Bring to a gentle boil. Reduce heat.

2. Crack egg into cup. Stir boiling water fast, creating whirlpool. Tip egg neatly into the whirlpool to shape it. Simmer 3–4 minutes.

3. Lift out carefully with a slotted spoon/fishslice once white is set, yolk still runny. Allow the water to drip off. Sit it on toast. Season.

YOU CAN
* substitute as the healthier option in full English breakfast
* slap on a bowl of Cheese & Onion Mash (pg 215) for a low-cost eat
* stick on Rosti (pg 214) or toasted muffins
* sit on a salad with crisp bacon and hot potatoes
* make Eggs Florentine. Spread cooked spinach in a buttered dish. Add 2 poached eggs. Sprinkle with cheese. Stick under grill. Or bake covered in cheese sauce (pg 90) till done and bubbling.

FEEDS 1 · £ · EXPRESS

Bit of butter
2 thin slices good ham
2 large eggs
Salt and black pepper

Fried Eggs & Ham

Tasty alternative to eggs 'n' bacon.

1. Melt butter over low heat in a frying pan.
2. Slide ham in. Turn after a minute.
3. Crack eggs in. Cook gently 1–2 minutes, kicking butter onto yolks with spatula. Eat with chutney, ketchup, coffee.

YOU CAN
* add a few thick slices tomato, mushroom
* team with Rosti (pg 214) or Frying Pan Crunchy Potatoes (pg 214)

Swiss Baked Eggs & Soldiers

Make a very fine tea or a special breakfast.

FEEDS 2 · **££** · **V** · **EXPRESS**

1. Preheat oven to 180°C/350°F/gas 4. Boil kettle.
2. Grease 4 ramekins/cups (approx 7.5cm/2¾in).
3. Spoon a little cream into each one. Crack an egg in. Season. Add more cream. Leave a bit of each yolk visible.
4. Sit ramekins in small roasting tin/dish with boiling water poured in to reach half way up sides. Bake 8–10 minutes till whites are set, yolks still a bit runny (prod one to test). Remove.
5. Sprinkle tops with cheese. Sit on a baking tray. Slip under preheated grill until tops are bubbling. Dip toast fingers in there.

YOU CAN

✱ add extras at step 3, e.g. diced cooked ham/gammon, chorizo, mushroom, pepper, finely chopped tarragon, chives, basil

Butter for greasing
4 tbsps cream, or milk
4 large eggs
Salt and black pepper
50–75g/2–3oz grated Gruyère, Parmesan/Cheddar
4 slices wholemeal toast, buttered, cut into fingers

61

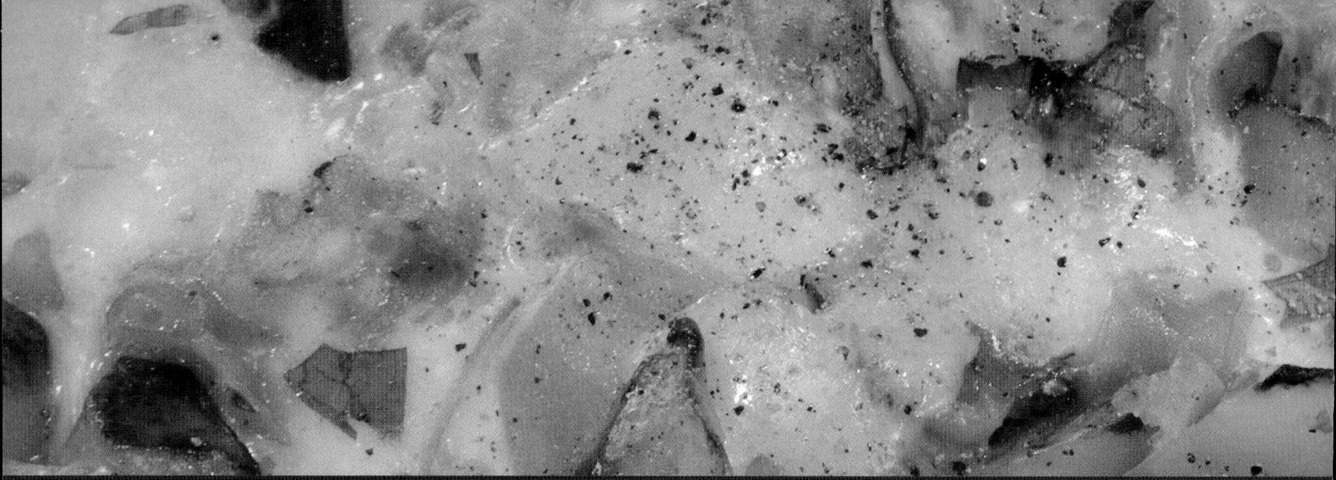

OMELETTES

The mark of a good chef is how good and fast their omelette is.
My record's 50 seconds. Beat it. Get creative with fillings.

FEEDS
1   £   **V**   EXPRESS

2 large eggs
2 tsps water
20g/¾oz butter
Salt and black pepper
Choice of filling

2 Hot Fast Omelettes

Team with warm bread, salads, fried spuds, deli meats or eat cold to-go in a salad box or sarnie.

1. Beat first egg in a bowl with 1 tsp water, salt, pepper.
2. Melt half the butter over a low heat in a 15cm/6in frying pan.
3. Add the egg. Swirl to cover base of pan. Allow it to set (not fry). Tilt the pan once or twice, holding the set edge back with a spatula/fishslice so the runny bit cooks.
4. Remove omelette while soft, only just set. Sprinkle half with choice of filling. Flip other half over. Repeat with second egg and filling.

YOU CAN
✻ fill with bit of grated Cheddar or Gruyère/cooked spinach/cream cheese, garlic and herbs/runny honey and lemon/diced fried chorizo with bit of tomato sauce/few prawns in mayo/skinned diced tomato with basil, dressing/pesto
✻ slap warm or cold into ciabatta/baguette with salad, chutney or dressing as food-to-go
✻ make loads, and serve up cold with various fillings for cheap simple party snacks
✻ add finely chopped herb of choice at step 1
✻ make in flat-based wok if no small frying pan

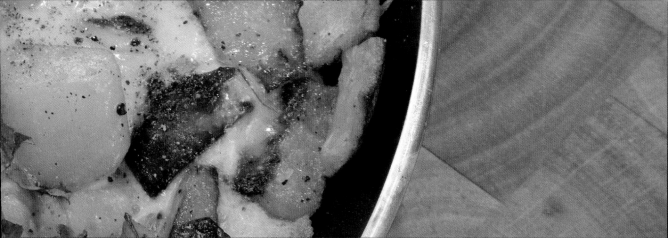

Ham & Potato Frittata

Basically a big fat omelette. A great stomach liner before a heavy night out or a tasty late breakfast. Go wild with filling combos. Eat hot, warm or cold later.

FEEDS
2
£

350g/12oz potatoes, waxy preferably (Charlotte, Pink Fir, Vivaldi) but any will do, peeled
1 tbsp olive oil
Butter
5 eggs, beaten
Few fresh herbs
Little salt and black pepper
4–6 slices ham or own gammon (page 133), chopped
Gruyère or Cheddar cheese, sliced

1. Chop potatoes into bite-size bits. Dry well. Fry in oil and bit of butter in 20.5–25.5cm/8–10in pan for 5 minutes. Reduce heat.
2. Cover pan. Cook for 10 minutes or till soft. Shake and stir occasionally to stop them sticking.
4. Beat the eggs, salt, pepper, herbs, bit of butter. Add ham. Pour into pan.
5. Cook slowly till set. **Either:** lay cheese on top. Flash under grill.
Or: slide out onto large plate. Invert. Return to pan. Cook other side. Don't overcook (it goes leathery). Great with tomato and onion salad (pg 210).

YOU CAN
* add a bit of rocket, spinach, sun-dried tomato
* beat a bit of cream cheese in with eggs
* layer in mushrooms/griddled veg with or instead of ham
* use cold left-over potatoes, butternut squash or leftover pasta
* really skint? Soak 1 thick slice crustless bread in 3 tbsps milk for 10 minutes. Squeeze dry. Beat in 3 eggs, season, add herbs and cheese. Fry. Delicious hot or cold.

110g/4oz plain flour
Pinch salt
1 large egg
300ml/½ pint milk
Splash of water
1 tbsp sunflower oil or melted butter
Butter for frying

Eat with: sugar and lemon juice ✱ maple syrup and orange juice ✱ chocolate sauce, melted jam, Nutella ✱ sliced banana, ice-cream and Butterscotch Sauce (pg 243)

Sweet Skint Crêpes

Tick all the boxes. Make the mix the night before if you want and stir before using. Get your crêpes well thin. The first one usually sticks. Just scrape it out and start over.

1. Sift flour and salt into a bowl. Make a hollow in it.

2. Crack the egg into the hollow. Add a good glug of milk.

3. Start beating hard using a balloon whisk or wooden spoon. Add the rest of the milk slowly, beating continually to get a smooth batter. Stir in the water and oil/melted butter.

4. Get a crêpe or frying pan well hot. Add a little butter. Swirl the pan so it spreads or brush it round for even coverage.

5. Pour or spoon in 2–3 tbsps batter. Swirl the pan again to make a big thin crêpe. Cook for 1 min or till it sets. Toss or turn with a spatula. Cook other side.

YOU CAN
✱ stack pancakes between greaseproof, keep warm till serving
✱ leave mix for 30 mins for lighter batter
✱ roll up, fold in half or quarters, or leave open
✱ sub a bit of cocoa into pancake mix for choc ones
✱ freeze crêpes

Quick Stuffed Crêpes

Sort out a more substantial meal with a richer batter. Fill with savoury bits (get creative) and bake in the oven.

1. Prep crêpes as basic method, see left. Add poppy seeds at step 3. Fry crêpes. Stack between bits of greaseproof paper.

2. Preheat oven to 220°C/425°F/gas 7. Lay crêpes out. Pile filling of choice into one corner. Try these:

Ham & Cheese: spread with mango chutney. Top with sliced ham, grated cheese.

Cheese & Spinach: cook spinach 3 mins in pan with ½ tbsp water. Drain. Mix with crushed garlic, low fat crème fraîche, grated Cheddar.

3. Fold in half. Repeat to make a triangle. Sit on a greased baking tray. Cook for 10 minutes or till hot and bubbling.

YOU CAN

✱ stuff with creamy mushrooms (pg 45) or ragu (pg 180). Slap in a dish. Top with cheese/tomato sauce. Bake for longer.

MAKES **8** | **££** | **V** OPTION | EXPRESS

175g/6oz plain flour
Pinch salt
2 eggs plus 1 yolk
425ml/¾ pint milk
2 tsps butter, melted
2 tsps poppy seeds

Ham & Cheese filling
Mango chutney
Ham, sliced
Cheese, grated

Cheese & Spinach filling
Spinach
Clove garlic, crushed
Low fat crème fraîche
Cheddar, grated

US Stacking Pancakes with Syrup & Bacon

Light and fluffy with a golden finish. Stack and style any way you want. Someone special over for breakfast? Delicious.

1. Separate eggs (pg 11). Beat yolks, milk, butter with a fork.

2. Sift flour, sugar, salt, baking powder into a separate bowl.

3. Add milk mix v. slowly to dry ingredients with a wooden spoon/balloon whisk for a smooth batter. Put bacon under grill.

4. Whisk egg whites till stiff. Fold gently into the batter (pg 10).

5. Brush a heated frying pan with melted butter. Drop individual tablespoons of batter in, leaving room between. Cook till the bottoms brown, bubbles show (1–2 mins). Turn. Cook till golden, puffy. Stack and top with bacon, berries, drizzle syrup and lemon.

YOU CAN

✱ skip bacon. Eat with jam and butter or smoked salmon and sour cream.

FEEDS **4** | **£** | **V** OPTION | EXPRESS

2 large eggs
150ml/½ pint milk
50g/2oz melted butter
110g/4oz plain flour
10g/½ oz caster sugar
Pinch salt
2 tsps baking powder
Extra melted butter

Stacking
Crispy grilled streaky bacon (optional)
Fresh berries
Maple/golden syrup
Lemon juice

SOUP

Grab a bowl full of gorgeousness. Soup's the ultimate comfort food. Go for hearty whole meal-in-one soups or fast-track snack soups. Slap in leftover veg to make them go further.

£ · V OPTION

Homestyle Stock (Meat & Veggie)

The real deal. Recycle a roast chicken for a great stock base for soups. Follow the formula without meat, just many more veg, herbs and seasoning for a veggie version. Easy, tasty, nutritious. Worth getting a big pan – use it for cooking pasta.

1 roast chicken carcass
2 onions, quartered
1 celery stick, chopped
1 carrot
1 leek, sliced (optional)
Few fresh herbs (optional)
2 garlic cloves, peeled
2.5 litres/4½ pints water

1. Chuck chicken bits, bones plus any gravy, jelly etc. into a large pan, breaking the carcass up if you need to. Discard any stuffing (it clouds the stock) except for lemons.

2. Add the washed veg, herbs, garlic. You don't need to peel them.

3. Add water to cover. Bring to the boil. Skim off any froth. Reduce heat. Simmer on a low heat for about 2 hours.

4. Strain everything through a colander/sieve into a bowl. Discard the carcass, veg.

5. To store stock, chill covered with clingfilm or freeze some for soup emergencies.

YOU CAN
* use as a base for risottos, stews, sauces, pies, gravy
* make from fresh with a chicken portion, less water
* peel any cooked chicken meat off carcass and reboil in stock for instant soup

Watercress Soup & Treacle Bread Fingers

Ridiculously healthy. Watercress has vitamins, folate, iron, but don't let that put you off. Team this light and gorgeous soup with toasted buttery Treacle Bread (pg 266) for a top taste combo. Note: a strategic eat at exam time.

1. Roughly chop watercress. Melt butter on low heat. Cook onions, leek, garlic very gently for 5–10 minutes till soft, not coloured. Stir sometimes.

2. Stir in potatoes. Cover pan. Cook very gently for 4 minutes.

3. Stir in half watercress. Cook 1 minute. Add stock, seasoning. Bring to the boil. Reduce heat. Simmer very gently for 15 minutes.

4. Stir in remaining cress. Simmer 5 minutes. Add cheese, lemon, mustard.

5. Blitz with handblender. Taste. Add optional crème fraîche.

6. Toast bread. Butter it. Cut into fingers. Eat neatly or dunk it.

FEEDS **4** £ **V** OPTION

225g/8oz young watercress
40g/1½oz butter
1 onion, chopped
1 leek, thinly sliced
2 cloves garlic, crushed
1 medium potato, peeled, diced small
900ml/1½ pints chicken/ vegetable/Marigold stock or water
Salt and black pepper
50g/2oz Cheddar/Stilton/ Parmesan/Lancashire cheese, crumbled or grated
1 tbsp lemon juice
2 tsps mustard
3 tbsps low fat crème fraîche or milk (optional)
4 slices Treacle Bread (pg 266)

My-Style Pot Noodle

Why buy it when you can make it better? Sort out this cheap and easy, healthy pot noodle…

1. Put noodles in a pan. Cover with cold water (or boiled from a kettle). Boil. Cook for 4 mins. Drain into a colander.

2. Heat up own ready-made stock in the pan. When really hot, add noodles, veg and optional chilli. Let the green stuff wilt a bit.

3. Tip into a bowl. Go eat it…

YOU CAN

✱ add sliced garlic, ginger, herbs, beansprouts

✱ add bits of cold cooked roast chicken/diced tofu. Heat well.

✱ use pre-cooked noodles (but it's more expensive)

✱ cheat. Use Knorr stock cube/Marigold stock made with water.

✱ chuck cooked noodles/leaves into organic miso soup

FEEDS **1** £ **V** OPTION EXPRESS

1 nest dry egg or pre-cooked noodles
1 bowl chicken or vegetable stock
2 spring onions, sliced
Green stuff (spinach, finely shredded pak choi/cabbage/ mangetout, optional)
Little chilli, deseeded and finely chopped (optional)

£ · V OPTION · FEEDS 4

3 tbsps butter
4–5 large brown-skin onions,
    peeled, thinly sliced into rings
2–3 cloves garlic, crushed
2 tsps sugar
300ml/½ pint white
    wine/cider/apple juice
1.8 litres/3 pints chicken/
    vegetable stock or water
Salt and black pepper

Croûtons
6 slices baguette/rough bread
110g/4oz Gruyère or Cheddar,
    grated

Classic French Onion Soup & Cheese Croûtons

A cheeky French classic that's packed with goodness (onions are high in vitamin C, folate, fibre, iron, calcium). Don't be tempted to rush the first cooking – onions need to caramelize slowly for fuller flavour. Made at a weekend, it keeps the week going.

1. Melt butter in big-ish pan. Add onion and garlic. Cover pan. Cook very gently on very low heat for 15 minutes. Stir occasionally.
2. Add sugar. Cook gently for a further 30 minutes till onion is reduced, soft and brown. Don't let it burn. Stir occasionally.
3. Increase heat. Whack in wine/cider/apple juice. Boil for 2 minutes. Add stock and seasoning. Boil again.
4. Reduce heat. Cover pan. Simmer gently for 20 minutes or so. Taste.
5. Toast baguette or bake in hot oven. Top it with grated cheese. Grill. Ladle soup into bowls. Get cheesy toasts on there…

Mushroom, Rosemary & Garlic

FEEDS 4   £   **V** OPTION

As soon as the garlicky herb base starts cooking you'll find everyone comes running. Smells and tastes delicious. Note: wipe mushrooms, there's no need to wash them.

1. Gently cook shallots/onion, garlic and a pinch of salt in oil and butter for 2 minutes, till soft, not coloured.

2. Chop or tear mushrooms. Stir into pan with rosemary. Cook very gently, covered, for 10 minutes.

3. Add bread, stock, nutmeg. Boil. Reduce heat. Cover. Simmer gently for 10 minutes (it looks disgusting but it's OK). Season.

4. Blitz with handblender till smooth. Add milk. Re-heat gently. Taste. Serve with warm buttered toast cut into fingers.

YOU CAN

✱ make giant cheese straws to eat with this. Lay sheet of defrosted butter puff pastry on board. Brush with beaten egg/milk. Cut into 1.5cm/½in strips. Holding each end, twist strip in opposite ways. Lay on baking tray. Sprinkle with grated cheese, sesame/poppy seeds or brush with pesto. Bake for 10 minutes at 220°C/425°F/gas 7.

3 shallots or 1 small onion, finely chopped
2 cloves garlic, crushed
50g/2oz butter
Drizzle sunflower or veg oil
350g/12oz flat mushrooms
Few rosemary leaves, chopped
2 slices crustless white bread, torn
1–1.5 litres/1½–2 pints chicken/veg stock or water
Grated nutmeg (optional)
Salt and black pepper
150ml/¼ pint milk

Mulligatawny

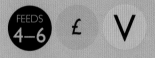

FEEDS 4–6   £   **V**

All the benefits of a curry night out in one bowl. As it cooks up, bang out a batch of impressive chappatis (pg 196).

1. Cook onion, salt in oil/butter over gentle heat for 3 minutes.

2. Add garlic, ginger, curry paste. Stir well. Cook for 6 minutes.

3. Add lentils. Stir in tomatoes, courgettes, potato. Reduce heat. Cover. Simmer very gently for 15 minutes.

4. Add stock, chutney, bit of coriander. Cover. Cook for 10–15 minutes. Adjust taste with lemon juice or chutney.

5. Blend in the pan with a handblender. Add water if it's too thick.

1 tbsp butter or groundnut oil
1 large onion, finely chopped
Pinch salt
2–3 cloves garlic, crushed
2.5cm/1in ginger, grated
2 tsps korma or other good curry paste
50g/2oz red lentils, rinsed
1x 400g/14oz can chopped tomatoes
450g/1lb courgettes, chopped
1 large sweet potato, peeled, chopped
1.2 litres/2 pints vegetable stock/water or 1 tsp Marigold stock in water
1–2 tsps mango chutney
Fresh coriander (optional)
Squeeze lemon juice

Knob of butter/bit of oil
1 large onion, finely chopped
Pinch salt
1 clove garlic, crushed
1 leek, sliced
2 potatoes, diced
3 carrots, diced
1 celery stick, sliced
Few sprigs fresh herbs (parsley, tarragon, sage, rosemary)
1.5 litres/2½ pints chicken stock
Lemon juice
Salt and black pepper

Blistering Chicken Soup

Not just a tasty meal in one, this low cal soup's the original comfort food. Also helps shift colds, hangovers. For fullest flavour, sweat the veg slowly till they're well soft. Customize till it's just as you want it…

1. Heat butter and oil in a large pan. Add onion and salt. Cook for 5 minutes over a very low heat without letting it colour.
2. Add garlic, other veg, herbs. Stir. Place a bit of butter/greaseproof paper on top. Cover pan with a lid. Sweat very gently for 10 minutes.
3. Add stock. Boil. Reduce heat. Simmer gently for 20–30 minutes. Taste. Add lemon. Adjust seasoning. Eat with good bread.

YOU CAN
✱ add in rice or pasta 10–15 minutes before soup is done
✱ add diced bacon at step 2. Then add 1 can chopped tomatoes, tomato puree, pinch sugar at step 3. Sprinkle with Parmesan. Eat with garlic bread.

FEEDS
2–3
££
EXPRESS

850ml/1½ pints chicken stock (homemade or Knorr)
7.5cm/3in ginger, peeled, thinly sliced
2 cloves garlic, crushed
2 red chillies, de-seeded, finely chopped
1 tsp lemon grass purée or 1 stalk, crushed, finely sliced
4 dried lime leaves, crumbled
110g/4oz white mushrooms
225ml/8oz coconut milk
2 tbsps Thai fish sauce
1 tsp sugar
225g/8oz skinless chicken breast, cut into small slivers
Juice of 2 limes or 1 lemon
Fresh coriander, chopped

Delicious Thai Chilli Chicken

Bored by the prospect of that same old griddled chicken breast? Don't be. Mix it up a bit. Transform it into this sensational Thai-style soup. It's bright, light and gorgeous.

1. Bring stock to boil in a pan with ginger, garlic, chillies, lemon grass, lime leaves.
2. Cover. Simmer on a reduced heat for 10 minutes.
3. Finely chop the mushrooms. Add to the pan with coconut milk, fish sauce, sugar. Return to the boil. Add the chicken. Cook on high heat for 2 minutes till white all through but still tender. Add lime or lemon juice.
4. Taste. Adjust seasoning. Bang into bowls. Scatter with coriander.

Chicken Ramen

FEEDS
4   ££

I'm slightly obsessed with this soup. So's everyone I've ever made it for. It's a Japanese-style whole meal. Think relaxing noodles, tasty broth, flavoursome meat, chilli finishing sauce.

1. Heat stock in a pan with garlic and ginger for 20–30 minutes over a low heat to get it well flavoured.

2. Meanwhile, flatten chicken. Thump with a rolling pin or flat of your hand. Slap it on a lightly oiled griddle or pan to cook 4–5 minutes per side or till white all through. Set aside.

3. Mix ingredients for sauce in a small bowl. Set aside.

4. Cook noodles in boiling water for 4 minutes. Drain. Set aside.

5. Finish soup. Add beansprouts and green leaf to flavoured stock. Simmer 1 minute. Sit noodles in bowls. Pour soup in. Top with onions, chilli, coriander, lime, sliced chicken. Drizzle your sauce in. Paradise.

YOU CAN

✱ top with Char Sui Pork (pg 135), griddled steak, prawns or salmon
✱ make veggie ramen: use veggie stock, top with pan fried tofu (pg 199)

850ml/1½ pints chicken stock (homemade or Knorr)
6 cloves garlic, sliced
10cm/4in ginger, sliced
2 chicken fillets
350g/12oz egg noodles
110g/4oz bean sprouts
4–6 spring onions, finely chopped
Bit of pak choi/Chinese leaf, shredded
1–2 red chillies, deseeded, finely sliced
½ red onion, thinly sliced
Fresh coriander
Chunks of lime

Sauce
1 tsp caster sugar
1 tbsp Chinese cooking wine/malt or white wine vinegar
1½ tbsps sweet chilli sauce
2½ tbsps fish sauce

FEEDS
2–3   £   V
                OPTION

450g/1lb floury potatoes
   (e.g. 4 medium-size Maris
   Pipers/King Edwards)
110g/4oz onions
50g/2oz butter
850ml/1½ pints water, mixed
   with ½ tsp Marigold veg
   stock or own veggie/chicken
   stock or water
Few sprigs fresh parsley
3 tbsps milk
Salt and black pepper
2 rashers grilled streaky back
   bacon (optional)

Skint Potato & Onion Soup (with Optional Crumbled Bacon)

Cheaper than chips and doubly impressive given the simple ingredients and subtle results. Use the base as a jumping-off spot for loads of other veg soups. Extra cash? Add toppings.

1. Dice potatoes into very small chunks. Chop onions very finely.
2. Melt butter in a pan. Add onion, salt. Cook, stirring, for 1 minute. Stir in potatoes.
3. Sweat them. Cover with piece of greaseproof paper or butter packet and the lid. Cook very gently for 10 minutes without colouring.
4. Remove paper. Add Marigold mix or stock or water. Bring to the boil. Reduce heat. Simmer very gently for 10 minutes.
5. Add parsley. Blitz with handblender. Stir in milk. Reheat. Season and taste. Adjust. Serve as is or with bits of crumbled bacon.

Everyday Brilliant Tomato Soup

Pull a fast one on your mates with this little beauty. One taste and they'll think you've been slaving for hours. It's made with tinned tomatoes and works with a stock cube.

1. Heat oil in a saucepan. Add onion and garlic. Cook gently for 5 minutes or till soft, not coloured. Tear the bread and add with all the other ingredients. Boil for 1 minute.
2. Reduce heat. Simmer gently for 20 mins. Taste. Adjust seasoning.
3. Blitz in a pan or jug with handblender or leave rough. Reheat gently.
4. Serve topped with extras or plate them up for the table.

YOU CAN

✱ make Bloody Mary soup: stir in a bit of vodka and a shake of Worcestershire sauce

✱ stir in bought or homemade pesto (pg 89)

✱ drop diced cheddar in at the end to boost your protein and calcium

1 tbsp oil
1 medium onion, finely chopped
1 clove garlic, crushed
1 x 400g/14oz can tomatoes
600ml/1 pint vegetable stock (own or mix ½ tsp Marigold stock in boiling water)
1 tbsp tomato purée
35g/1½ oz crustless bread
Fresh basil leaves or pinch dried oregano
Salt and black pepper

Optional toppings
Finely diced red pepper, cucumber, hard-boiled egg, fried bread, torn basil

1 big tomato
1 stick celery, thinly sliced
1 carrot, diced small
2 potatoes, diced small
2 tbsps olive oil
3 fat cloves garlic
1 shallot or chunk of onion
Tiny pinch chilli flakes
1.2 litres/2 pints chicken/
   Marigold vegetable stock
Handful random pasta bits
   (e.g. spaghetti, tagliatelle,
   macaroni, penne, broken
   lasagne)
1 x 400g/14oz can cannellini
   beans
Squeeze or two lemon juice
Black pepper
Fresh parsley
Freshly grated Parmesan/
   Cheddar

End-of-Term Pasta & Bean Soup

A great cupboard-clearer. Whack in those bits of broken pasta lurking at the bottom of the pack. Light, yet filling soup. Windowsill herbs keep the cost down.

1. To skin the tomato: nick it with a knife, sit it in a bowl, cover with boiling water, leave 1–2 minutes, drain – and peel skin. Cut in half. Remove and discard seeds. Chop flesh.

2. Prep vegetables, cutting into very small dice.

3. Heat oil in a pan. Fry garlic and shallot very gently till soft, not coloured. Stir in celery, carrot, potatoes, tomato flesh, chilli flakes. Add the stock. Simmer for 10 minutes.

4. Add random pasta and beans. Simmer till just soft. Add lemon, seasoning, herbs. Taste. Serve with grated cheese and Garlic Bread (pg 206).

YOU CAN
∗ use haricot or butter beans
∗ use dried beans to save money (see pg 7)

Spanish-Style Chorizo & Potato Complete Meal Deal

Don't be thinking soup can't fill you up. This bad-boy bowlful's a complete meal deal. Spicy chorizo gets it hot and kicking. Potato and veg sort out layers of flavour...

1. Gently fry the chorizo in a bit of oil in a medium saucepan for 2–3 minutes. Remove the chorizo and set aside.

2. Add the onion, garlic, salt to the same pan. Cook gently for 5–10 minutes till soft, not coloured. Add the potatoes with enough water to cover without swamping. Increase the heat. Boil for 30 seconds.

3. Reduce heat. Simmer everything very gently for 10 minutes.

4. Slap in cabbage, chorizo, drained tomatoes with just enough extra water to cover everything. Simmer very gently on low heat for 15 minutes, till potatoes are well soft and broth fully flavoured.

5. Add a bit of water if needed. Taste. Adjust seasoning.

YOU CAN
* add a few cannellini beans, chickpeas
* drizzle with a bit of olive oil
* add a pinch of smoked paprika and chopped parsley

FEEDS
3–4   ££

110g/4oz chorizo sausage,
  skinned, sliced
Drizzle of olive oil
1 large onion, finely chopped
2–3 cloves garlic, crushed
2 large floury old potatoes,
  peeled, cut into large
  bite-size bits
Water
4–5 cabbage leaves, finely
  shredded
1 x 400g/14oz can plum
  tomatoes, drained
Salt and black pepper

PASTA
& PIZZA

Turn your student staples into something glorious.
Pasta's cheap, easy and these bad boy sauces
whack the flavours in. Check out the pizzas –
made my way they're faster, healthier and
cheaper than takeaways.

HOW TO COOK PASTA

1. Get dried pasta, not fresh (it's cheaper and stores for a year). Measure the amount you need (usually 110g/4oz per person).

2. Read the directions on the pasta pack for cooking times. Work out when you need to start cooking it in relation to sauce preparation time.

3. Boil up plenty of water with 1 teaspoon salt in a large pan – pasta needs room to spread or it gets gluey. Add to the pan when boiling vigorously. Stir…

4. Boil for designated cooking time but test before it's due. Bite a bit. Eat "al dente" – with a bit of bite – or softer. Never overcook. Drain in a sieve/colander.

5. Team with sauce or salad dressing or use in recipe at once or it cools/spoils. Toss any extra in a few drops of oil. Chill. Re-use in frittatas, layer up in ragu (pg 97) or tomato sauce (pg 83).

FEEDS **2** | £ | **V** | EXPRESS

110g/4oz linguine or spaghetti
50g/2oz Parmesan cheese
½ tsp black peppercorns
Little pasta water (or olive oil)
Salt

Skint Cheese & Cracked Pepper Pasta

As simple as you can get with pasta while keeping it interesting. Pasta's a great source of complex carbohydrates for slow release during your sport and recovery later.

1. Cook pasta as above.
2. Crack the peppercorns roughly in a pestle and mortar, or bash in a bag, or buy it ready cracked.
3. Drain pasta. Save a bit of water. Chuck pasta back in pan. Add cheese, pepper, bit of water (or olive oil). Stir well. Serve.

YOU CAN
✱ add a bit of cream, crème fraîche, Dijon mustard, peas, crisp bacon
✱ skip the pepper. Add more grated cheese and a knob of butter.

Tomato Lifesaver Pasta (with Vodka Option)

Student staple – evolved from years of brother and sister student life. Subject to many tasty variations. Cook it – maybe add a bit of vodka if there's any going.

1. Make sauce: heat oil gently in pan. Stir in chopped onion, garlic, salt. Cook to soften over low heat for 5–10 mins without colouring.

2. Stir in tomatoes, sugar. Simmer very gently for 15–20 minutes. Stir occasionally. Season, taste, adjust balance of flavour by adding lemon, herbs, optional vodka. Cool sauce for later or use immediately.

3. Meantime cook pasta. Drain. Slap back into pan and add a bit of butter/oil and optional vodka if not used in the sauce.

4. Stir hot sauce in. Or slap onto naked pasta. Or put in heatproof bowls, top with cheese and pesto. Grill till bubbling.

YOU CAN

✻ blitz sauce with blender for a smooth version

✻ stir in 2 tbsps double cream, mascarpone or Philadelphia at step 3 for touch of luxury

✻ skip the onion. Garlic only gives a softer taste.

✻ chop bacon and chilli in at step 1 for a punchy pasta

✻ add 1–2 chopped, de-seeded red/orange peppers at step 1

✻ grate a bit of fresh ginger in at step 1 to lift the taste

✻ dice a bit of mozzarella into hot sauce just before serving

✻ bake it. Layer up any cooked or left-over pasta, sauce, grated cheese, fried sliced aubergine. Top with grated cheese or cheese sauce (pg 90). Cook 30 minutes at 200°C/400°F/gas 6.

FEEDS 3–4 £ V

Basic tomato sauce
2 tbsps olive oil
1 medium onion, very finely chopped
2 cloves garlic, crushed or very finely chopped
Pinch salt
2 x 410g/14oz cans chopped tomatoes
Pinch sugar
Sea salt and black pepper
Squeeze lemon
Fresh or dried basil/thyme/ oregano (optional)
Vodka (optional)

350g/12oz penne
Butter or extra oil
Parmesan/Cheddar, freshly grated (optional)
Pesto (optional)

225g/8oz white or wholewheat
  spaghetti
2–3 tbsps olive oil
3 cloves garlic, sliced
50g/2oz tin anchovies, drained,
  chopped
½ dried chilli, crumbled
Little lemon rind (optional)
Parsley, finely chopped
  (optional)
Black pepper

Dare to Eat Anchovy

It's the sauce that packs the punch. Anchovies melt down in garlicky chilli oil to sort out your bland pasta.

1. Put pasta in to cook. Four minutes before it's ready heat the oil gently in a small pan. Add garlic. Stir to soften it without colouring.
2. Add anchovies, chilli, lemon, parsley, pepper to garlic and oil. Stir as it all melts together (don't boil it).
3. Tip over drained pasta. Stir well. Serve.

YOU CAN
✱ Dare to Eat Chilli: at step 2 omit anchovies, add 1–2 de-seeded finely chopped chillies

Hot Pasta, Cool Salsa

Perfect alfresco eating. Sit yourself down in the sunshine, music on, beers out and chow down. Simple…

1. Slice tomatoes open. Scoop seeds out with a spoon and discard. Roughly chop the flesh. Using cherry tomatoes? Just slice them.
2. Mix marinade ingredients. Taste. Adjust. Add to tomatoes.
3. Cook and drain pasta. Slap back into pan. Fling tomato salsa on top. Tip onto plates. Enjoy yourself.

YOU CAN
* slip a bit of sliced shallot, red onion, chopped garlic into salsa
* add tin of drained tuna, finely chopped red onion, or tin of drained beans
* chuck some baby croûtons on top for a crunchy texture

2 handfuls good tomatoes
 (cherry, vine, whatever)
225g/8oz spaghetti/penne

Marinade
2 tbsps extra virgin olive oil
Splash balsamic or wine
 vinegar
Pinch sugar
Salt and black pepper
Fresh basil
Black olives

Make What You Want of It Pasta Salad

Just a framework for your tastes (or what you've got in). Work out your combos – check they're compatible. Sometimes less is more when it comes to flavour…

1. Put pasta on to cook. Make dressing. Prep other ingredients.
2. Drain pasta. Shake well to dry. Tip into a bowl. Dress immediately.
3. Leave to cool a bit. Toss in your salad bits. Serve.

YOU CAN
* eat as a side dish or customize for mains – add one or more of the following…

* cubed cheese
* griddled halloumi (pg 124)
* feta
* roast peppers (pg 210)
* hard-boiled egg (pg 59)
* tuna (fresh/tinned)
* ham
* bits crispy bacon/pancetta
* cooked green beans

* butter/canellini beans/chickpeas
* chorizo
* salami
* cooked chicken
* baby potatoes
* spinach
* watercress
* sundried tomatoes
* croûtons (pg 203)

175g/6oz penne or other
 short pasta
3 tbsps My Sparky Dressing
 (pg 211) or Pesto (pg 89)
2–3 tomatoes, chopped, or
 handful cherry tomatoes
Some cucumber, chopped
A bit of red onion, peeled,
 sliced
Few black olives
Fresh parsley/basil/
 coriander, chopped or torn
Salt and black pepper

FEEDS 1 · £ · V · EXPRESS

Cheeky Chilli Garlic Eggs on Ribbon Pasta

110g/4oz tagliatelle/
  pappardelle/spaghetti
1 tbsp olive oil
1 tsp butter
1 clove garlic, thinly sliced
1 or 2 large eggs
Sprinkle dried chilli flakes or
  shake pepper sauce/Tabasco
Salt and black pepper
Freshly grated Parmesan/
  Cheddar
Bit of fresh windowsill herb

Pub, club, late-night study session? Sort yourself out with this neat pasta snack. Take the chilli. It makes all the difference.

1. Put pasta in to cook. Four minutes before it's done, heat oil/butter in a small frying pan. Add garlic. Stir to soften without colouring.

2. Crack egg into pan. Fry 2 minutes, flicking garlicky oil over yolk with a spatula.

3. Drain pasta. Tip back into pan with a few chilli flakes, cheese, seasoning, herbs. Tip onto plates. Top with egg, garlicky juices. Sprinkle more chilli.

Hot Sexy Tuna with Spaghetti

A store-cupboard meal that's alive with flavour – and it's nutritionally balanced. Love it…

1. Put pasta on to cook.

2. Mix tuna, tomato purée and water in a bowl.

3. Squash garlic with blade of a knife until cracked.

4. Heat oil in small pan. Toss garlic in. Cook till browned. Discard garlic – it's a flavouring. Stir in chilli and tuna mix.

5. Cook, stirring on very low heat 10 minutes. Add extra water/oil if needed. Add optional extras to heat through. Taste. Adjust. Mix into drained pasta.

FEEDS 3 · £ · EXPRESS

350g/12oz spaghetti/linguine
185g/6 ½oz can tuna, drained
3 tbsps tomato purée
2–3 tbsps water
1 clove garlic
2–3 tbsps olive oil
Sprinkle crushed chilli flakes
   or finely chopped, de-seeded
   red chilli
Optional extras
Fresh parsley/basil
2 tsps capers, drained
Few black olives, pitted,
   chopped

Suave Spaghetti & Mussels

Don't be afraid of this dish (or of cooking mussels). It's really simple to do. We're talking restaurant-style food and bold flavours.

1. Prep mussels (see pg 172). Put pasta on to cook.

2. Melt butter, oil in saucepan big enough to take mussels.

3. Fry onion, garlic, briskly stirring so they don't colour.

4. Add wine. Boil for 2–3 minutes with lid on.

5. Throw mussels into the pan. Replace lid. Boil 4–5 minutes or till all opened. Shake pan. Don't overcook. Discard any closed or cracked shellfish.

6. Drain pasta. Return to pan. Throw mussels, juice, parsley over. Eat with bread to soak up juices.

FEEDS 2 · ££ · EXPRESS

225g/8oz spaghetti/linguine
20 mussels, prepped (pg 172)
Oil/butter
1 small onion
2–3 cloves garlic, sliced
Glass white wine
Chopped parsley

FEEDS
1
£
V

4–5 small salad potatoes
1–2 nests tagliatelle
Handful fresh thin green
   beans, ends trimmed
Bit of pesto – homemade (pg
   89) or bought
Salt and black pepper

Garlic breadcrumbs
1 slice crustless white bread,
   fresh or stale
1 clove garlic, crushed
Dollop of butter

Optional Parmesan or veggie
   equivalent

Slap-It-In-The-Pan Veg & Garlic Crumb Pasta

Veg and pasta cook up in the one pan for this great eat so there's less washing-up, which is never a bad thing. Garlic breadcrumbs give it a wonderful texture. Italians invented the idea to give texture and taste to pasta instead of having to use expensive Parmesan. Your choice.

1. Boil potatoes in large pan of lightly salted water.

2. Meantime, blitz bread into crumbs with handblender.

3. Melt butter in frying pan. Add garlic and crumbs. Fry gently, stirring over low heat till crispy. Remove.

4. When potatoes are just tender (test with a knife), add pasta to pan. 3 minutes before pasta's ready, add beans.

5. Drain contents of pan well. Tip back in. Season with pepper. Stir in 1–2 tsps pesto. Serve sprinkled with crumbs, and have extra grated cheese on the table.

Welsh Rarebit-Style Baked Pasta

OK, not one for every day but something to look forward to. Think luxurious velvety taste and well relaxing…

1. Cook pasta. Preheat oven to 200°C/400°F/gas 6.
2. Drain penne. Slap in bowl with few drops of oil.
3. Grease 2 small/1 medium shallow dish with butter. Rub with cut garlic. Divide penne between dishes – no more than 2 bits deep.
4. Mix crème fraîche, mustard, cheese, seasoning. Tip evenly over penne. Top with breadcrumbs. Dot with butter.
5. Bake 10–15 minutes till hot and bubbling. Or grill slowly.

175g/6oz penne
Few drops olive oil
10g/½oz butter
1 cut clove garlic
200g/7oz crème fraîche
½ tsp Dijon or grain mustard
50g/2oz Gruyère/Cheddar/
    Lancashire cheese, grated
Salt and black pepper
10g/½oz white breadcrumbs
    (see opposite)

Cracking Own Pesto

This herby little sauce smells, looks and tastes brilliant. Get a herb garden going on your windowsill – makes it well cheap. Slap it in everything. If buying pesto, go for tubs rather than jars if possible.

110g/4oz fresh basil
150ml/5fl oz olive oil
25g/1oz pine nuts (optional)
2 plump cloves garlic
50g/2oz Parmesan or veggie
    equivalent, grated

1. Blitz basil, oil, nuts, garlic in processor or with handblender or bash in pestle and mortar.
2. Stir cheese into mix. Chill. Stir into any cooked pasta.

YOU CAN

* make it with coriander
* stir into mash, baked spuds, tomato soup, rice and pasta salads. Stir loads into hot trofie pasta, for a pasta-to-go box with salad bits
* spread on tart bases
* spread on chicken or white fish
* store in fridge for 1 week

1 tsp oil (add to boiling water)
225g/8oz macaroni
50g/2oz butter
50g/2oz plain white flour
600ml/1 pint semi-skimmed
  milk
200g/7oz strong Cheddar,
  grated
1 tsp English mustard
1 tbsp lemon juice
Salt and black pepper
Extra cheese for topping

Good Old Macaroni Cheese

The cheesy sauce is the key to this. Get it down and smooth and you'll be mastering loads of other dishes.

1. Boil macaroni hard for 15 mins or till soft. Drain. Preheat oven to 200°C/400°F/gas 6.

2. Melt butter in a saucepan for cheese sauce. Add flour. Stir over low heat with wooden spoon to make a paste ball (roux). Don't let it burn. Stir for 2 minutes. Remove from heat.

3. Beat milk into paste just a bit at a time to ensure sauce is smooth. Use a balloon whisk or wooden spoon. If your sauce goes lumpy – sieve or blitz with a handblender.

4. Return pan to low heat, stirring until it boils and thickens. Add a splash more milk if you think it needs it. Reduce heat.

5. Simmer sauce gently for 5–10 minutes. Beat in cheese, mustard, juice, seasoning. Taste. Adjust.

6. Stir into pasta. Tip into buttered ovenproof dish/tin. Top with grated cheese. Bake for 20–30 minutes.

YOU CAN

✱ top with 2 tbsps fresh breadcrumbs or drizzle with garlic butter
✱ slap cooked, drained spinach on base of tin/dish before macaroni cheese
✱ add chopped ham/bacon/cooked mushroom/onion
✱ use penne instead of macaroni
✱ use boiled/steamed cauliflower or broccoli instead of pasta

Orecchiette & Crunchy Broccoli

A cacophony of flavour and texture – and it looks cute. You get crunchy garlic-butter breadcrumbs nestling in tiny pasta ears and superfood broccoli. Nice one…

1. Put pasta on. Prep and cook garlic breadcrumbs (pg 88).

2. Boil separate pan of water. Add broccoli 4–5 minutes before pasta's ready and boil till just tender (you want bite and colour). Drain.

3. Drain pasta. Tip back into warm pan. Add broccoli, extra oil/butter, lemon rind, salt and black pepper, ¾ of the crisp crumbs. Stir well.

4. Tip into bowls. Top with more crumbs and cheese.

YOU CAN

✳ add a bit of crisp bacon/crumbled feta, stir in cream/crème fraîche

1 tsp oil (add to boiling water)
175g/6oz orecchiette pasta
2 cloves garlic, crushed
4 tbsps fresh breadcrumbs
175g/6oz broccoli florets
2–3 tbsps olive oil or oil/
   butter mix
Bit grated lemon rind
   (optional)
Salt and black pepper
Handful freshly grated
   Parmesan or Cheddar

91

FEEDS 2   **££**

4 best sausages
175g/6oz penne
10g/½oz butter
150ml/5oz cream, crème
  fraîche (low-fat's OK) or
  sour cream
Salt and black pepper
2 tsps Dijon, wholegrain or
  English mustard
50–75g/2–3oz Parmesan or
  other hard cheese, grated
Fresh parsley/coriander/sage/
  tarragon, finely chopped
  (optional)

Banging Bangers on Creamy Penne

Everyone starving and your turn to cook? Give this a go – you'll be well popular and they'll be well fed. Hearty and great for winter. Balance it out with a crunchy salad.

1. Preheat oven to 220°C/425F/gas 7. Slap sausages on baking tray. Cook 15–20 minutes, turning once. (Or fry gently till sticky, or grill slowly.) Slice when done.

2. Meantime, cook and drain pasta. Save 2 tbsps water.

3. Tip pasta back into warm pan with cream, butter, mustard, pepper. Stir over very low heat to warm through. Chuck in sausage, ½ cheese, herbs, pasta water if too dry. Tip into bowls. Top with more cheese.

YOU CAN

✱ slice up chorizo and fry gently. Add instead of standard banger.

✱ grill/bake/fry 2–3 Portobello mushrooms with oil, garlic, herbs. Slice and slap into sauce instead of sausage.

Sausage Power Pasta

A bit of a banger blow-out. Breaking the sausage down and teaming it with fennel makes this special. Eat with wholemeal garlic bread and a crunchy salad with mustardy dressing.

1. Cook onion, garlic, chilli, fennel seeds in a large pan over low heat for 5 minutes till onion's soft but still uncoloured.

2. Strip skin off sausages. Crumble meat into onion. Cook over higher heat till browned. Add mushrooms.

3. Reduce heat. Stir and cook for 5–10 minutes.

4. Increase heat. Add wine/water/stock. Boil for 3 minutes.

5. Add tomatoes, purée, sugar, lemon juice, herbs. Boil.

6. Reduce heat. Cook on a gentle simmer for 15–20 minutes.

7. Cook pasta. Drain. Slap back into pan with bit of butter or oil. Stir sausage ragu in or tip on top when plated. Top with grated cheese.

YOU CAN
* stack left-over sauce on baked potatoes
* shove in pancakes with grated cheese and bake (pg 65)

FEEDS
4   ££

1 tbsp olive oil
1 medium onion, finely chopped
3 cloves garlic, peeled, crushed
1 small red chilli, de-seeded, finely chopped (or pinch chilli flakes)
½ tsp fennel seeds
6 Italian-style or spicy pork sausages
225g/8oz chestnut mushrooms, roughly chopped
150ml/5fl oz wine, water or stock
1 x 400g/14oz can chopped tomatoes
1 tsp tomato purée
Pinch sugar
Squeeze lemon juice
Bit of fresh parsley, thyme, basil, finely chopped
350g/12oz tagliatelle, penne, or other pasta
Parmesan or Cheddar, grated

225g/8oz spaghetti, linguine or
penne
225g/8oz best bacon (back or
streaky), cut into bite-size
bits
2 tsps olive oil
2–3 large eggs
Lots of Parmesan, grated
Black pepper and salt
A little butter
1 clove garlic, crushed

All-Day Breakfast Pasta (Carbonara)

Watch the sauce make itself as the heat from the pasta pulls
it together. Get it creamy – don't let it scramble. You can sub
kipper fillet or pancetta for bacon, or add peas and stir a bit
of cream in. Make it your own dish – enjoy yourself.

1. Put pasta on to cook. Meantime, heat oil in a frying pan.

2. Fry bacon till crisp. Remove and keep warm.

3. Beat eggs, half Parmesan, pepper, salt in a bowl.

4. Drain pasta. Tip back in warm pan. Add bacon, a little butter,
crushed garlic, toss in the egg mix.

5. Sit pan back on very low heat for a few seconds. Stir till sauce
coats pasta and warms through – don't let it scramble. Serve with
more cheese.

Chic Lemon Tagliatelle with Cheese & Spinach

FEEDS
2   £   V   EXPRESS

175g/6oz tagliatelle/spaghetti
1 lemon
1–2 tbsps crème fraîche
Salt and pepper
Few baby spinach leaves
Parmesan, grated

Pasta triggers feel-good hormones so it's perfect to eat when you're stressed (exams, love life, whatever). Team with lemon and spinach for sharp tastes and goodness.

1. Slap pasta on to cook. Grate lemon rind into a bowl. Mix with crème fraîche, salt, pepper.

2. Drain pasta well. Tip back into warm pan with spinach – to wilt it – and add some Parmesan.

3. Stir lemon juice into crème fraîche sauce. Mix into hot pasta. Serve in bowls topped with Parmesan.

95

400g/14oz spaghetti

Meatballs
1 thick slice white bread
    (crustless)
2–3 tbsps milk
450g/1lb good minced
    beef/pork/lamb or a mix
2–3 cloves garlic, crushed
Small onion, finely chopped or
    grated
1 tbsp fresh parsley, thyme,
    coriander, or 2 pinches dried
Grated lemon rind (optional)
Cubes Cheddar/Mozzarella
    (optional)
Plain flour with salt and black
    pepper
Olive/sunflower oil for frying

Sauce
1 x tomato sauce (pg 83)

Topping
Freshly grated Parmesan/
    Cheddar

Spaghetti, Meatballs & Tomato Sauce

Got the lads (ladettes) round, footie on, a few drinks (or not). Make this. Just the smell of it'll get them dribbling…

1. Start by making meatballs. Soak bread in milk. Leave 5 minutes. Squeeze dry. Mix in meat, garlic, onion, seasoning, herbs, lemon rind, with a fork. Chill mix to let flavours develop.
2. Make tomato sauce (pg 83). Set aside.
3. Roll meatball mix into golf-balls, or flat patty shapes if stuffing. Put a cube of cheese in the middle. Pull meat up round cheese. Pinch to seal. Roll in lightly seasoned flour. Set aside.
4. Put pasta on to cook.
5. Meantime, fry meatballs gently in oil, turning frequently till cooked through. Or simmer gently in tomato sauce in a lidded pan.
6. Pile heated sauce and meatballs onto spaghetti. Top with Parmesan. Eat with a green salad.

YOU CAN
✳ add cinnamon to tomato sauce and meat mix for Morrocan-style variation
✳ add grated ginger and coriander to meat for Chinese style
✳ make meatloaf: slap meatball mix into greased or foil-lined 900g/2lb loaf tin. Bake at 190°C/375°F/gas 5 for 1–1¼ hours. Eat hot with tomato sauce, or cold with baked spuds and salads.

Spaghetti Bolognese

You've got to have this sauce (ragu) in your repertoire. It multi-tasks and freezes. With spaghetti, it's the definitive student dish. Use the best ingredients, season well. The taste develops if you don't rush it.

1. Gently fry bacon in oil for 2–3 mins. Add onion, carrot, garlic, bay leaf.

2. Cook for 5 minutes or till onion softens, without colouring.

3. Slap mince in. Cook till browned on a higher heat for 4–5 minutes, breaking meat up with a wooden spoon.

4. Add wine, water or stock, herbs, tomato purée, lemon juice, sugar, pepper. Boil and stir for 2 minutes. Reduce heat to very low.

5. Simmer 30–40 mins, covered, stirring and tasting sometimes. Adjust seasoning. Add extra water to loosen or tomato purée to thicken.

6. Meantime cook and drain pasta (put water on 20 minutes before sauce is due to be ready). Slap it back into pan with a bit of oil or butter. Mix sauce in or spoon onto buttery pasta. Serve with grated Parmesan/Cheddar.

YOU CAN

✻ get it tomatoey: use tinned chopped tomatoes or passata, instead of stock

✻ mix with cooked rice. Stuff and bake aubergines, tomatoes (pg 191), peppers (pg 190).

✻ use reheated left-over sauce on mash, baked potatoes, in pancakes

✻ layer sauce with any cooked or left-over pasta: cover with cheese sauce (page 90) or 1 large tub of plain yogurt mixed with 2 beaten eggs, top with 225g/8oz grated Cheddar, and bake at 180°C/350°F/gas 4, 30–40 minutes

✻ stuff into large cooked pasta shells, sit them on tomato sauce (pg 83), cover with grated cheese or cheese sauce. Bake at 200°C/ 400°F/gas 6 for 30 mins.

FEEDS 4   ££

Meat ragu

3–4 rashers bacon or pancetta, chopped small
1–2 tbsps olive oil
1 onion, finely chopped
1 carrot, grated
3 cloves garlic, crushed
1 bay leaf
450g/1lb best lean minced beef/steak
150ml/5fl oz red wine
100ml/3½fl oz water or beef/chicken/veg stock
Dried or fresh thyme, oregano, parsley
3 tbsps tomato purée
Squeeze lemon juice
½ tsp sugar
Salt and black pepper

350g/12oz spaghetti/tagliatelle
Grated Parmesan/Cheddar

1 x meat ragu (pg 97)
1 x cheese sauce (pg 90)
9–12 sheets fresh/dried/
   no-pre-cook lasagne
Extra cheese (Cheddar/
   Parmesan/Mozzarella) for
   topping

Choice Lasagne

Layers of lush meat sauce stacked between sheets of soft flatpack-style pasta with a cheesy sauce topping. Eat with garlic bread (pg 206). Classic.

1. Make meat sauce (pg 97). Make cheese sauce (pg 90).

2. If using no-pre-cook lasagne, soak in cold water for 10 mins. Drain.

3. Preheat oven to 200°C/400°F/gas 6. Grease oblong lasagne dish or any ovenproof dish or tin that's at least 5cm/2in deep.

4. Layer up lasagne. Spread base of dish thinly with meat sauce. Sprinkle a little grated cheese on top. Cover with a single layer of pasta. (Break it up if you need to.) Drizzle with a little cheese sauce. Repeat this sequence. Finish with a layer of pasta and a thick covering of cheese sauce. Top with grated cheese.

5. Bake 40 minutes. Cover with foil for the first 30. Let lasagne settle for 10 minutes before serving.

YOU CAN
* make it a few days ahead for parties
* make up a batch of roast ratatouille (pg 185) and layer it with cheese sauce and lasagne sheets. Bake.
* freeze it

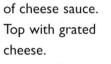

Veg Lasagne

Making and eating lasagne's a therapeutic pursuit. Feel free to customize this chic veggie version. Layer in different cooked pasta (penne, macaroni, leftover spaghetti) and veggies.

1. Make tomato sauce (pg 83) with additional onion, tomatoes.
2. If using no-pre-cook lasagne, soak in cold water for 10 minutes.
3. Slap spinach into a saucepan with a few drops of water. Heat for a few seconds to wilt. Drain in sieve. Use spoon to press out moisture.
4. Mix spinach, ricotta, Parmesan, egg, garlic, seasoning, lemon rind, basil, optional nutmeg together with a fork. Taste. Adjust. Add a little grated Mozzarella.
5. Preheat oven to 200°C/400°F/gas 6.
6. Grease a lasagne or ovenproof dish/tin, at least 5cm/2in deep.
7. Layer up with tomato sauce, layer of pasta sheets (break to fit neatly or drain if soaked), the cheese and spinach mix, bit of grated mozzarella. Repeat twice.
8. Finish with layer of pasta. Top with grated Mozzarella and Parmesan.
9. Bake 30 minutes or till golden. Rest for 10 minutes before serving.

YOU CAN
* top with cheese sauce (pg 90) for a creamier finish
* add layers of griddled courgettes and aubergines
* add a bit of grated Cheddar or feta to the ricotta

FEEDS 6–8 **££** **V**

Sauce
1 x tomato sauce (pg 83) made with addition of 1 large onion and 1 x 400g/14oz tin chopped or plum tomatoes, squashed

Filling
Good handful spinach leaves
2 x 250g/8oz tubs ricotta
50g/2oz Parmesan, grated
1 egg
1–2 fat cloves garlic, crushed
Salt and black pepper
Bit of grated lemon rind (optional)
Bit of fresh basil, chopped
Pinch nutmeg (optional)
Pasta
9–12 sheets lasagne

Topping
225g/8oz Mozzarella, grated from a block
Parmesan, grated

PIZZA SYSTEM

1. Make easy dough (below). See pg 11 for kneading technique.

2. Before first rising, tear a bit off to make Turbocharge griddled pizza (thin and crispy).

3. Let the rest rise for Lush Night In (see opposite) or other pizzas.

4. Roll and freeze extra dough for emergency bases. Saves time later.

450g/1lb strong white bread flour
1 tsp salt
1 tsp caster sugar
2 x 7 g sachets fast action dried yeast
300ml/½ pint warm water
2 tbsps olive oil

1 lump pizza dough made till end of step 4
Olive oil for griddle pan
2–3 tbsps tomato sauce (pg 83)/passata mixed with crushed garlic/chopped raw tomatoes with oil and garlic
Few black olives
Few basil leaves or dried oregano
Freshly grated Parmesan/ Cheddar or sliced Mozzarella
Ham/salami/pepperoni (optional)
Drizzle olive oil

Cracking Pizza Dough

Proper olive oil dough. Great taste and workout.

1. Sift flour, salt into large bowl. Add sugar, yeast, water, oil. Work to a soft dough using your hand. Add more water if dry, or flour if sticky.
2. Chuck dough onto flat surface. Knead for 10 minutes (see pg 11) till soft and elastic. Got machine with dough hook? Knead for 8 minutes.
3. Tip big dough ball into a bowl. Cover with a teatowel. Leave to double in size in warm place. Could take 1 hour but check regularly.
4. Knead again for 2 minutes. Now dough is ready to roll and top for specific pizzas…

YOU CAN
* make doughballs. Add 3 cloves chopped garlic and rosemary at step 1. End of step 4, roll into balls. Brush with milk. Bake at 220°C/425°F/gas 7 for 15 mins. Dunk in garlic butter or salsa.

Turbocharge Pizza… No-rise & Griddle It

Speedy, crispy option. Slightly charred, wood-fired oven style. Ridiculously delicious.

1. Tear off a bit of freshly kneaded dough (made to end of step 2).
2. Roll into thin pizza base on lightly floured surface.

3. Brush griddle pan with oil. When scorching hot, slap on thin dough to cook for 1 minute. Prick with knife if it puffs up. Turn, cook a further minute.

5. Spread with a thin layer of garlicky tomato sauce. Scatter toppings. Drizzle oil.

6. Cook under pre-heated grill 1–2 minutes till a bit charred, crisp and sizzling.

Lovely Lush Night In Pizzas

Proper thick pizza. Make this classic Margherita or vary your toppings. Tastier than takeaways (faster too with frozen bases).

1. Make dough to end of step 4. Pre-heat oven to 230°C/400°F/gas 6.

2. Roll dough out to make 4 thin pizza shapes. Leave to rise 10 mins in warm place on lightly oiled baking trays. Cover (I use carrier bags).

3. Mix garlic into sauce/passata. Spread over bases. Scatter with olives, basil, Mozzarella, Parmesan. Drizzle with olive oil.

4. Bake 15–20 minutes till base crisp, top bubbling. Eat hot or cold.

FEEDS **2–4** ££ **V**

1 x pizza dough made till step 4, or frozen bases

Basic topping
8–12 tbsps tomato sauce (pg 83) or passata
2 cloves garlic, crushed
A few black olives
Fresh basil leaves
Sliced Mozzarella from a block
Freshly grated Parmesan
Olive oil to drizzle

Other topping choices
Ham, chorizo, prosciutto, pepperoni, spinach, seafood, tuna, griddled veg, rocket, egg

1 x pizza dough (pg 100) made to end of step 4, or frozen or bought base
2 medium-size old potatoes, peeled
Sprinkle fresh thyme/finely chopped rosemary/dried oregano
Sprinkle sea salt
Sprinkle grated cheese (optional)
Olive oil

Skint Chip-Butty Pizza

Make something great out of pretty much nothing.
This pizza's a French classic and tastes pretty beautiful.
Slice spuds nice and thin for looks, taste and texture…

1. Make dough to end of step 4. Preheat oven to 230°C/400°F/gas 6.
2. Roll pizza out and leave to rise on tray for 10 minutes. Or use a good bought or frozen base.
3. Slice potatoes mega thinly. Arrange over base overlapping each other just a bit. Scatter herbs, salt, optional cheese. Drizzle olive oil.
4. Cook for 20 minutes or till base is crisp, spuds soft and browning. Drizzle more oil. Eat. Also good cold.

YOU CAN
✳ rub a cut garlic clove over base before arranging spuds
✳ forget the spuds. Cover base with thinly sliced Mozzarella and serve with tomato/olives on the side for deconstructed Margherita.

1 x pizza dough (pg 100) made to step 4
Olive oil

Filling 1
1 x tomato sauce (pg 83) or passata mixed with garlic
Sliced ham, salami
Few olives
Any cheese, sliced, grated
Basil leaves

Filling 2
1 x tomato sauce (pg 83) or passata mixed with garlic
Load of mushrooms, sliced and fried
Garlic, sliced or crushed
Basil or thyme
Any cheese, sliced/grated

Beach-Party Pasty

Great to munch on. No knife and fork needed. Cross between calzone and a pasty.
Customise the fillings. Take it anywhere…

1. Roll dough out into a large rectangle to fit baking tray.
2. Sit lower half on tray. Let the upper half hang over.
3. Spread lower half with tomato sauce, then scatter filling.
4. Fold upper half of dough over to make a pasty. Press edges to seal, moisten with a little milk if it helps. Leave to rise for 20 minutes. Brush top with olive oil, salt.
5. Bake 10–15 minutes at 220°C/425°F/gas 7.
6. Cool it. Slice it. Pack it. Take it.

Industrial Party Pizzas

Having a house party? Keep everyone happy by getting a few of these turned out. Cheap and tasty crowd-pleasers.

FEEDS 8–10 | ££ | V OPTION

1. Make pizza dough (pg 100) to end of step 4.
2. Roll out to fit 1 or 2 greased baking trays at least 32.5cm/12in x 32.5cm/12in.
3. Leave to rise until doubled – maybe 1 hour.
4. Topping 1: fry onions and garlic gently in olive oil 15–20 minutes or till really soft.
5. Topping 2: make tomato sauce (pg 83).
6. Preheat oven to 220°C/425°F/gas 7. Spread onions, olives over pizza 1 (arrange anchovies in lattice shape if using). Spread tomato sauce, olives, herbs, cheese over pizza 2.
7. Bake 20 minutes or till base is crispy.

1 or 2 x pizza dough (pg 100)

Topping 1
700g/1½lb onions, peeled and sliced
2–3 cloves garlic, crushed
2 tbsps olive oil
12 black olives
1 small can anchovies (optional)

Topping 2
1 x tomato sauce (pg 83) or passata mixed with garlic
Dried oregano/fresh basil
12 black olives
Freshly grated Parmesan/ Cheddar
Sliced Mozzarella

NOODLES RICE, GRAINS & LENTILS

Cracking Asian, Italian and Middle Eastern meals, made from basic ingredients, pack in plenty of proteins, energy and top flavours. Simple to cook and easy on the budget.

HOW TO COOK NOODLES

1. Get thin, medium or large dried noodles (egg or rice). Read pack for preparation times.

2. For egg noodles: bring a large pan of water to the boil. Measure how much you need (usually 75g/3oz per person or see recipe). Add to the water. Boil again until done – usually 3–4 minutes. Stir occasionally to separate strands. Drain. Put directly into soup. Or stir-fry in a hot wok with a little sunflower/sesame oil, garlic etc, tossing/scooping with a large spoon, adding further ingredients as per recipe.

3. For rice noodles: put in a bowl. Cover with boiling, hot or cold water for as long as pack directs. Drain well. Stir-fry or use in noodle salads.

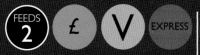

150g/5oz dried egg noodles

Sauce
¾ tbsp soy sauce
½ teaspoon sesame oil
2½ tbsps hot water or stock

Stir-fry
¾ tbsp groundnut/sunflower
   oil, plus splash of sesame oil
½ tbsp peeled, grated, finely
   chopped ginger
3–4 cloves garlic, finely sliced
110g/6oz beansprouts
4 spring onions, finely sliced

Chop Suey Noodles

Stir-fry for beginners. Master this one and you'll bang through the others… Eat alone or as part of a banquet.

1. Cook noodles according to packet instructions. Drain well.
2. Mix sauce in a small bowl.
3. Heat wok (or pan). Add oil. Stir-fry ginger, garlic for a few seconds, using a large spoon to quickly scoop and toss.
4. Add beansprouts, onions. Stir-fry 1 minute.
5. Add sauce, noodles. Stir-fry till heated through (don't overdo).
6. Pile into bowls. Eat with chopsticks.

YOU CAN
* add canned water chestnuts, bamboo shoots
* make garlic noodles. At step 2 finely chop 8 cloves garlic. Stir-fry lightly. Skip ginger, beansprouts, onions. Add noodles. Stir-fry 2 minutes. Add sauce with additional oyster sauce and chopped spring onion.
* store beansprouts in fridge 2–3 days wrapped in kitchen paper in freezer bag

My Top Chicken & Noodles with Oyster Sauce

Based on a great little dish I ate in Amsterdam at 2 in the morning a bit bleary-eyed. A beautiful clean-tasting meal with some really healthy ingredients. Sorted me out…

1. Cook noodles as packet instructions. Drain well.

2. Mix soy sauce, sugar, rice wine, oyster sauce in a bowl.

3. Heat a wok or pan. Add 1 tbsp oil. When hot, stir-fry garlic, ginger, chilli, spring onions for 30 seconds. Add rest of oil. Chuck in chicken, chorizo if using, pak choi or broccoli. Stir-fry, tossing quickly, for 3–4 minutes till chicken is cooked (white and moist).

4. Add oyster sauce mix, noodles, beansprouts. Heat through.

YOU CAN

✱ stir-fry baby corn and sliced mangetout to mix in

✱ use black bean sauce for an earthy taste, or hoisin sauce for a sweet one

FEEDS **2**   ££   EXPRESS

175g/6oz egg or rice noodles
Sauce
1 tbsp soy sauce
1 tsp sugar
1 tbsp rice wine
1 tbsp oyster sauce
Stir-fry
2 tbsps vegetable oil, plus splash sesame oil, mixed
2 cloves garlic, sliced
Bit of fresh ginger, grated
Bit of red chilli, finely chopped
1–2 spring onions
1 large/2 small chicken breasts, cut into thin bite-size bits
Bit of chorizo sausage, sliced (optional)
1 head pak choi, sliced, or tenderstem broccoli, chopped small
Handful beansprouts

200g/7oz rice noodles
4 tsps groundnut/sunflower oil
2 eggs, beaten
1 tbsp tamarind paste
1 tbsp brown sugar
Juice ½ lime
2 tbsps fish sauce
1 shallot or small onion, finely chopped
2 cloves garlic, crushed
1 sliced, de-seeded red chilli or pinch chilli flakes
Handful cooked prawns (optional)
Handful beansprouts
Fresh coriander, chopped
3 tbsps roast salted peanuts, roughly chopped
Splash soy sauce

Gorgeous Pad Thai, Gap-Year Style

Tamarind paste gives this Thai stir-fry a sharp, rich kick. Get it from Asian stores and supermarkets – or sub lemon juice. Sort when you're back or before you go travelling.

1. Cook rice noodles according to instructions. Drain well.

2. Heat wok. Add 2 tsps of oil. Tip beaten egg in, swirling to make thin omelette. Cook 1 minute or till set. Remove. Roll. Slice in thin strips.

3. Mix tamarind and sugar with a little water, lime, fish sauce.

4. Reheat wok. Add remaining oil. Add shallot/onion, garlic, chilli. Stir-fry for 30–60 seconds. Add prawns. Toss for 30 seconds.

5. Add noodles, tamarind mix. Mix well. Add beansprouts. Serve topped with coriander, peanuts, egg strips, soy sauce.

YOU CAN

✳ sling cooked chicken, Char Sui Pork (pg 135) or tofu into this instead of prawns

✳ using uncooked prawns? Add at start of step 4.

FEEDS 2–3 · £ · V · EXPRESS

225g/8oz rice vermicelli
4 tsps groundnut/sunflower oil
2 eggs, beaten
1 onion, thinly sliced
2 cloves garlic, crushed
Little fresh ginger, grated
2 red chillies, de-seeded and chopped
Char Sui Pork (pg 135, optional), diced
Few cooked prawns (optional)
225g/8oz beansprouts
Pinch curry powder
2 tbsps soy sauce

Curried Singapore Fried Noodles

Noodles need to rule this Indian-style Chinese, so get your bits finely chopped. Tasty.

1. Cook vermicelli as packet instructions. Drain well.

2. Heat wok on high heat. Add 2 tsps oil. Swirl. Add egg to make an omelette. Remove. Roll, slice in thin strips. Reheat wok. Add rest of oil.

3. Add onion, garlic, ginger, chillies, pork, prawns. Cook 1 minute. Chuck in beansprouts. Cook 30 seconds. Add noodles, curry powder, soy sauce. Cook 1 minute.

4. Serve. Top with egg.

One-Bowl Egg & Veg Stir-Fry

Well easy. Bang all the bits into one bowl and you're ready to wok and roll. Try varying the veg (green beans, pak choi, sugar snaps). Halfway to your 5-a-day…

1. Cook noodles as packet instructions. Drain well.

2. Mix sauce ingredients.

3. Tip sauce, noodles, everything else into one large bowl. Mix well.

4. Heat wok or pan. Add oil. Swirl it round a bit. Tip in contents of bowl.

5. Stir-fry over high heat for 3 minutes, turning quickly, till veg is cooked. Spoon into bowls. Eat with chopsticks.

FEEDS **2** ££ V EXPRESS

225g/8oz soba, egg or rice noodles (½ in thick)

Sauce
2 tbsps soy sauce
1 tsp sugar/runny honey
Little grated ginger

Stir-fry
1 red pepper, de-seeded, finely sliced
Mangetout, finely sliced
Beansprouts
2–3 cloves garlic, finely sliced
1 red onion, peeled, finely sliced
6 spring onions, finely sliced
Few chestnut/button mushrooms, wiped, finely sliced
2 large eggs, beaten
2 tbsps vegetable or sunflower oil and 1 tsp sesame oil (optional) for frying

109

Thai-Style Chicken Noodle Salad

It's like your mouth lights up, this is so refreshing. Thai flavours lift soft noodles. NB Soak noodles for long enough. If the pack underestimates, boil for 1–2 minutes.

1. Prepare noodles as packet instructions. Drain well. Blot dry.
2. Add to bowl with prepped salad and chicken.
3. Mix dressing. Toss into salad bowl. Toss again.

YOU CAN

＊ add chopped roast peanuts
＊ simmer a chicken breast covered in water for 10 minutes. Cool in liquid. Shred with two forks. Toss into salad. (Use poaching liquid as a soup stock.)

Char Sui Chow Mein

Western style Chinese classic. Roast up a pork fillet in a sweet barbecue-style sauce. Bang it up on a mountain of carb-rich noodles and healthy stir-fry. Veggies check out the tofu option. More protein than meat plus low cal, low fat.

1. Marinate and roast the pork (pg 135) or get cooked from fridge.
2. Cook the noodles as packet instructs. Set aside.
3. Mix stir-fry sauce. Set aside. Prepare stir-fry vegtables.
4. Heat a wok or large frying pan. Mix the oils and add to heat.
5. Add and stir-fry the garlic, spring onion, ginger. Toss for 1 minute without colouring. Add carrot and mushrooms. Toss 1–2 minutes. Add beansprouts, green veg and the sauce. Let everything boil to wilt.
6. Add the noodles to heat through or remove veg and keep warm and stir-fry noodles briefly in a little oil. Slice pork. Lay out on noodles and veg. Drizzle with hoisin you've thinned with water.

YOU CAN

＊ drain tofu. Press under plate/board for 30 mins. Drain again. Cube. Marinate in char sui sauce (pg 135). Pan fry with sliced garlic. Slap on chow mein.
＊ make mushrooms the main event: stir-fry 170g/6oz torn shiitake mushrooms with a few sliced chestnut ones. Add baby corn and sugar snaps for texture.

FEEDS
2
££
EXPRESS

2 bunches thin rice noodles

Salad
1 handful beansprouts
1–2 cooked chicken breasts or cold roast chicken, shredded (pg 156)
1 red onion, thinly sliced
6 spring onions, thinly sliced
1–2 red chillies, finely chopped
1 red pepper, de-seeded, cut in thin lengths
Bit of fresh coriander/mint

Dressing
1 clove garlic, crushed
1 tbsp fish sauce
1 tbsp lime juice
1 tsp caster sugar
Splash of rice/malt vinegar

Hot tip: make noodle cake. Cook egg noodles. Toss in a bit of sesame oil. Fry in hot oil both sides till crisp. Slap char sui on top – or griddled steak/tuna with Ginger Lime Drizzle (pg 115).

FEEDS
3–4   £££

450g/1lb char sui pork
(pg 135)
225g/8oz egg noodles

Sauce
6 tbsps water
2 tbsps soy sauce
2 tbsps rice wine
2 tsps sesame oil
2 tsps cornflour
Pinch sugar/dribble honey

Stir-fry
2 tbsps veg/groundnut oil
Splash sesame oil
2 cloves garlic, sliced
4–6 spring onions
Bit fresh ginger, grated
Carrot, chopped in sticks or
ribboned with peeler
Few mushrooms, sliced
75g/3oz beansprouts
Few mangetout, sliced
Chinese leaf/cabbage/pak
choi/bok choy, finely
shredded

Drizzle
2–3 tbsps hoisin sauce or
plum sauce
Water for thinning

HOW TO COOK RICE

1. Get long grain rice: **basmati** (fine grains, faster cook), **jasmine** (sticky, works with chopsticks), **brown** (wholegrain, retains nutrients) or other. Measure 50g/ 2oz per person or see recipe.

2. Wash and rinse thoroughly under cold water to remove excess starch or it can get gluey.

3. Stir into pan of boiling water. Cook for as long as pack directs. White usually takes 10 minutes. Brown up to 30. Bite a grain to test it. Drain well.

4. Use jasmine directly. Tip others into a sieve/colander. Rinse in boiling water to get it light. Drain. Cover hot rice with a cloth for 3 minutes. Fluff with a fork to separate the grains. Serve or use in recipe.

5. Safety alert: cold rice gets toxic fast. Cool on a tray. Refrigerate immediately.

FEEDS **2** £ EXPRESS

2 chicken breasts, very thinly sliced
110g/4oz basmati/long-grain rice

Marinade
2 cloves garlic, thinly sliced
1½ tbsps lemon juice
1 tbsp cornflour
6 drops soy sauce
Little egg white

Stir-fry
½ tbsp veg/groundnut oil
4 drops sesame oil
1 clove garlic, thinly sliced
1 tbsp lemon juice
2–3 spring onions, chopped

Luscious Lemon Chicken Rice Bowl

Use basmati as the base for this light and lemony chicken stir-fry. Really delicious.

1. Mix marinade ingredients. Stir into thinly sliced chicken.

2. Cook rice as basic method. Drain. Cover and rest 3 minutes.

3. Heat wok or pan. Add oils and heat up. Stir-fry garlic for 20 seconds without browning.

4. Add chicken. Stir-fry briskly for 3 minutes till cooked white all through. Reduce heat. Add lemon juice, spring onion. Cook 1 minute. Taste. Adjust seasoning. Slap rice into bowls. Sit lemon chicken on top.

YOU CAN
* serve on noodles instead of rice
* eat it cold to-go on rice or noodle salad

Hot Sticky Chicken Rice

Teriyaki your chicken. It makes great sticky finger food. Get your chopsticks into the rice bowl. Also great cold on noodle or rice salad.

FEEDS
3–4   ££

Teriyaki sauce
4 tbsps soy sauce
1½ tbsps Chinese rice wine
2 tbsps rice vinegar
1 tbsp caster sugar
¾ in piece fresh ginger, grated or chopped
Few drops sesame oil
Or
Kikkoman's Teriyaki Marinade

8 chicken thighs
225g/8oz basmati or long grain rice
Pinch salt

1. Preheat oven to 220°C/425°F/gas 7. Mix teriyaki sauce ingredients.
2. Simmer gently for 5–10 minutes in small pan. Remove. Tip two-thirds into a bowl for the marinade. Save the rest to drizzle at end.
3. Prep chicken: pull skin off. Leave the bone in (holds together better and tastes sweeter).
4. Spread foil on baking tray/shallow roasting tin (stops sauce baking on). Brush meat with marinade. Sit on foil in single layer. Slap in oven.
5. Brush with marinade every 5 minutes for 20–25 minutes. Remove.
6. Meantime, cook washed rice as basic (for brown, start earlier).
7. Preheat medium grill. Grill chicken 5 minutes till sticky brown, but white inside. Leave it to relax. Drain rice. Cover with a cloth for 3 minutes. Fluff with a fork.
8. Pile rice into bowls. Top with chicken. Drizzle with saved one-third of marinade.

YOU CAN
✳ marinate chopped chicken breast in teriyaki for 30 minutes. Thread on skewers. Grill, turning and brushing, for 5–7 minutes or till cooked white through. Sit it on rice. Gorgeous.

175g/6oz basmati rice
Sauce
1 tbsp malt vinegar
2 tsp sugar/runny honey
1 tbsp tomato ketchup
1½ tbsps soy sauce
Stir-fry
4–6 rashers bacon, chopped
1 medium onion, peeled, cut in
  half-moons
1 red/orange pepper
  de-seeded, cut in lengths
Vegetable oil
3 eggs, lightly beaten
Fresh basil/parsley (optional)

110g/4oz Thai sticky rice
1½ tbsp soy sauce
1 tsp runny honey/sugar
5 cloves garlic, sliced
2 tbsps groundnut/
  sunflower/vegetable oil
2 fat shallots or 1 small onion,
  finely chopped
1 small red chilli, de-seeded,
  finely chopped
110g/4oz chestnut
  mushrooms, quartered
110g/4oz fine green beans,
  trimmed, chopped
½–1 red pepper, de-seeded,
  cut in long thin slices
2–3 cabbage leaves, finely
  shredded (optional)
Handful cashew nuts
  (optional)
Finely chopped fresh coriander
Few fresh basil leaves
  (optional)

English Breakfast Rice Bowl

All the benefits of a fry-up (bacon, egg, ketchup) with a twist
of the oriental and a lovely rice base.

1. Cook rice as basic (pg 112). Drain. Cool on a plate. Chill.

2. Mix vinegar, sugar/honey, ketchup and soy sauce together in a small
bowl.

3. Heat wok or large frying pan. Add bacon. Fry without oil. Stir on
low heat for 5 minutes without browning.

4. Add onion, pepper, few drops of oil (only if bacon was dry). Fry
very gently for 5 minutes. Add eggs. Stir until almost set.

5. Add a drop more oil and increase heat. Chuck rice in. Stir quickly
to get everything hot and to crisp it up.

6. Tear herbs in. Tip onto plates. Drizzle with sauce.

Firecracker Sticky-Rice Bowl

This one can be very hot, so watch it. The rice may look
innocent but it holds the chilli scorch. Gorgeously sticky
integrated rice dish.

1. Cook rice as basic (pg 112). Drain. Cool on a plate. Chill.

2. Mix soy and honey/sugar together to make sauce.

3. Fry three of the sliced garlic cloves very gently, in a small pan in a
few drops of oil till just colouring. Set aside for garnish.

4. Make stir-fry. Heat wok. Add oil. Heat again. Add and stir-fry
remaining garlic, shallots, chilli for 2 minutes. Add mushrooms, beans,
pepper, optional cabbage and stir-fry for 2–3 minutes.

5. Add rice and optional nuts. Mix and heat through till it's all
blistering hot. Add sauce and coriander.

6. Tip into bowls. Top with fried garlic slices and optional basil.

YOU CAN
✱ cool down chilli mouth with yogurt/milk drink. Water/beer won't do it.

Egg-Fried Rice & Ginger Lime Drizzle

FEEDS 1   **£**   **V**   **EXPRESS**

Whenever you have left-over rice, let it cool and get it into the fridge ready to throw this cheeky number together. When you're less skint, add cooked prawns, diced chicken, gammon. Tasty. Packed with brain boosters – top exam food.

1. Get rice from fridge or make fresh as basic (pg 112).
2. Mix drizzle ingredients in bowl.
3. Pour boiling water over peas to defrost them. Drain.
4. Beat eggs in a bowl. Add half spring onion.
5. Heat a wok. Add oils. Reduce heat. Add the egg, stirring, so it just starts to scramble. Tip rice in before it sets.
6. Increase heat. Stir mix with a fork to break it up. Add peas, remaining spring onion. Heat for 1 minute. Sprinkle coriander, if using.
7. Pile into a bowl. Pour over drizzle (or soy sauce/ketchup).

Fried rice
200g–225g/7–8oz chilled cooked basmati/long-grain rice (or cook 75–110g/ 3–4oz rice from scratch)
50g/2oz frozen peas
2 eggs
1 spring onion, chopped
2 tbsps sunflower oil
Dash sesame oil
Fresh coriander (optional)

Ginger Lime Drizzle
1 tsp caster sugar
2½ tbsps soy sauce
1½ tbsps rice vinegar
Little fresh grated ginger
Squeeze lime juice

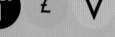

FEEDS 1 · £ · V · EXPRESS

50g/2oz basmati rice, white/
  brown

Sauce
Soy sauce
Pinch sugar/runny honey
Water/rice wine/lemon juice

Stir-fry
½ tbsp groundnut/sunflower
  oil mixed with 1 tsp
  sesame oil
2–3 cloves garlic, sliced
1 head pak choi, base
  trimmed, leaves stripped and
  sliced

Tea
Pinch of Good Luck,
  Gunpowder, Jasmine or
  other green/Chinese tea
Boiling water

Chill-Out Rice with Garlic Pak Choi & Green Tea

Relax with a little bowl of healthy green tea and this pukka rice stunner. Pak choi's like a wonder veg – it packs good flavour and loves the garlic. Experiment with green teas.

1. Cook rice as basic (pg 112).
2. Meantime, mix sauce ingredients.
3. Drain and rest the cooked rice in a pan, covered with a tea towel.
4. Heat wok. Add oil. Stir-fry garlic for a few seconds without browning. Add pak choi. Stir-fry for 1–2 minutes.
5. Add the sauce. Heat for 1 minute.
6. Pile rice into bowl. Top with stir-fried veg.
7. Put a pinch of tea in a cup/mug. Top with boiling water.

YOU CAN
* top rice with tenderstem broccoli, stir-fried tofu for other calm eats

Nasi Goreng Tasty Rice Bowl

Thick rice and onion mix with cool extras. First time I ate this I was on a filmshoot. I loved it, recreated it. Wok it up anytime – makes a great breakfast.

1. Use cooled left-over rice from fridge or cook as basic (pg 112) and cool. Prepare cucumber garnish. Have prepped vegetables handy.

2. Heat wok. Add half the oils and heat up. Add onion, garlic, ginger, chilli powder, shrimp paste (if using). Stir-fry for 2 minutes or till onion's soft.

3. Add rest of oil. Add rice after 5 seconds. Stir-fry for 3 minutes. Add soy, oyster sauce (if not using shrimp paste), optional sugar if you want sweet browned rice. Add prawns, if using. Stir through to heat.

4. Fry eggs in separate pan or plate the rice and re-use the wiped wok.

5. Top rice with fried eggs, coriander, prawn crackers, cucumber.

YOU CAN

✱ skip prawns and use veggie oyster sauce

✱ add bits of cold char sui

✱ top with strips of omelette (pg 108) instead of fried egg

Cooled cooked rice from fridge (or cook fresh 75–110g/3–4oz basmati long-grain or Thai)

1½ tbsps groundnut oil

½ tsp sesame oil

1 medium onion, peeled, sliced into long half-moon shapes

1 clove garlic, crushed

Bit of fresh ginger, grated

Good pinch chilli powder

½ tsp shrimp paste or ½ tbsp oyster sauce

Soy sauce

1–2 tsps brown sugar (optional)

Few cooked shrimps/prawns (optional)

Garnish

2 eggs

Fresh coriander, chopped

Prawn crackers

Bit of cucumber, peeled, de-seeded, chopped into half-moons (optional)

117

1.2 litres/2 pints chicken/veg
  stock/water and stock cube
50g/2oz butter
1 onion, finely chopped
1 clove garlic, crushed
350g/12oz Arborio/Vialone
  Nano risotto rice
  (unwashed)
1 small glass white wine
50g/2oz Parmesan plus extra,
  freshly grated, for garnish
Knob of butter
Salt and black pepper

Skint Risotto Parmigiana

Risotto's like a great thick, creamy rice soup, soaking up all kinds of flavours and textures. Even the simple ones reward patience. Get creative by adding extras. Like fresh herbs, the juice and rind of a lemon, left over roast chicken.

1. Boil up stock in a pan for a few minutes. Reduce heat to a simmer.
2. Melt butter in a second pan. Add onion. Cook gently 7–10 minutes till softened, not coloured. Add garlic, if using.
3. Add rice (unwashed). Stir with a wooden spoon for 1 minute. Increase heat. Add wine. Stir till almost absorbed.
4. Reduce heat to medium. Add a ladleful of hot stock. Once absorbed, add another. Keep going till it's all in, the rice is soft and creamy, the risotto soupy (can take 10–15 minutes). Add extra liquid if needed.
5. Add Parmesan and knob of butter. Season. Stir well. Cover. Rest risotto for 3 minutes. Serve in bowls, with extra Parmesan to add at the table.

YOU CAN
∗ make sausage risotto: at step 2 add meat from 4 de-skinned sausages and

½ tsp fennel seeds, and use red wine instead of white
* make pea and bean risotto: at step 4 add a handful of peas and broad beans
* make prawn or salmon risotto: at step 5 add cooked prawns or smoked/hot smoked salmon
* make risotto Bolognese: at start of step 4 add left-over ragu (pg 97)
* make suppli (stuffed rice balls): chill risotto left-overs, mix with a bit of egg, mould into small flat circles. Put cubes of Mozzarella/Cheddar inside, and mould into sealed balls. Dunk in beaten egg, breadcrumbs. Fry.

Blow-Out Mushroom Risotto

Great date food. Chat while you stir – get them to pour the hot stock in. Dried mushrooms pack a punch. OK, they cost a bit more but make up for it in flavour.

1. Get pan of stock simmering as previous recipe.
2. Stick dried mushrooms in a bowl with 3 tbsps hot stock. Leave to rehydrate.
3. Melt butter in large pan on low heat. Add onion, pinch salt. Cook for 5 minutes without colouring. Add garlic.
4. Increase heat. Add rice (unwashed). Stir to coat. Cook 1 minute. Add wine. Stir as the rice crackles. When the moisture's almost absorbed, add rehydrated mushrooms with soaking liquid, fresh mushrooms, bit of chosen herb. Add a ladleful of hot stock.
5. Stir till liquid's nearly absorbed. Add another ladleful. Continue for 10–15 minutes till stock is used, rice creamy, risotto soupy. Add lemon juice, more wine or stock if needed.
6. Remove from heat. Stir in half the cheese, soy, seasoning, butter/ cream/crème fraîche, if using. Cover. Rest it for 3 minutes. Top with torn herbs, extra Parmesan.

YOU CAN
* use Knorr chicken stock cube in place of (or as well as) own chicken stock
* make salmon, cheese and green-leaf risotto: skip the mushrooms, and at end of step 5 add 225g/8oz hot smoked salmon, in large bits, plus a handful of spinach/rocket

FEEDS 4 · ££ · V OPTION

1.2 litres/2 pints chicken or vegetable stock
10g/½oz dried mushrooms, chopped
50g/2oz butter (or 2 tbsps oil)
1 medium onion, finely chopped
2–3 cloves garlic, crushed
350g/12oz Arborio/Vialone Nano rice (unwashed)
150ml/5fl oz white wine
350g/12oz mushrooms (including chestnut), roughly chopped
Fresh tarragon/thyme/parsley, chopped
Juice ½–1 lemon
50g/2oz freshly grated Parmesan plus extra
1 tsp soy sauce
Salt and pepper
Extra butter/1 tbsp cream/ crème fraîche (optional)

HOW TO COOK LENTILS

1. Weigh out lentils according to recipe. Wash and rinse under running water, removing stray husks, stones, bits.

2. Boil in lots of water according to type (check packet). Generally:

Brown lentils cook in 25–30 minutes (soak in cold water for 1 hour to reduce cooking time).

Green lentils cook in 20 minutes.

Puy lentils: add to cold water. Bring to boil. Cook for 10–15 minutes.

Red and yellow lentils: cook as recipe.

3. Boiling lentils hard for first 5 minutes makes for easier digestion. Drain. Use as per recipe. Substitute a few cooked lentils for meat in sauces (ragu, shepherd's pie, chilli) to save cash and in vegetable sauces for cheap protein.

FEEDS 2–3   ££

1 tsp olive oil
1 onion, finely diced
1 clove garlic, crushed
2 rashers bacon, diced
Few mushrooms, chopped
4 good sausages
110g/4oz Puy or green lentils
200ml/7fl oz stock/water
100ml/3½fl oz red wine/cider/
    stock
Fresh/dried thyme/oregano
Salt and black pepper
Single cream/crème fraîche
    (optional)

One-Pan Lentil & Sausage Dinner

There's something about a bubbling hot pot of bangers, lentils and wine that does it for me. Give it a go – keep your diet varied. NB Lentils are packed with protein and carbs, so well good for you.

1. Heat oil in a large frying pan over low heat.
2. Fry onion, garlic, bacon for 5 minutes till soft. Add mushrooms. Fry 5 minutes. Increase heat.
3. Add sausages, turning so they colour. Add lentils. Stir, to coat them in oil. Add stock, wine/cider, herbs. Boil briefly. Reduce heat. Simmer very gently for 20–25 minutes.
4. Check and stir regularly, adding more liquid if you need to. Season. Stir in a bit of cream/crème fraîche if you want to.

Skint Lentils, Rice & Lovely Sticky Onions

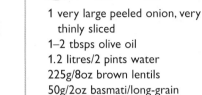

FEEDS 3–4 £ V

1 very large peeled onion, very thinly sliced
1–2 tbsps olive oil
1.2 litres/2 pints water
225g/8oz brown lentils
50g/2oz basmati/long-grain rice
Salt and black pepper

So simple – caramelized onions lift earthy-tasting lentils and rice to a different level. Surprisingly gorgeous. A top skint number. You can top with sliced hard-boiled egg, yogurt. Great with a tomato and onion salad (pg 210).

1. Fry onion very gently in olive oil over low heat till it caramelizes (don't let it burn). This could take 20–30 minutes.

2. Meanwhile boil water in a pan. Add lentils. Cook for 20–25 minutes or till almost tender. Add washed rice.

3. Cook rice and lentils for another 10 minutes or till tender and water absorbed. Drain in a colander if this doesn't happen.

4. Leave covered with a tea towel for 5 mins. Tip on a plate. Stir in most of the onions, leaving a good few on top. Season.

YOU CAN
✱ use green lentils: add rice sooner as green lentils cook faster

FEEDS 3–4   £   V

225g/8oz Puy lentils
850ml/1½ pints water
4–6 spring onions, finely sliced
1 medium red onion, finely
  chopped
Handful cherry tomatoes cut
  in half, or 4–6 large
  tomatoes, chopped
Freshly chopped parsley/mint/
  coriander/basil
Salt and black pepper

Dressing
½ tsp caster sugar/honey
½ tsp mustard (Dijon/English/
  wholegrain)
1 tbsp vinegar (red or white
  wine/cider/balsamic)
5 tbsps good olive oil

A Proper Lentil Salad

Puy lentils cost a tad more but they've got a certain something – like a chic taste, cool look, loads of nutrients. Spritz them up with some jazzy little salad bits. Eat with cold deli meats, cheeses, griddled veg, hardboiled eggs with mayo.

1. Wash and prep lentils. Slap in a pan with water. Bring to boil. Boil 15 minutes till cooked with a bit of bite. Drain. Tip into a bowl.
2. Mix dressing ingredients by shaking in a jar or whisking together.
3. Mix onions, tomatoes, herbs, lentils, seasoning. Pour dressing over. Leave to cool.

YOU CAN
* add olives or chopped sun-dried tomatoes
* mix in bits of cooked ham/gammon/crumbled cooked bacon, diced Mozzarella/Swiss cheese/crumbled feta/Lancashire cheese
* use other brown/green lentils – watch they don't collapse as you boil them

Bulgur Wheat Salad with Vit-Boost Pomegranate

FEEDS 2–3 ££ V

A right riot of tastes and colours – plus it's pretty damned healthy. Herbs aren't just cute leaves. They're medicinal. Bulgur packs iron, protein, B vitamins and zinc. Top off with the pomegranate – an exotic antioxidant.

110g/4oz bulgur wheat
600ml/1 pint boiling water
2–3 tbsps extra virgin olive oil
Juice of ½–1 lemon
Salt and black pepper
1 clove garlic, crushed
Handful mint, finely chopped
Handful parsley, finely chopped
3 tomatoes, diced small
Length of cucumber, diced small
1 red onion, diced small
1 pomegranate/pack of pomegranate seeds/drizzle pomegranate molasses

1. Put bulgur wheat in bowl and pour on freshly boiled water. Cover and leave to soak for 15–30 minutes till soft. Drain well. Squeeze excess moisture out in a tea towel: put the wheat in the centre, bunch towel and twist. Or just spread out to dry a bit while you prep other ingredients.

2. Chuck wheat into a bowl with oil, lemon juice, seasoning, garlic, herbs. Fork it up. Add salad bits or slap dressed wheat onto a plate, surrounded by separate heaps of salad.

3. Top wheat with pomegranate seeds or stir in a bit of fizzy pomegranate molasses.

Eat with: flatbreads ✳ mezze ✳ kebabs ✳ cream cheese (pg 47) ✳ hard-boiled eggs ✳ griddled halloumi

YOU CAN
✳ skip the pomegranate. Chop bits of satsuma in there.
✳ no fresh herbs? Toss in chopped rocket, watercress or baby spinach.
✳ crumble feta on top
✳ chuck in a box for healthy to-go salad
✳ cook wheat in a pan of simmering water for 10 minutes if hurrying

Couscous
225g/8oz couscous
300ml/½ pint boiling water
Salt and black pepper
4–5 tbsps olive oil
1 tbsp lemon juice

Salad
2 big fat ripe tomatoes, chopped small (or lots of cherry tomatoes)
1 red pepper, de-seeded, chopped small
3 spring onions, sliced, or 1 small red onion, diced, or both
Few black olives, pitted, chopped (optional)
Fresh coriander/parsley/mint, finely chopped

Marinade
Garlic, crushed
Lemon juice
Olive oil

Griddle
Choice of:
6 thick slices halloumi cheese
4–6 lamb cutlets
2 small chicken fillets, diced into bite-size pieces

Classic Couscous Salad with Fast Citrus Griddle

This cheeky little grain is a masterpiece, linking all the beautiful strong flavours together. Team with your top griddle – or make the lot for a blow-out party.

1. Tip couscous into heatproof bowl. Cover with boiling water then tea towel. Leave for 5 minutes. Tip onto large plate. Separate grains with fork. Cool for 2 minutes. Season. Drizzle with oil, lemon juice.

2. Mix salad ingredients into it, or pile them on top.

3. Prep griddle: mix garlic, lemon, oil. Tip this mixture over cheese, chicken or lamb. Leave to marinate.

4. Heat griddle pan on high. **Cheese:** slap onto the heat. Sizzle it. Turn after 1–2 minutes. Cook other side till char-grilled and melty.

Chicken: toss bits onto the griddle for 2–3 minutes, turning quickly, until golden outside, white all through. **Lamb:** cook each side 2–3 minutes till crispy brown outside, pink and tender in the middle. Season.

5. Pile onto couscous. Team with green leaves and flatbread.

YOU CAN
* spice up chicken with cumin/chilli powder/coriander
* add chilli/lime to halloumi
* treat lamb to mint/rosemary/oregano
* tomato-up your couscous: mix 150ml/5fl oz tomato juice, 50ml/2fl oz olive oil, juice 1 lemon, 2 tbsps boiling water. Tip over dry couscous. Leave for 1 hour or longer.
* fry chicken bits in a pan. Grill lamb and halloumi.
* slap couscous salad and griddled chicken in a healthy box to go

Couscous with Bite
(& Vegetable Skewers)

FEEDS 3–4 | £ | V | EXPRESS

Hot harissa's the star of the show in this one, transforming timid couscous. Skewering vegetables is a brilliant way of cooking them. Fun to eat – great for sharing.

1. Soak couscous in boiling water for 5 minutes, covered with cloth. Tip out onto plate. Separate grains with a fork. Season.

2. Tip dressing ingredients into a bowl. Leave to marinate.

3. Tip prepped vegetables into a bowl. Turn them in a mix of olive oil, garlic, lemon. If using wooden skewers, soak them in water.

4. Preheat grill. Thread veg onto metal/wooden skewers. Turn regularly under heat till browned and just tender.

5. Mix dressing into couscous. Sit skewers on top. Season.

YOU CAN

✱ make chicken or lamb kebabs (pg 159) instead of veggie skewers
✱ cook thin lengths of courgette, pepper, aubergine on a griddle pan if you've no grill. Slap onto couscous and drizzle with dressing.

300ml/½ pint water
225g/8oz couscous

Dressing
50ml/2fl oz olive oil
2 tbsps lemon juice
2 tsps red harissa paste
Lemon rind
2 tbsps parsley/coriander
25g/1oz raisins, chopped
25g/1oz dried apricot, chopped
Salt and black pepper

Skewers
Cherry tomatoes
Red onion, cut into chunks
Courgettes, sliced
Button mushrooms
Olive oil
Garlic
Lemon juice
Salt and pepper

3 tbsps olive oil
110g/4oz onion, finely chopped
2 cloves garlic, peeled and
   crushed
1 small dried chilli, crumbled
1 tsp ground cumin
1 tsp ground coriander
¼ tsp turmeric
1 tsp lemon grass paste or ½
   piece fresh, finely chopped
200g/7oz chestnut
   mushrooms, finely chopped
Juice of 1 lime
1 x 400g/14 oz can chickpeas,
   drained
75g/3oz fresh breadcrumbs
Few shakes Tabasco sauce
2 tbsps fresh coriander, finely
   chopped
Salt and pepper

White flour for coating
Olive oil for frying

Stack
Griddled, toasted or warmed
   bun or ciabatta
Guacamole (pg 18)
Thinly sliced tomato
Mayo mixed with sweet chilli
   sauce
Rocket
Shredded spring onion

Chickpea Burgers

Chickpeas are a cheap and easy source of protein and fibre – and low in fat. Smash them into this great burger that even hardcore carnivores will love. Great for sport and brain training. Stack creatively…

1. Heat olive oil in pan. Cook onion and garlic very gently for 5 minutes till soft, not coloured.
2. Add chilli, cumin, coriander, tumeric, lemon grass. Cook and stir for 3 minutes. Add mushrooms, lime juice. Cook for 5 minutes. Remove from heat.
3. Crush chickpeas with a fork or semi-blitz with handblender. Fork into fried veg with breadcrumbs, Tabasco, coriander, salt and pepper.
4. Spread coating flour on plate. Flour hands. Shape mix into 6 burgers, handling gently. Roll in flour to coat. Chill in fridge for 15 minutes – or longer, till needed.
5. Fry in a little olive oil for 5 minutes per side or till cooked through. Sit on salad leaves or stack.

Homestyle Baked Beans & Polenta

Team your beans with crisp fingers of griddled polenta. This Italian grain is well fast and multi-tasks. Eat it griddled or while hot and soft. Match with stews and sauces. No polenta in? Slap these sweet beans onto toast then.

FEEDS **2** ££ **V**

1. **Polenta:** boil water, salt in large pan. Add polenta in steady stream. Stir on low heat 5 minutes as it spits and thickens. Add butter, cheese if using, garlic, optional herbs. Pour into lightly oiled tin or onto baking paper. Cool. Chill. Mark into fingers.

2. **Beans:** fry onion very gently in hot oil for 5 minutes. Add garlic. Cook 2 minutes. Add tomatoes, stock, soy sauce. Simmer very gently for 10–15 minutes. Add mustard, Worcestershire sauce, sugar, beans. Simmer another 5 minutes. Taste for balance. Adjust.

3. **Finish:** Brush polenta fingers with olive oil. Cook for a few minutes per side on scorching griddle, or grill till hot and crispy. Serve.

YOU CAN

✱ use left-over polenta with ragu (pg 97). Or top with roasted mushrooms or halved baked beef tomatoes.

Polenta
1.2 litres/2 pints water
½ tsp salt
200g/7oz fast-cook polenta
50g/2oz butter
2 big handfuls grated Cheddar/ Parmesan (optional)
2 cloves garlic, crushed
Fresh herbs (optional)
Oil for griddling

Beans
1 tbsp olive/sunflower oil
1 small onion, finely chopped
1 clove garlic, crushed
1 x 200g/7oz can tomatoes
150ml hot water mixed with 2 pinches Marigold veg stock
2 shakes soy sauce
1–2 tsps made mustard
Shake Worcestershire sauce
1 tbsps brown sugar
1 x 400g/14oz can cannellini/ mixed/haricot beans

MEAT

Can't beat it (unless you're a vegetarian, of course). Get yourself some quality eating without blowing a hole in your pocket. Some old-school favourites and gorgeous new ones.

4–6 best pork or pork and
apple sausages

Onion gravy
Knob of butter
1 large onion, very thinly sliced
Pinch salt
Pinch sugar
1 clove garlic, crushed
½ tbsp plain flour
300ml/½ pint chicken/veg
stock/Marigold stock/Knorr
stock cube in water
Good shake Worcestershire
sauce
Splash balsamic vinegar
Fresh sage, chopped (or pinch
of dried)
Salt and black pepper

Mash
450g/1lb old potatoes (e.g.
Maris Piper/King Edward)
peeled, quartered
50–75ml/2–3fl oz skimmed
milk, warmed
Bit of mustard
Dollop of butter
Salt and pepper

Sticky Pan Sausage & Mash with Sweet Onion Gravy

A sumptuous classic – if you put the effort in. Get some proper nice sausages from the butcher's or farmers' market. Make creaming the mash a workout. Finish it off with an onion gravy…

1. Gravy: melt butter in pan. Add onions, salt, sugar, garlic. Cook very gently without colouring for 10 minutes.

2. Add flour. Stir for 2 minutes (removes floury taste). Gradually add stock, stirring. Add sauce, balsamic vinegar, herbs. Season.

3. Simmer on very low heat for 15 minutes. Taste. Adjust seasoning.

4. Mash: boil potatoes till tender. Drain. Dry over heat for 1 minute. Mash with hot milk, mustard, butter. Or try creamy extras (pg 215). Season well.

5. Sausages: grill, fry or bake the sausages slowly. Grill on low setting, turning regularly. Or bake at 200°C/400°F/gas 6 for 20 minutes. Or fry in a little oil over very, very low heat for about 20 minutes for the stickiest sausage. Eat with brown sauce, apple chutney, red cabbage (pg 213).

YOU CAN

✱ use red onions for the gravy. Substitute a bit of the stock with Guinness and add ketchup to beef it up. Or drizzle bangers with melted onion marmalade.

Banging Sausage Casserole

The smell of this one bubbling away does it for me. Layer up some of your favourite ingredients and bang them in for a good long bake and soft, beautiful flavours. One for sharing – a good winter warmer.

1. Preheat oven to 190°C/375°F/gas 5.

2. Heat oil and butter in frying pan. Fry sausages for a few minutes, turning till browned all over. Remove to a plate.

3. Repeat with bits of bacon. Fry till just browned. Remove to plate. Add onions to pan. Fry lightly for 5 minutes or till just softening.

4. Layer up casserole: cover base with a third of the onion and potato slices. Sprinkle herbs. Season lightly. Add half the bacon and 4 sausages.

5. Layer the next third of onions and potatoes, herbs, rest of the bacon, sausages. Finish with onions, then potatoes.

6. Pour stock/water over the lot. Cover with lid/foil. Bake for 50 minutes. Uncover. Bake for 15 minutes till browning. Gorgeous.

YOU CAN

✱ add mushrooms at step 3
✱ add a few baked beans at step 5
✱ add a sliced apple with the potatoes
✱ add a few chunks of black pudding

FEEDS
4

££

1 tbsp sunflower oil
½ tbsp butter
8 great fat best bangers
8 slices unsmoked bacon, cut into big bits
3 large onions, thinly sliced
700g/1½lb floury spuds (King Edward, Maris Piper), thinly sliced
Fresh herb of choice, chopped (or pinch of dried)
850ml/1½ pints stock/Knorr stock/cider/water or mix
Salt and black pepper

Batter
4 eggs
300ml/½ pint milk or milk/
    water mix
Salt and pepper
225g/8oz flour

1 tbsp oil
8 best sausages

Yorkshire Toad in the Hole

A God's Own County classic but you've got to get it to rise. One rule: get the tin and fat good and hot before chucking in your batter. It's that simple. Eat with creamy mash (pg 215) and cabbage (stir-fried in butter, garlic). Enjoy yourself.

1. Start batter: using handblender/mixer/whisk, beat eggs, milk and seasoning till frothy. Leave 20 minutes. Heat oven to 220°C/425°F/gas 7.
2. Heat oil in roasting tin (mine's 30x20x7cm/12x8x3in) for 5 minutes. Add sausages. Cook 10 minutes.
3. Finish batter: if using machine, sift flour into milk mix and whisk till smooth. If doing by hand, sift flour into bowl, make well in it, then use wooden spoon or balloon whisk to beat in egg/milk mixture very gradually till smooth.
4. Pour mix over sausages. Cook 20–40 minutes till well high, golden, delicious.

YOU CAN
* cook for 20 minutes in 4-hole Yorkshire-pud trays – one banger per hole
* wrap rasher of bacon round bangers before browning
* veggie option: substitute chunks of butternut squash/red onion/grilled Portobello mushroom for bangers

Champion Cider-Baked Gammon

This gorgeous gammon got my brother Tom through uni. OK it takes a bit of time and process – boil it up in something sweet then roast it off in a sticky glaze. But it's great for crowds and would last you a week. Brilliant taste and worth the effort. Recycles hot and cold in lots of ways.

FEEDS 8 **££**

2kg/4½ lb gammon or bacon, tied with string to keep shape
Water to cover
300ml/10fl oz cider, ginger beer, orange or apple juice plus extra for roasting
1 onion, peeled, halved

Jammy glaze
1 tbsp English mustard
1–2 tbsps chunky marmalade/ apricot jam/runny honey
1 tbsp soft brown sugar
Load of whole cloves

Eat with: roast/baked spuds
* cauliflower cheese (pg 212)
* baked red cabbage (pg 213)

1. **Day(s) before:** sit meat in large bowl. Cover with cold water to get excess salt out. Fridge it.
2. **On the day:** drain. Put in pan with cider/juice/ginger beer. Cover with water. Add onion.
3. Boil gently for 1 hour. Meantime mix glaze (not cloves).
4. Preheat oven to 200°C/400°F/gas 6. Drain meat over bowl. (Keep the stock to use for soup if not too salty.)
5. Cut skin from ham leaving fat exposed. Cut across in diamond pattern with sharp knife. Stud all over with cloves.
6. Sit meat in baking dish/tin with extra juice/cider. Smear two-thirds of glaze over. Cook 45 minutes. Brush with extra glaze a few times. Relax meat for 10–15 minutes before carving.
7. Make jammy gravy: slap extra cider/juice in meat tin. Boil and stir bits in.

YOU CAN
* keep a vacuum-packed joint in the fridge for weeks. Buy when you're flush, bake when you're hard up.
* chuck into stir-fries, crêpes, omelettes, salads, sarnies

FEEDS 2 ££

Ribs
8 large spare ribs
½ can cola
2 cloves garlic
Bit of fresh ginger, chopped
Water

Marinade
5 tbsps ketchup
2½ tbsps soy sauce
2½ tbsps rice wine vinegar
1½ oz brown sugar
2 cloves garlic, crushed
Little grated fresh ginger
½ tsp dried chilli flakes or
   shake of Tabasco sauce
Dash of cola

Fizzy Chilli Cola Spare Ribs

One good use for cola. Stick it in a marinade. Let it tenderize your spare ribs then bake them. Great finger-licking food.

1. Stick ribs into big pan with cola, garlic, ginger, water to cover.

2. Bring to boil. Reduce heat. Simmer for 20 minutes. Spoon off froth.

3. Remove from heat. Cool ribs in water for 10 minutes. Drain well.

4. Mix marinade, adding cola – but keep it thickish. Tip over ribs, turning. Leave for as long as you've got.

5. Heat oven to 200°C/400°F/gas 6. Lay foil over baking tray/tin. Arrange ribs in single layer. Brush with marinade. Cook for 15 minutes. Turn. Repeat. Don't overcook – they dry out quickly.

YOU CAN

✱ cook indoors to step 4, then finish on barbie

✱ use this marinade for pork chops before frying

✱ make half as much marinade again for a pouring sauce

✱ experiment with marinade combos – Barbecue-style Chicken marinade (pg 150) and Char Sui Pork marinade (see right) work with spare ribs

My All-Time Favourite Char Sui Pork

Pork fillet's a great lean meat for soaking up sweet Chinese flavours. Marinate overnight or do it in the moment. Veggies: try this marinade with tofu (pan-fry it).

1. Stick the pork fillets into the mixed marinade. Turn. Leave for as long as you have. Preheat oven to 200°C/400°F/gas 6. Lay foil in roasting tin. Sit grill rack on top.
2. Roast meat on rack for 20 minutes or till cooked through. Brush with marinade occasionally. Remove. Rest it in a warm place for 5 mins.

YOU CAN
* eat cold in lunch-box-to-go with noodle salad (pg 205)
* slice up in Chinese pancakes with hoisin sauce, cucumber sticks, spring onion

FEEDS 4   **££**

2 x 450g/1lb pieces pork fillet

Marinade
2 tbsps runny honey
2 tbsps soy sauce
2 tbsps hoisin sauce
1 tsp sesame oil
Pinch of five-spice powder

Eat with: stir-fry * rice * noodles

Powerhouse Pork Chop & Salsa

Gym-goers' delight. Pork's packed with protein and thiamine to get the energy out of your carbs. Breadcrumbs keep the meat sweet. A crunchy salsa works with the rich flavours.

1. **Pork:** bash chops with a rolling pin to flatten a bit. It's trickier with the bone in, but go with it.
2. Blitz bread and garlic to crumbs with handblender. Put on a plate.
3. Mix egg, mustard, herbs, seasoning on another plate.
4. Dunk each chop into the egg mix to coat well. Dip into crumbs till well covered. Chill for later or cook now.
5. Heat oil or oil/butter mix in a pan. Add chops once hot. Fry a few minutes per side till cooked but still juicy inside, crunchy outside. Test with a knife. Rest meat while making salsa.
6. **Salsa:** dice tomatoes and apple. Mix lemon juice, oil, mustard, sugar, seasoning. Drizzle over.

YOU CAN
* do powerhouse chicken: bash a chicken fillet and treat it the same way

FEEDS 2   **££**   **EXPRESS**

2 pork chops (bone in) or boneless loin steaks
2 thick slices bread, crusts removed
1 clove garlic, crushed
1 egg, beaten
1 tsp Dijon mustard
Pinch dried sage/rosemary/oregano
Salt and pepper
Oil and/or butter

Apple salsa
2 tomatoes
1 apple
Lemon juice
Olive oil
Mustard
Pinch sugar
Salt and pepper

1 piece of belly pork (6 ribs or
   as big as you like)
2 tsps sea salt
1–2 tsps fennel seeds
Fresh herbs – thyme/
   rosemary/sage
3 apples, cut in half

Gravy
Water/apple juice/cider

Awesome Roasted Belly Pork with Apple Gravy

I don't know where to start with this one – there's so much going on. Best gravy I know ... sweet melty meat ... crunchy crackling. Pork belly's the chef's secret. Feeds loads and takes very little effort. Enjoy with mash or roasties and trimmings.

1. Preheat oven to 220°C/425°F/gas 7. Wipe meat dry with kitchen paper.
2. For crackling: score skin deeply at 1cm/½ in intervals with kitchen/Stanley knife then pierce all over (or ask butcher to do it).
3. Rub salt and fennel seeds between cracks. Stick herbs in/on.

4. Roast in a tin for 30 minutes without oil. Lower the temperature to 180°C/350°F/gas 4 and roast for another 45 minutes–2 hours or longer till meat's almost melting.

5. About 20 minutes before finish, add apples, cut side down.

6. Rest meat 15 minutes. Remove from tin and lose apples before carving. Pour water/cider into tin with juices. Boil and stir for brilliant appley gravy.

YOU CAN

✱ make crispy Chinese-style belly pork. At step 3 rub in 1 tsp each of five-spice powder and sea salt. Sit uncovered in fridge to help flavour (day before is OK) or cook immediately at 230°C/450°F/gas 8 on rack in tin for 20 minutes. Reduce temperature as above. Cook till crispy. Rest. Smash into chunks with knife/cleaver.

Bacon, Cheese & Potato Tartiflette

All your favourite basics on meltingly hot and softly gorgeous form. An easy one-pan classic. There's one rule – don't rush it.

1. Heat oil in large frying or sauté pan. Fry bacon till just crispy. Remove. Add butter. Fry onion, garlic gently for 10 minutes till softened and just colouring.

2. Meantime, slice potatoes very thinly for speedy, even cooking. Add to pan with the bacon, onion, garlic. Sprinkle thyme. Cover.

3. Leave pan on low heat for 15–20 minutes or till spuds are soft. A knife should pass through easily. Grate/slice cheese over top.

4. Replace lid. Cook a few minutes more till cheese has melted. Scrummy. Good with a sharp salad.

FEEDS **2–3** £

Olive oil
4 rashers good bacon, chopped
Bit of butter
1 onion, thinly sliced
2 cloves garlic, thinly sliced
450g/1lb potatoes, waxy style are best (Charlotte, Wilja), peeled weight
Fresh or dried thyme
110g/4oz Gruyère/Cheddar

3 medium potatoes, peeled,
  chopped bite-size
2 tbsps olive oil
1 large onion, roughly chopped
2 cloves garlic, crushed
Pinch chilli powder
175g/6oz corned beef
Juice of ½ lemon
Few leaves fresh or dried
  thyme
Dash Worcestershire sauce
Salt and black pepper

US 24-Hour-Diner-Style Corned Beef Hash

Store-cupboard special. Get it for breakfast, late night, anytime. Adding lemon and thyme lifts it out of the ordinary. Note: dried herbs are stronger than fresh – 1 tsp dried equals 1 tbsp fresh ones.

1. Boil potatoes in lightly salted water for 7–10 minutes till just tender. Drain well. Cover with a cloth.

2. Meantime, heat oil in large frying pan and gently fry onion, garlic, chilli and salt for 5–10 minutes till soft, not coloured.

3. Add potatoes with extra oil if needed. Stir to coat. Cook 10 minutes or till browning. Stir in crumbled corned beef, lemon juice, thyme, Worcestershire sauce, seasoning.

4. Cook till crusty or slap into a dish and sit under a hot grill till the top browns. Add a fried or poached egg if you like.

YOU CAN
* substitute corned beef with cooked ham, bacon, roast beef or pork, fried chorizo, mushrooms, drained tinned tuna, gammon
* roll spuds in a bit of mustard before frying
* chuck some cheese in there

The Burger...
(& Options)

Beats Maccy-D's any day. Use good minced steak. Get everyone to customize their burger.

FEEDS 4 £ EXPRESS

700g/1½ lb best bought minced beef steak, or mince it yourself
Salt and black pepper
Herbs of choice, chopped
1 tbsp light olive oil or butter
1 medium onion, finely chopped
2 cloves garlic, crushed
4 burger buns

Binding – choice of
Bit of beaten egg
1 tbsp cream
Mayo
Ketchup
Dijon mustard
Beer
Guinness

Stacking – choice of
Chorizo sausage, sliced and fried
Grated cheddar
Grilled smoked bacon
Iceberg lettuce, shredded
Tomato, thinly sliced
Red onion, thinly sliced
Ketchup
Mayo
Mustard
Rocket

Extras
Big chips (pg 178)
Coleslaw (pg 210)
Green salad (pg 210)

1. Slap mince into bowl. Season. Add herbs.
2. Heat oil/butter in pan. Fry onion and garlic very gently for 5–10 minutes to soften, not colour.
3. Tip in with meat. Mix with a fork. Add binding of choice – but not too much.
4. Shape meat firmly for 4 fat or 8 thin burgers. Ideally, chill for 1 hour.
5. Preheat grill (you can also fry/griddle/barbie).
6. Cook 3–4 minutes per side depending on taste for rare/medium/ well done.
7. Warm buns. Or slice, then griddle cut side. Stack with fillings just as you like. Team with any extras.

YOU CAN
✱ dice and blitz rump steak in processor for best mince
✱ substitute one-third of the meat with breadcrumbs if skint
✱ do pork burger. At step 1 use minced pork. At step 2 add grated fresh ginger and chopped coriander, grated apple. Stack with beansprouts, mayo, cucumber/spring onion sticks, sweet chilli sauce.
✱ do lamb burger. Use good lamb. Add fresh mint. Add prepped bulgur wheat if skint.
✱ do cheeseburger. Dip slices of goat's cheese in beaten egg, seasoning. Coat in garlic breadcrumbs (pg 88). Chill. Griddle aubergine slices. Fry goat's cheese both sides in bit of oil. Layer mayo, aubergine, cheese, rocket in griddled bun.
✱ do tuna burger for 2. Chop 225g/8oz fresh tuna in tiny bits, add crushed garlic, Dijon mustard, fresh herb, pinch cayenne, Tabasco. Chill. Fragile – fry gently.

Cottage Pie (the Beef)

Originated in the north sometime in the 18th century as a cheap meal to feed huge families, apparently — so then, perfect for your house. Try varying the basics every time you do it. Makes it interesting. Tasty comfort food.

1. Put oil into a big pan. Heat gently. Add onion with pinch of salt. Cook for 5 minutes till soft. Add garlic, carrot. Cover. Sweat very gently for 5 minutes or till the carrot softens.

2. Increase heat. Add meat. Stir briskly till well browned up. Stir flour in. Add stock/water/wine, tomatoes, purée, sugar, sauce, herbs, seasoning. Boil 2–3 minutes.

3. Reduce heat. Simmer, lid on, for 30 minutes. Meantime make mash topping (pg 215).

4. Preheat oven to 200°C/400°F/gas 6. Taste meat and adjust seasoning. Tip into 1 large pie/ovenproof dish or 4 small ones (freeze uneaten extras). Cover with well-flavoured-up fluffed-up mash.

5. Cook for 30–40 minutes or till golden, hot and bubbling.

YOU CAN

* add grated Cheddar to mash
* use a bit of mashed sweet potato/parsnip in topping
* do shepherd's pie: good minced lamb instead of beef
* do spicy keema. At step 1 omit carrots, grate in a 3cm/1½in chunk ginger. At step 4 add 1 finely chopped de-seeded chilli, 1 tsp garam masala. Cook till step 5. Add defrosted peas, lemon or lime juice, fresh coriander. Eat with rice or chapattis (pg 196), yogurt (pg 46).
* make moussaka. At step 2 add 2 pinches cinnamon, dried oregano, more red wine. At step 3 fry slices of aubergine in oil till browned/soft. At step 4 layer meat sauce, grated cheese, aubergine. Repeat layers. Finish with aubergine. Top with cheese sauce (pg 90). Awesome.

FEEDS
4–6   ££

1 tbsp light olive/sunflower oil
1 large onion, very finely chopped
Pinch salt
2–3 cloves garlic, crushed
1–2 carrots, very finely diced
450g/1lb best minced steak
1 tbsp plain white flour
275g/10oz stock/water/bit of red wine
1 x 400g/14oz can chopped tomatoes
2–3 tbsps tomato purée
Pinch sugar
2 tsps Worcestershire sauce
Herbs of choice, chopped
Salt and black pepper

Topping
900g/2lb floury potatoes (e.g. King Edward, Maris Piper)
2 tbsps milk
Dollop butter
1 tsp mustard
Salt and pepper

Best Beef Chilli

Having a movie marathon/poker night/party? Sort this out. Make it a couple of days ahead if that helps. Let the flavours develop. Chuck loads of chilli in (maybe a bit of chocolate, Mexican-style). Pile on the extras and get the beers in.

1. Heat olive oil gently in a big pot. Fling in onions, garlic. Cook gently till soft, not coloured (5–10 minutes).

2. Add the chilli or chilli flakes, cumin, coriander, red peppers. Increase the heat and stir. Chuck the beef in. Stir briskly till it's browned up.

3. Add tomatoes, ketchup, purée, sugar, cinnamon, beans, stock or water, lemon/lime juice, salt and pepper. Stir well.

4. Bring slowly to boil. Reduce heat. Simmer very gently, covered, for 1–2 hours. Stir occasionally. Taste, adjust seasoning. Add coriander and Tabasco.

2 tbsps olive oil
2 big onions, finely chopped
2 cloves garlic, crushed
2 chillies, de-seeded, finely chopped, or 1 tsp chilli flakes
1 tsp cumin
1 tsp coriander
2 red peppers, de-seeded, chopped small
900g/2lb best minced beef
2 x 400g/14oz cans chopped tomatoes
4 tbsps ketchup
4 tbsps tomato purée
1 tsp sugar
1 pinch cinnamon
1 x 400g/14oz can red kidney beans
1 x 400g/14oz can haricot beans
200ml/7fl oz stock/water
Juice of 1 lemon/lime
Salt and pepper
1 tbsp coriander, chopped
Hot pepper sauce or Tabasco (optional)

Extras
Guacamole (pg 18)
Sour cream
Grated Cheddar
Nachos
Cornbread or muffins

YOU CAN

✱ make traditional cornbread or muffins. Mix 110g/4oz plain flour, 1 level tbsp baking powder, 110g/4oz polenta, 75g/3oz grated Cheddar. Add 300ml/10fl oz milk, 2 beaten eggs, 50g/2oz melted butter. Bake in greased muffin tin (12–15 minutes) or 900g/2lb loaf tin (40–50 minutes) at 200°C/400°F/gas 6.

Speedy shortcurst pastry
(or buy good all-butter one)
225g/8oz plain white flour
Pinch salt
110g/4oz cold butter
2–3 tbsps very cold water
Beaten egg/milk

Filling
225g/8oz lean beef steak
(rump or best stewing)
1 medium onion, finely
chopped
2 medium potatoes, diced
small
2 tbsps stock or oil
Pinch dried thyme
1 tbsp parsley, chopped
Salt and black pepper

Houseparty Steak Cornish Pasties

My mate Tom got me into these when I was staying at his place. I had one every day for breakfast (OK – lunch by the time we were up). Think gorgeous meaty filling, crumbly pastry. PS They freeze well.

1. Preheat oven to 200°C/400°F/gas 6. Make pastry (pg 238). Chill it.
2. Cut meat into small bits. Mix with onion, potato, stock/oil, herbs, seasoning to make filling.
3. Cut pastry into four. Roll one bit out in a square on lightly floured surface. Sit a 15cm/6–7in plate on it. Cut round it. Or guess. Repeat for 4 circles. Roll a bit thinner if you want to.
4. Pile filling onto circles. Don't overfill. Damp edges with water. Pull opposite sides up over filling, pinching firmly to seal well. Brush with beaten egg/milk. Sit on baking trays. Cook 15 minutes. Reduce heat to 190°C/375°F/gas 5 and cook for another 15–20 minutes. Cover with paper if browning. Eat with brown sauce, ketchup, pickle, baked beans.

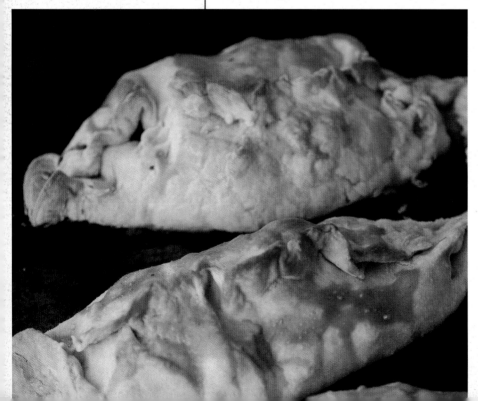

YOU CAN
fill with …
* veggie chilli (pg 33)
* ragu (pg 97)
* gammon (pg 133) and veg
* Cauliflower Cheese
(pg 212)
* Champion Cheese
Mushrooms (pg 45)
* veg: diced potato, onion, garlic, cauliflower, sweet potato, swede, carrot, beans, peas. Fry briefly. Add drizzle of Marigold stock, herbs, seasoning.

Blow-Out Steak Dinner

Special. Head for your trusty local butcher or farm shop and get a quality steak for your money. Team with dauphinoise (best potato dish ever invented), ginger drizzle and salad.

1. Start dauphinoise ahead: preheat oven to 180°C/350°F/gas 4. Butter oven dish.
2. Slice potatoes very thinly. Swirl in cold water. Rinse. Dry. Lay half in dish. Season.
3. Mix garlic, cream, milk. Pour half over potatoes in dish. Top with remaining potatoes. Season. Top with rest of cream mix.
4. Cover with foil and bake for 1 hour. Remove foil. Bake for 30 minutes or till soft.
5. Meantime, get steak to room temperature. Bash to thin it a bit if very thick. Snip fat at edge to stop curling.
6. Mix drizzle ingredients if using. Prep any salad, extras.
7. Rub garlic, oil, pepper into steak. Heat griddle pan or heat oil/butter in frying pan.
8. Griddle or fry steak for 2 minutes per side. (Or more: depends on thickness and your taste. Stick knife in – best pink, not raw or leathery.) Rest meat for a few minutes. Salt it. Eat with dauphinoise, drizzle, green salad.

YOU CAN

* skip dauphinoise. Make big chips (pg 178).
* mix wine into pan juices. Boil and stir. Add cream and stir. Pour over steak.
* mix herbs, garlic, lemon juice into soft butter. Put onto greaseproof paper. Roll like a Christmas cracker. Chill. Slice and top cooked steak.
* mash Roquefort/other blue cheese. Melt on steak.
* gin-and-tonic it. Rub a bit of gin, pepper, oil, thyme into rump steak. Chill in freezer bag for up to 3 days. Get it to room temp. Griddle.

FEEDS **2**   £££

Dauphinoise
450g/1lb floury potatoes (e.g. King Edward, Maris Piper), peeled
3 cloves garlic, crushed
150ml/5fl oz cream plus bit of milk
Salt and black pepper

Ginger drizzle (optional)
1 tsp caster sugar
1 tbsp sweet chilli sauce
1 tbsp malt/wine vinegar
2 tbsps fish sauce
Little grated ginger

Steak
2 x 175g/6oz fillet or 225g/8oz rib-eye or sirloin steaks
1 clove garlic, cut in half
A little olive oil/butter for frying
Salt and pepper

Roast Beef & Yorkshires

Magnificent meat … and a great excuse to make Yorkshires. Get everyone chipping in for this one. Enjoy leftovers in sarnies/salads.

1. Get beef to room temperature (1–2 hours). Weigh. Calculate cooking time (see below).

2. Preheat oven to 230°C/450°F/gas 8. Sit beef in tin. Run knife down fat, scoring it lightly at intervals. Season. Rub oil in. Cook for 15 mins. Halve/quarter or leave pre-boiled spuds whole. Add to the tin.

3. Reduce heat to 180°C/350°F/gas 4 for rest of cooking time. Baste meat with juices once or twice.

4. Get Yorkshires going – make batter exactly as for Toad in the Hole (see pg 132).

5. Stick oil in Yorkshire-pud tin (30x20x7cm/12x8x3in) or in two 4-hole Yorkshire trays. Put into oven to preheat for 5 minutes (key to rising).

6. Remove beef from tin when done. Leave to relax in warm place. Leave spuds in oven to crisp. Increase heat to max.

7. Pour batter into tins. Cook Yorkshires 20–30 minutes till puffy.

8. Remove potatoes from roasting tin. Sit tin on hob. Add water/stock/wine. Boil and stir for a lovely thin beef gravy.

YOU CAN

✱ calculate cooking times. Start with a 15-minute blast, then reduce heat as follows…

On bone: 12 mins per pound (rare)/15 mins (medium)/20 mins (well done)

Boned joint: 10 mins per pound (rare)/12 mins (medium)/15 mins (well done)

✱ coat top of joint with mustard, cracked black pepper, or rub in grated ginger

✱ make skint pot roast. Flour and then brown a 1.8kg/4lb joint of beef brisket/topside in oil/butter. Sit in casserole dish with chopped carrots, onion, herbs. Pour over stock/wine/beer/water to cover two-thirds of meat. Season. Boil. Reduce heat. Cook, covered, at 170°C/325°F/gas 3, for 3 hours plus. Add dumplings (pg 145) 20 minutes before eating.

FEEDS
6   £££

1.8kg/4lb beef rib on bone or 1.3kg/3lb boned rib joint
2 tbsps olive oil
Salt and black pepper
Roasties
2–3 medium potatoes per person (Maris Piper or King Edward), peeled, boiled 10 minutes, drained
Yorkshires
4 eggs
300ml/½ pint milk or milk/water mix
Bit of oil
225g/8oz flour
Salt and pepper
Extras
Horseradish sauce
Mustard
Cauliflower Cheese (pg 212)
Carrots and broccoli

Beef in Guinness or Red Wine

Cheaper cuts of meat tenderize with long, slow cooking. Customize this classic casserole. Makes loads so freeze some.

FEEDS
4   ££

25g/1oz butter
2 tbsps oil
2 large onions, chopped
1 clove garlic, crushed
4 carrots, chopped
Little ginger, grated (optional)
900g/2lb stewing or chuck
    beef, cut into 4cm/1½in bits
1½ tbsps plain flour
Salt and black pepper
250ml/8fl oz Guinness/red
    wine
250ml/8fl oz stock/water
1–2 tbsp Worcestershire sauce
2 tsps tomato purée
1 tsp sugar
1 bay leaf
Thyme, fresh or dried
Splash balsamic vinegar
Bit of orange rind (optional)
Mushrooms (optional)
Lemon juice (optional)

1. Heat butter and half of oil in large casserole. Fry onion, garlic, carrot, ginger on low heat for 10 minutes. Remove from pan.

2. Roll chunks of meat in seasoned flour to coat. In batches, fry in rest of oil for 3–4 minutes max. Turn for even browning.

3. Remove meat from pan. Add Guinness or wine, stock, sauce. Boil up on increased heat, scraping the base, stirring in any crusty bits.

4. Return meat and veg to pan. Add tomato purée, sugar, herbs, balsamic, orange rind (if using). Boil briefly.

5. Simmer on very low heat or cook at 180°C/350°F/gas 4 for 2–3 hours till well tender. Add optional mushrooms 30 mins before finish.

6. Taste. Adjust flavour balance. You may want to add more sugar, some lemon juice, another herb, seasoning. Too much gravy? Remove meat. Boil it down a bit. Put it back together.

Eat with: bits of toasted baguette spread with mustard
* baked garlic croûtons for crunch * mash * green veg
* herby dumplings

YOU CAN
* cover with puff pastry and bake in a pie
* replace Guinness/wine with stock or water
* use red wine, beef stock, soy sauce at step 4. Add 2 star anise, 2 tsps honey, 1 tbsp wine vinegar instead of Worcestershire sauce for Chinese casserole.
* replace Guinness with cider, beef with pork. Add apple and prunes to onions.
* casserole chicken bits. At step 1 coat chicken joints in flour. Fry. Cook in stock/water/cider/chopped tomatoes.
* add dumplings…
Mix 110g/4oz sifted self raising flour, pinch salt, 50g/2oz vegetable suet, fresh chopped/dried herbs with splash water. Make 12 balls. Add at end of step 5. Cook for 15–20 minutes.

3–4 small waxy potatoes
1 chicken fillet, sliced diagonally
Length of cooking chorizo
   sausage, peeled, sliced
2–3 tbsps butter beans
2 cloves garlic, sliced
A bit of passata, or tomato
   purée thinned with a bit of
   water
Splash of wine/cider/sherry/
   stock/apple juice
Sprinkle dried oregano
Drizzle of olive oil
2 tbsps crème fraîche/sour
   cream (optional)
Salt and black pepper

FEEDS
1   ££

4 small potatoes
1–2 carrots, sliced in
   matchsticks
Few green beans
1 chicken breast, sliced
   diagonally
½ lemon, sliced
Basil/rosemary/parsley
2 cloves garlic, sliced
Salt and black pepper
Bit of white wine/stock/apple
   juice

Two Chicken Ready Meals

Homestyle ready meals. Make up either of these neat parcels ahead of time or the night before. Get them into the oven as soon as you're in … low stress. Feel free to customize.

Chicken, Bean & Chorizo Ready Meal

1. Boil potatoes for a few minutes to get them started. Drain. Squeeze gently to bruise/crack them.

2. Lay a large sheet of foil out in front of you. Fold edges up a bit before setting out the components of your ready-meal.

3. Set out chicken slices neatly on foil. Arrange potatoes, chorizo, beans, garlic around. Spoon in a bit of passata/thinned tomato purée for sauce. Drizzle in wine/stock/juice, add herb, olive oil. Add crème fraîche/sour cream (or serve after cooking). Season.

4. Pull foil up and over. Scrunch top firmly to parcel. Chill for later/next day, or cook 20 minutes at 220°C/425°F/gas 7 (open and test chicken with knife). From chilled may take longer. Open foil at table.

YOU CAN

✱ add a melting cheese, feta, olives, use tomato sauce (pg 83)

Classic Chicken Dinner Ready Meal

1. Boil potatoes for 4 minutes. Add carrots, beans and boil for further 2 minutes. Drain. Squeeze potatoes as above.

2. Spread foil out as above.

3. Lay out chicken pieces. Slip lemon slices in between. Arrange veg, herbs, garlic around. Season.

4. Drizzle in wine/stock/juice, bit of olive oil. Close parcel and cook as above.

YOU CAN

✱ add a bit of ham/bacon, peas, broad beans, cream, asparagus

✱ do a Chinese-style ready meal on foil/baking paper. Parcel up chunks of chicken in mixture of oyster/hoisin sauce, crushed garlic, bit of sesame oil, rice wine, spring onions. Bake 20 minutes at 220°C/425°F/gas 7. Delicious.

FEEDS 3–4 £ EXPRESS

4 good chicken breasts
Plain white flour for coating
3 good pinches chilli powder
Salt and black pepper
1–2 eggs, beaten
Polenta (plain or with bits of
   dried vegetable)

Dips
Sweet chilli sauce
Salsa (pg 18)
Ketchup
Garlic mayo (pg 211)

FEEDS 1 ££ EXPRESS

1 chicken fillet
Butter
½ glass white wine
A little fresh tarragon, finely
   chopped, or pinch dried
2–3 tbsps cream
Salt and pepper

Eat with: crunchy spuds
* salad

Chicken Strippers

Dunk and dip these crunchy strippers anytime (the polenta does it). Whack into bowls for party-style munchies.

1. Preheat oven to 200°C/400°F/gas 6.

2. Lay chicken fillets on board between sheets of clingfilm. Bash to flatten.

3. Cut into strips – at least 8cm/3in or longer.

4. Make coating: slap flour, chilli powder, seasoning onto one plate, beaten eggs on another, polenta on a third.

5. Coat chicken strips in flour, egg, polenta. Sit on greased baking tray.

6. Cook for 10 minutes till white and moist right through. Dip them.

YOU CAN

* fry 2–3 minutes per side, in a little oil/butter

* serve retro chicken and chips. Make big chips (pg 178). Slap in a paper bag with chicken strips, salt, vinegar, ketchup.

Creamy Tarragon Butterfly Chicken

Haute cuisine meets student life: chicken, tarragon, wine, cream – pretty cheap and bloody tasty.

1. Find flap under chicken. Open breast out like butterfly wing. Bash to flatten with mallet/rolling pin/flat of hand (between clingfilm sheets if you want to).

2. Heat a bit of butter in a pan. When it sizzles, slap chicken down. Cook a few minutes per side till white all through. Test with a knife. Remove and keep warm.

3. Chuck wine into pan. Boil, stirring to include bits and juices. Add tarragon, cream, seasoning. Reduce heat. Bubble for 2 minutes. Pour over chicken.

YOU CAN

* add ½ tsp mustard to sauce

* coat chicken in seasoned flour to make schnitzel. Serve with tarragon or fresh tomato sauce (pg 83).

Lime Sherbet Butterfly Chicken

Brilliant tasty, lean meat. Good to eat during exams etc. The tryptophan in chicken triggers serotonin, chills you out and gives you focus. Team with salad if eating midday (keeps you awake). Rice or pasta in the evening (chilling). Good cold in a salad bowl or box to go ... saves cash.

1 chicken fillet
Bit of ginger, grated
1 clove garlic, crushed
Lime juice
Olive oil
Coriander, chopped
Sea salt

1. Open and bash chicken as Tarragon Butterfly Chicken, opposite.
2. Make a dressing with ginger, garlic, lime juice, oil, coriander, salt.
3. Rub half the dressing into the chicken. Heat griddle pan.
4. Slap meat down. Cook both sides till white all through.
5. Slice diagonally. Drizzle with rest of dressing.

YOU CAN
* drizzle with pomegranate molasses for extra fizz

FEEDS
4   ££

8–12 chicken bits on bone
Sauce
1 medium onion, chopped
Little oil
4 tbsps honey
2 tbsps brown sugar
1 tbsp Worcestershire sauce
2 tbsps soy sauce
4 tbsps ketchup
4 tbsps wine vinegar
2 cloves garlic, crushed
1 tsp ground/fresh ginger
2 tsps mustard
2–3 tbsps orange juice
Pinch paprika

Extras
Salad
Frying Pan Crunchy Potatoes
  (pg 214)

FEEDS
3–4   ££

8–12 chicken bits on bone
Black pepper
2 lemons
1 head garlic
Olive oil
Sprinkle of dried tarragon
Sea salt
Sprigs rosemary or sage leaves
1 large glass wine

Easy Barbecue-Style Chicken in a Tin

Every state in America has its favourite barbecue sauce – this is mine. Works harmoniously with the chicken (loves pork and lamb too). Finger-lickingly irresistible.

1. Fry onion in a little oil till soft. Mix with all other sauce ingredients.
2. Slap sauce over chicken. Leave to marinate for up to 1 day.
3. Preheat oven to 200°C/400°F/gas 6. Stick chicken onto foil in roasting tin. Cover with more foil. Bake for 30 minutes. Remove top foil. Baste. Bake for further 15 minutes or till chicken bits are white all through (test with knife – drumsticks take the longest).
4. Remove to plate. Thin any remaining sauce with a bit of water and drizzle over.

YOU CAN
✱ use this sauce to barbie spare ribs (pg 134), pork or lamb chops (pg 161)

Easy Lemon & Rosemary Baked Chicken

Another classic combo – the lemon and rosemary complement each other so well. I reckon they could pack the flavour into even a dull bird.

1. Preheat oven to 200°C/400°F/gas 6.
2. Chuck pepper-seasoned chicken into roasting tin. Squeeze lemons over it and add to tin. Drop in garlic. Drizzle with olive oil. Sprinkle tarragon. Slap in the oven for 30 minutes.
3. Remove. Sprinkle with salt, rosemary/sage. Cook another 10 mins.
4. Pour wine into hot tin so it sizzles. Cook another 5 minutes.

YOU CAN
✱ stir a bit of crème fraîche into sauce
✱ roast chicken bits in tin for 25 minutes with parboiled potatoes, peeled carrots. Add 6 sausages. Cook a further 20 minutes.

Irresistible Five-Spice Baked Duck Legs

Think crisp, salty duck. Five spice twist. Fruity sauce. The long slow cook draws the fat off (perfect for making five spice roast potatoes, so store in the fridge – don't waste it).

1. Preheat oven to 200°C/400°F/gas 6.

2. Chuck duck into roasting tin/dish in single layer.

3. Prick all over with fork (releases fat). Rub with five-spice, salt. Poke rosemary, garlic, star anise under. Bake 1 hour. Pour fat off regularly.

4. Meantime, melt jelly/jam in pan. Whisk in wine/juice, water. Simmer for a few minutes. Remove from heat.

5. Reduce heat to 180°C/375°F/gas 4. Pour sauce over duck. Cook 15 minutes or till tender yet crispy.

YOU CAN

✳ shred duck meat and eat in Chinese pancakes/wraps with smear of hoisin, spring onion, cucumber. Use iceberg lettuce leaves if no pancakes.

✳ shred and add to noodle soup (pg 73)

FEEDS
2   ££

4 duck legs
Five-spice powder
Sea salt
2 sprigs rosemary
6 cloves garlic
4 bits star anise

Jelly Sauce
2 tbsps redcurrant jelly/ cherry jam
150ml/5fl oz red wine/ apple/pomegranate juice
4 tbsps water

FEEDS
3—4 ££ EXPRESS

Cakes
1 knob ginger, grated
4 cloves garlic, crushed
1 tbsp lemon grass paste or
  1 finely chopped stick
450g/1lb skinless chicken thigh
  or breast fillets, chopped
Good pinch salt
2 tbsps fresh coriander
¾ red chilli
5 spring onions, trimmed,
  chopped
6 canned water chestnuts,
  drained

Frying
Groundnut oil plus splash of
  sesame
Dried breadcrumbs (pg 11)

Little Thai Chicken Cakes

I'm a great fan of gyoza (Japanese dumplings) but the outside is tricky to make, so I nicked the filling idea and make these cakes instead. Very easy, tasty and good for dipping…

1. Using machine: blitz ginger, garlic, lemon grass in processor. Add chicken. Process briefly. Add salt, coriander, chilli. Process again. Add onions, water chestnuts. Process very briefly for rough texture. By hand: chop everything finely. Mix together.

2. Test flavour: heat a little oil in pan. Fry off a bit of mix. Taste. Adjust main mix. Roll into 12 small cakes. (Handmade option may need bit of egg white/sesame oil to bind.) Roll in dried breadcrumbs to coat.

3. Heat more oil in pan. Fry cakes a few at a time, turning, till cooked through. Dip into chilli sauce or Ginger Lime Drizzle (pg 115).

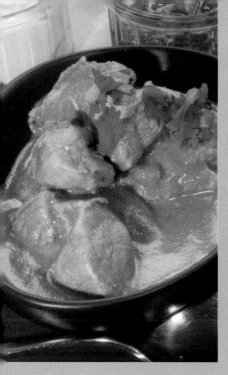

Red Butter Chicken Curry

Curry-house standard for student-house eating. Get the Cobras in and make yourself up a banquet (make chapattis).

1. Melt butter in large casserole/pan. Add onion, garlic, salt. Cook gently for 2 minutes. Add spices. Cook till onion is well soft.
2. Tip in passata, mango chutney, tomato purée, vinegar, ginger. Stir well and bring to boil. Reduce heat and simmer for 10 minutes.
3. Chuck chicken bits in. Stir, adding cream, yogurt. Lower heat. Simmer very gently for 10 minutes till chicken's white all through and still tender. Cook rice in meantime (pg 112). Stir coriander into chicken. Taste. Adjust seasoning. Serve with chapattis (pg 196), raita, mango chutney, dhal (pg 21).

FEEDS 4   £££

75g/3oz butter
1 medium onion, finely diced
4 cloves garlic, crushed
Pinch salt
½ tsp cayenne pepper
½ tsp chilli powder
3 tsps sweet paprika
2 tsps garam masala
2 tsps ground coriander
1 cinnamon stick
4 cardamom pods, crushed
700g/1¼ pints tomato passata
1–2 tbsps mango chutney
2 tbsps tomato purée
2 tbsps red wine vinegar
1 tbsp fresh grated ginger
6 large skinless chicken
   breasts, diced
200ml/7fl oz double cream
150ml/5fl oz natural yogurt
225g/8oz Basmati or other
   long grain rice
Fresh coriander

Quick & Tasty Thai Green Curry

Classic Thai curry, gastropub-style. Team it with jasmine sticky rice. You can use chicken breast (a bit leaner and more expensive) or thigh (cheaper, richer, darker, chef's choice).

1. Heat oil in wok/pan. Fry onion gently for 2 minutes to soften. Add curry paste, optional chilli. Stir and cook for 1 minute.
2. Continue stirring, adding coconut milk and water/stock. Prepare and cook rice (pg 112).
3. Increase heat. As mix boils, stir in chicken, mushroom, beans, lime leaves. Reduce heat. Simmer gently for 15 minutes.
4. When meat is cooked through and white (test), stir in lime juice, sugar, fish sauce. Top with basil. Pile onto rice. Eat with chopsticks.

FEEDS 3–4   £££

1 tbsp groundnut oil
1 onion, chopped
2 tbsps green curry paste
½ mild red chilli (optional)
375ml/12fl oz coconut milk
150ml/5fl oz water or stock
50g/2oz sticky rice per person
450g/1lb chicken thigh/breast,
   chopped into bite-size bits
6 mushrooms, thinly sliced
Handful fine green beans, each
   cut into 3
4 kaffir lime leaves
Juice of 1 lime
2 tsps brown sugar
1 tbsp fish sauce
Basil leaves, torn

4 chicken breasts, chopped
    into large bite-size bits
Bit of flour
Salt and black pepper
1 tbsp olive oil/bit of butter
1 small onion, finely chopped
1 clove garlic, crushed
2 carrots, chopped
425ml/15fl oz chicken
    stock/water or Knorr stock
    cube and water
Splash white wine (optional)
Pinch dried tarragon
½ tsp Dijon mustard
1 pack all-butter flaky pastry,
    defrosted
A little beaten egg or milk

Eat with: mash (pg 215)
✳ broccoli ✳ green beans
✳ carrots ✳ gravy – heat extra
liquid from pie

Flaky Bird Pie

Sometimes only a pie will do. This chicken job is basic but delicious. The tarragon lifts it. Use all-butter puff pastry or make speedy shortcrust (pg 238). Get mates round…

1. Chop chicken. Roll in mix of flour, little salt, pepper to coat well.
2. Heat oil and butter in a large pan/casserole dish. Add onion, garlic. Cook very gently for 5–10 minutes till soft, not coloured. Add chicken. Increase heat. Stir quickly for 1–2 minutes. Add carrot. Reduce heat.
3. Gradually add stock, wine, tarragon, stirring well. Boil on increased heat to thicken a bit. Simmer, covered, on low heat for 20 minutes.
4. Remove from heat. Stir in mustard, seasoning. Tip into 1-litre/2-pint or available pie dish (or small dishes). Include enough liquid to cover meat.
5. Preheat oven to 220°C/425°F/gas 7. Roll pastry out on floured surface to fit pie dish, plus extra. Lift pastry over and down onto dish with a rolling pin. Press and pinch down edges to seal. Trim carefully with a knife (not too neatly as pastry can shrink). Cut two slits in top to release steam if no funnel. Brush with beaten egg/milk. Cook for 15 minutes. Reduce heat to 180°C/ 350°F/gas 4 and cook for another 15 minutes till hot and bubbling.

YOU CAN
✳ make leek and chicken pie. At step 2 fry 1–2 leeks till soft. Add to mix.
✳ make chicken and mushroom pie. At step 2 fry a few choice mushrooms. Add them.
✳ make chicken and veg pie. At step 2 add sliced carrots, squash, asparagus, peas, potatoes.
✳ make chicken and ham pie. At step 3 add diced cooked gammon/ham or bacon.
✳ add orange juice to stock
✳ make steak and mushroom pie. At step 1 coat 600g/1½lb stewing/skirt steak, cubed, in flour. At step 3 add Worcestershire and tomato sauce, red wine. Simmer meat very, very slowly on hob or in very low oven for 2 hours. Add more stock/water if needed. Cool. Cover. At end of step 5 bake for 30 minutes.

1 very large chicken
1 lemon, in 4 bits
Loads of garlic cloves
Sea salt and black pepper
Fresh rosemary/sage/tarragon
3–4 rashers streaky or back
   bacon/pancetta
Olive oil
Water/wine/stock

Roasties
2–3 medium potatoes per
   person (Maris Piper or King
   Edward), peeled, boiled 10
   minutes, drained

Eat with: cauliflower cheese
✶ carrots ✶ stir-fried broccoli
✶ beans ✶ carrots cooked in
foil parcel with orange juice
and butter ✶ salad

A Brilliant Lemon Roast Chicken

Not just for Sundays – there's nothing wrong with a midweek roast if there are loads of you chipping in. Buy free-range if you can and get everyone helping to prep the trimmings… No bacon? Keep top of the bird well oiled/buttered. Classic.

1. Preheat oven to 190°C/375°F/gas 5.

2. Sit chicken in roasting tin. Squeeze 2 bits lemon over. Drop in tin. Stuff other 2 bits into bird. Drop garlic in tin.

3. Season with salt and black pepper. Lay bacon over breast.

4. Drizzle all over with oil, leaving a glug in the tin (use extra if no bacon). Tuck fresh herbs between joints or sprinkle top with dried.

5. Roast for 20 minutes per 450g/1lb weight, plus another 20 minutes.

6. Halve/quarter the pre-boiled spuds or leave whole. Add to the tin after first 20 minutes to get them roasting.

7. Baste bird with juices a couple of times, turning spuds. Prep any side dishes.

8. Test for doneness. Leg should be loose. Juices should run clear, meat look white when pierced with knife. Remove bird and garlic from tin and rest in warm place.

9. Increase heat to get roast spuds crispy brown (10 minutes). Remove from oven and from tin.

10. Stick tin on hob. Add water/wine/stock to remaining juices. Boil up, stirring bits in. Serve it all up. Gorgeous.

YOU CAN

✶ stuff chicken with half an apple. Add the other half to tin, cut side down, 20 minutes before end. Use juices for making good gravy with apple juice or cider.

✶ make stock/soup from carcass, odd bits, gravy, jelly (see pg 88)

✶ recycle chicken in pies, risotto, sarnies, wraps, salads, stir-fries, soup, noodle and rice dishes

✶ roast carrots/sweet potato chunks/chicory in with chicken

✶ mix bit of cream cheese (pg 47), garlic and herbs, and slip under skin of breast – also works with chicken-leg joints. Or stuff cream cheese into slashed chicken breasts with a bit of pesto. Season. Drizzle oil. Cook as is or wrap in Parma ham. Bake in shallow dish at 190°C/375°F/gas 5 for 30 mins/till white through, tender.

Easy Roast Duck

My favourite game bird. Cooking it this way does it justice – soft sweet dark meat with crispy salty skin. OK it takes time but the oven does the work. Perfect. Snack on leftovers.

1. Preheat oven to 220°C/425°F/gas 7.
2. Stab duck all over with fork. Rub salt into skin.
3. Roast in a tin (on rack if you have one). Pour fat off regularly. Save for cooking potatoes.
4. Reduce heat after 20 minutes to 190°C/375°F/gas 5. Cook another 2 hours plus till skin is crispy and bird tender.
5. Rest bird. Cut into 4 with scissors/big knife. Make sauce: bubble up cherry jam, red wine in a pan. Pour over. Eat with green salad, potatoes.

FEEDS 3–4 ££

1 duck
Sea salt

Sauce
3 tbsps morello cherry jam
1 glass red wine

157

FEEDS 4   ££

4 lamb shanks
Bit of flour
Salt and pepper
Oil
2 white/red onions, sliced
2 carrots, chopped
3 cloves garlic, crushed
Bit of rosemary, chopped
275ml/½ pint red/white wine
275ml/½ pint water
1 tbsp balsamic vinegar
  (optional)
Mash (pg 215)

Eat with: green beans stir-fried in bit of olive oil and balsamic vinegar

Melting Lamb Shanks & Creamy Mash

Another long slow-cook job. Chuck in any seasonal vegetables (get down to the market). Play the waiting game till it's all fully tender, then jump in.

1. Preheat oven to 170°C/325°F/gas 3. Roll lamb in flour and seasoning.

2. Heat oil in large casserole. Fry lamb gently, turning to brown all over. Remove from pan.

3. Add veg and garlic to oil in pan. Fry lightly. Sit browned lamb on top. Add herb, wine, water, vinegar if using. Bring to brief boil.

4. Stick it in the oven (or let it simmer on low heat on the hob). Cook 2 hours minimum. Start making creamy mash 25 minutes before eating time. Taste meat sauce. Adjust flavouring. If too liquid, remove meat and veg and boil it down a bit.

YOU CAN

✱ make it a day ahead. Remove fat before reheating.

✱ cook for much longer to get meat melting

✱ do Greek lamb stew: at step 3 add chunks of aubergine to fry, then add can chopped tomatoes, tomato purée, pinch cinnamon and oregano, pinch sugar

FEEDS 4   £   EXPRESS

450g/1lb minced lamb
2 fat cloves garlic, crushed
1 tbsp fresh mint/oregano/
  coriander, finely chopped
1 tsp ground cumin
1–2 tsps ground coriander
Salt and black pepper

Eat with: flatbreads ✱ yogurt
✱ tomato and red onion salad
✱ tzatziki (page 16)
✱ couscous

Gorgeous Quick-Cook Lamb Koftas

Turn out a production line of these for parties, barbies, cool alfresco summer-term eating. So fast...

1. Mix everything together with a fork.

2. Split into 6. Mould into sausage shapes.

3. Thread onto pre-soaked wooden/metal skewers. Brush with oil.

4. Cook under a preheated grill or on a searing hot griddle pan or barbie for a few minutes per side, till browned and delicious.

YOU CAN

✱ make these with beef

✱ serve in wraps or pittas with hummus

Lamb Kebabs & Greek Salad

Why bother wasting cash on rip-off fast food kebabs? Bang out these inside or on the barbecue. Marinate ahead for deeper flavours. Greek salad's a stand-alone classic.

1. Turn meat in marinade ingredients.

2. Leave to marinate in fridge or cook now.

3. Preheat grill or barbie. Get meat to room temperature.

4. Thread onto pre-soaked wooden or metal skewers. Sit on rack under grill/over charcoal. Turn every 1–2 mins, brushing with marinade. Get lamb browned outside, still pink inside. Sprinkle with salt.

5. Make Greek salad: mix lettuce, tomato, cucumber, black olives, crumbled feta with squeeze of lemon and a little olive oil.

YOU CAN

✶ wrap in flatbread with hummus, lettuce, red onion

✶ slash the cash: substitute half the meat with chunks of courgette, red onion

✶ treat lamb chops/cutlets to this marinade. Sizzle, turning on the griddle.

FEEDS 4 · ££ · EXPRESS

900g/2lb cubed lamb
shoulder/leg/fillet
Sea salt

Marinade
4 cloves garlic, crushed
2 tsps dried oregano
1 lemon (juice and rind)
Pinch of cinnamon (optional)
2½ tbsps olive oil
Black pepper

Greek salad
Lettuce leaves
Tomato, chopped
Cucumber, chopped
Black olives
Feta cheese, crumbled
Lemon juice
Olive oil

159

1 shoulder of lamb, boned,
   rolled, string-tied
4 cloves garlic, cut in slivers
Few sprigs rosemary
½ lemon
Olive oil
Salt and pepper
Bit of water/wine/cider/stock
Sprinkle of flour

Eat with: mash * stir-fried
broccoli * mint sauce * foil-
baked carrots with orange
juice and butter * gravy

Skint Lamb in a Bag

If you're wanting to do a good big roast for loads of mates
that's a bit cheaper, go for this. Wrap it in foil and cook till
meltingly tender — full of herb and garlic flavours.

1. Preheat oven to 220°C/425°F/gas 7.

2. Sit lamb on a large piece of foil in roasting tin/tray. Slip some garlic,
rosemary and lemon underneath.

3. Cut slits all over meat, sticking bits of garlic and rosemary in as you
go. Squeeze lemon over it.

4. Rub oil into meat. Season well. Drop the squeezed lemon in. Pull
foil edges up. Seal securely at the top.

5. Put meat into oven. Reduce heat to 170°C/325°F/gas 3. Cook 3
hours or till meltingly tender.

6. Open foil. Remove meat to rest it. Tip
juices into tin. Sit it on hob. Stir up sticky
sediment with a bit of water/wine/cider/
stock, a sprinkle of flour. Stir till smooth,
taste, adjust seasoning. Carve meat.

YOU CAN
* cook at lower heat — leave for 6 hours
* slap garlic, rosemary, peeled spuds, carrots
in tin. Sit meat on top. Add a glass of white
wine/cider. Cover with foil. Cook as above.
* rub cumin, cinnamon, coriander and oil into
lamb. Serve on couscous.
* shred lamb with 2 forks instead of slicing.
Eat in wrap with tzatziki, salad.
* make fast lamb. Stuff herbs, garlic into cuts in
leg/half leg of lamb. Drizzle oil, sprinkle salt
over. Or smush anchovies, garlic, oil and rub
over. Roast 220°C/425°F/gas 7 for 20 minutes.
Reduce heat to 190°C/375°F/gas 5 and cook a
further 20 minutes per pound, or as you like it.

Lamb Chops & Salsa Verde

Salsa verde is well refreshing, packed with good herby flavour and has an acidity that cuts through your neat lamb chops. Great spring or summer eating.

1. Make salsa: blitz all ingredients in processor or with blender. Or chop herbs, garlic, capers finely, then stir in mustard, vinegar, oil. Taste. Adjust. Store in fridge. Keeps ages.

2. Rub oil, herbs, garlic, seasoning into lamb. Leave.

3. Melt jelly in pan, stirring. Add red wine. Stir. Leave.

4. Heat grill or griddle. Grill: cook lamb 3 minutes per side for thinner cuts. Thick take longer. Lamb is best still pink, not red raw or leathery. Griddle: slap down on hot plate. Cook and turn till done as you like it. Rest for 2 minutes. Drizzle with jam. Dip into salsa to eat.

YOU CAN

✱ serve salsa with chicken, white fish, tuna, vegetable skewers

FEEDS **2**   ££   EXPRESS

Salsa verde
1 bunch parsley
1 bunch basil
3 cloves garlic
1½ tbsps capers
1 tbsp Dijon mustard
1 tbsp white wine vinegar
6–8 tbsps olive oil

Lamb
2 lamb steaks or lean chops or 6 cutlets
1 tbsp olive oil
Fresh mint/sage/rosemary/ thyme or pinch dried
1–2 cloves garlic, crushed
Salt and pepper

Jam
2 tbsps redcurrant jelly
½ glass red wine

161

£19 kg
LEMON SOLE
from BRIXHAM
grill it first and serve
with olive oil, lemon
and sea salt

£19 kg
WILD LINE-CAUGHT
SEA BASS
A really beautiful fish
roast with rosemary
and enjoy it as it is.

£43 kg
TURBOT
the king of all fish
simply roast and serve
with Hollandaise
a treat

£13.50 kg
FARMED SEA BASS

FISH

Dive in. There's nothing better. It's low fat, has omega 3s, is fast and easy. Go for sustainable (ask a proper fishmonger).

FEEDS 4 · £ · EXPRESS

450g/1lb skinned white fish (pollack, coley, sustainable cod, haddock)
White flour
Salt and pepper
110g/4oz breadcrumbs (pg 88)
2 eggs, beaten
Sunflower or light olive oil
Any good bread, baguette, ciabatta, wrap, pitta
Tartar sauce (pg 166)/garlic mayo (pg 211)/ketchup/ brown sauce
Iceberg lettuce, shredded (optional)
Squeeze lime/lemon juice
Malt vinegar

Fish Finger Sandwich

This one reminds me of back in the day when life was as easy as this little recipe. Relive your kiddie days with an irresistible fish finger sarnie. If you can, get sustainable white fish. Helps preserve fish stocks.

1. Lay fish on board. Check for bones (tweeze out). Cut into fingers.

2. Mix flour, salt and pepper on plate. Tip breadcrumbs onto another.

3. Beat eggs. Tip onto another plate. Dip each finger into flour, then egg, then breadcrumbs.

4. Pour oil into frying pan. Fry fingers, turning, on medium heat for a few minutes till golden, fish white and flaky. Drain on kitchen paper.

5. Slather bread/wrap with garlic mayo/tartar sauce/ketchup/brown sauce. Fill with fingers and optional salad. Add squeeze of lime/lemon and dash of vinegar.

YOU CAN
* cheat. Use good bought fish fingers.
* flavour breadcrumbs up with paprika, garlic, lemon rind, Parmesan
* forget bread. Plate with peas/chips/baked beans.
* sandwich a whole fillet instead of fingers

Salmon Teriyaki Wrap

A great fusion wrap – Asian meets Tex-Mex. Salmon's packed with omega 3s so a strategic eat at exam time. Teriyaki cuts through the fish and lifts flavour.

1. Check fish is bone-free. Pull any strays out with tweezers.

2. Mix up own teriyaki sauce (pg 113) or measure bought. Brush onto fish.

3. Heat griddle pan. Brush with a little oil. Slap fish in pan, skin side down. Cook for 2 minutes or till crisped up.

4. Turn. Cook for a few more minutes till fish is opaque. Brush 2–3 times with teriyaki sauce. Pierce with a knife to check fish is done. Get it out of the pan (it keeps cooking).

5. Warm wraps in foil in the oven for 10 minutes, or in a dry frying pan for 10 seconds.

6. Spread wraps with chilli sauce, mayo, salad. Break fish up. Divide between them. Fold, roll or wrap.

YOU CAN

* use yogurt, tzatziki (pg 16), raita, or tartar sauce (pg 166) instead of mayo
* cook noodles, pak choi (pg 116). Top with whole fillets and drizzle on more teriyaki.
* break griddled salmon into big flakes – sit on a bowl of ramen (pg 73)
* bake fillets in sauce at 200°C/400°F/gas 6 for 5–10 minutes
* scrunch up fillets, sauce, spring onion in foil parcels and bake for 10 minutes

FEEDS 2   ££   EXPRESS

2 good sustainable salmon fillets
1–2 tbsps teriyaki sauce (pg 113) or Kikkoman's
Sunflower or olive oil

Wrap
4 soft tortillas (pg 266) or flatbreads (pg 24)

Spreads
Sweet chilli sauce
Garlic mayo (pg 211)

Stacking salad
Rocket/watercress/spinach/ lettuce
Tomatoes (big or cherry), sliced

225g/8oz potato, peeled, diced
225g/8oz flaked cooked
 salmon (pg 171) or 1 x
 212g/7½ oz can red salmon
Salt and black pepper
Bit of grated lemon rind
Squeeze lemon juice
1 tsp butter
1 tbsp parsley/dill/coriander
 (optional)
1 egg, beaten

Coating
Bit of flour
Rest of beaten egg plus 1 tsp
 water
Dried breadcrumbs (pg 11) or
 polenta
Olive or sunflower oil for
 frying

Tartar Sauce
3 tbsps own/Hellmann's mayo
1 tbsp chopped gherkin
1 tbsp chopped capers
2 good squeezes lemon
Lemon rind
Parsley, finely chopped
½ shallot, finely chopped
5 drops Tabasco/pepper/
 Worcestershire sauce

Old-School Salmon Fishcakes

Canned fish works as well as fresh in these tasty little cakes. Team with tartar sauce or stick with ketchup. Leave out the fish and season well for skint potato cakes.

1. Boil potato in lightly salted water for 10 minutes or till tender. Drain. Mash or press through sieve.

2. Bung in a bowl with flaked fish, seasoning, lemon rind, juice, butter, herbs.

3. Mix gently, adding a little egg to bind. Cool it.

4. Mix tartar sauce ingredients together, or mayo with garlic and lime.

5. Flour hands. Shape mix into 2.5cm/1in-thick cakes. Dip cakes in egg/water mix, then in breadcrumbs/polenta till well coated.

6. Fry for a few minutes per side till golden, cooked through.

YOU CAN
* replace salmon with smoked mackerel/kipper, herbs
* make tuna fishcakes: drain can of tuna. Add to mash with crushed garlic, lemon, splash of chilli sauce, grated Cheddar, dill/parsley. Chill. Fry.
* make skint tuna fishcakes: mix drained tuna with handful of breadcrumbs, crushed garlic, ketchup, chopped spring onion, seasoning. Shape. Chill. Fry.
* lose the fish. Use cooked bacon/ham, cheese, cabbage, lightly fried mushrooms.

FEEDS
2–3 £

225g/8oz sustainable white fish
  (pollack, hoki etc.)
2 cloves garlic
Good grating fresh ginger
½ red chilli
Good pinch salt
Good squeeze lemon juice
1 slice crustless bread
Little fresh coriander

Coating
Plain white flour
Salt and pepper
Sunflower oil for frying
1 egg, beaten

Dipping
1 x Ginger Lime Drizzle
  (pg 115)
Sweet chilli sauce
Mayo mixed with wasabi/
  crushed garlic

Thai White Fishcakes with Wasabi Mayo & Dipping Sauce

Show off your oriental cheffy skills with these little beauties. Serve them as nibbles to dip with or plonk onto a bit of salad or hot or cold noodles as a whole meal.

1. Cut fish into small bits. Slap into processor (or use a bowl and handblender).

2. Add garlic, ginger, chilli, salt, lemon, bread, coriander.

3. Blitz to a stiff paste. Mould into little cakes.

4. Coat each cake in a little seasoned flour.

5. Heat oil in a frying pan.

6. Dunk each cake in turn into beaten egg.

7. Fry a few minutes per side till cooked through. Dip into sweet chilli sauce, Ginger Lime Drizzle or mayo mixed with wasabi paste.

Mash
1.2kg/2½lb floury potatoes,
  such as Maris Piper
50g/2oz butter
125ml/4fl oz milk
Salt and pepper
Handful grated cheese
  (optional)

Filling
900g/2lb white fish fillets (or
  mix with a bit of undyed
  smoked haddock and/or
  salmon)
750ml/1¼ pints milk
Chunk of onion
Bayleaf (optional)

Sauce
75g/3oz butter
50g/2oz plain flour
1 tsp mustard
Squeeze lemon juice
Fresh parsley, finely chopped
  (optional)

Big Old-Fashioned Fish Pie

This is my dad's favourite so if he comes knocking on the door of your student flat looking for me, give him this. It's a great filler, and relatively cheap to make if you split costs.

1. Make mash (pg 215). Preheat oven to 200°C/400°F/gas 6.

2. Put fish, milk, onion, bayleaf in an ovenproof dish or tin. Bake till just cooked (7–10 minutes) or poach on hob (pg 171).

3. Lift fish out (save milk). Skin it. Fork into large chunks. Check for stray bones – tweeze any out.

4. For sauce: melt butter in a pan. Stir in flour. Cook gently for a few minutes. Gradually whisk in the fish milk, beating as you go for a smooth sauce. Boil, then reduce heat. Simmer gently for another 5 minutes, beating as it thickens. Taste. Add mustard, lemon juice, parsley.

5. Pour sauce over fish. Mix gently. Tip into pie dish. Top with mash. Cook for 30–40 minutes.

YOU CAN

✱ add cooked prawns or mushrooms, chopped hard-boiled egg, a few capers, a few cooked mussels (pg 172)

✱ add grated cheese or white wine to sauce

✱ make sauce much thinner. Cover with all-butter puff pastry instead of mash. Bake in pie tin.

✱ cover pie with garlic breadcrumbs (pg 88) instead of mash or make half the mash and pipe it round the edges. Cook at slightly lower temperature.

✱ use frozen fish from a supermarket multipack. No need to defrost.

Cheat's Smoked Fish Pie

All nice. Sweet little pieces of smoky haddock topped with gorgeous mash. Just like that. Cooks fast and with little fuss. Try to eat undyed haddock.

1. Make cheese mash, other favourite mash (pg 215), or use leftovers.

2. Preheat oven to 220°C/425°F/gas 7. Grease an ovenproof dish/tray/tin.

3. Sit the bits of fish on the tray. Smear with a bit of butter. Season with pepper. Spread a layer of mash neatly over each fish.

4. Bake till done. Check after 10 minutes: pierce with knife to check it's just cooked through/flaky.

5. Sprinkle more cheese, finish under hot grill for crunchy topping if you like.

YOU CAN

✳ make this with fillets of white fish. Rub a bit of salt into them and leave for 20 minutes to firm them up a bit

✳ slap fish in a dish. Top with rarebit mix (pg 36) and cook as above – gorgeous.

✳ cut large tomatoes in two. Season. Drizzle with olive oil. Bake with fish.

FEEDS 2

££

Cheese mash
450g/1lb potatoes, peeled, cut
  into chunks
1 clove garlic, peeled
25g/1oz butter
2 tbsps milk
1 tsp mustard
Good handful Cheddar/
  Gruyère, grated
1–2 spring onions, finely
  chopped
Salt and black pepper

Pie
2 x 175g/6oz pieces smoked
  haddock
Bit of extra butter
Black pepper
Extra cheese for topping

2–3 tbsps olive oil/butter
4 cloves garlic, finely sliced or
   chopped
350g/12oz large prawns,
   peeled, de-veined
Parsley/coriander, finely
   chopped (optional)
Salt and black pepper

Garlic Prawns

Great speedy tapas-style starter. Mop up the garlicky juices with good bread or chuck onto salad/rice or into a lunch box.

1. Heat oil/butter in frying pan or wide saucepan.
2. Add garlic. Cook 1 minute, stirring.
3. Add prawns. Cook 1–2 minutes, stirring. Cover and shake until prawns are white and tender. Sprinkle optional herbs. Season.

YOU CAN

* add 4 tbsps white wine at step 3
* add finely chopped chilli or 2 pinches chilli flakes
* can't afford prawns? Mash tin of sardines with Tabasco, ketchup, Worcestershire sauce. Season. Eat on hot toast. Tasty health boost.

Salmon in a Pan

Get yourself a good-looking salmon steak. Poach it in a pan for a minute or so with a bit of flavouring. It's that simple and pretty damned tasty. Eat with mayo or maybe a watercress sauce with veg, baby spuds and a sparky salad.

1. Fill small frying pan two-thirds full of water or water/wine mix. Add peppercorns, bayleaf. Add salmon steak.

2. Heat till liquid just starts to simmer (not boil). Turn off heat. Cover pan. Leave for 10 minutes. Remove fish. Ready to eat now.

YOU CAN

✱ cook 2 steaks. Leave second in liquid till cool. Remove. Chill. Eat in salad/ sarnie.

✱ make peppered salmon in a pan. Brush salmon steak with mustard. Press a few cracked black peppercorns all over. Fry in a little butter/oil for 2 minutes. Turn. Splash white wine into pan with pinch of dried tarragon. Cook till almost reduced. Add good glug or two of cream. Heat through. Adjust seasoning.

✱ make Cajun salmon. Rub Cajun spice into fish (pg 35). Griddle. Eat with sour cream.

FEEDS 1 £££

Water
Glug of white wine (optional)
Few peppercorns
Bayleaf
1 salmon steak

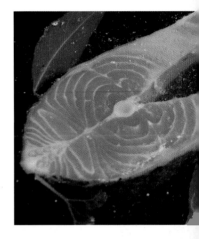

Chic Fish Salad

Healthy and a bit gorgeous. Cook from fresh or make up with leftovers from a hot salmon (pg 181). Eat with Treacle Bread (pg 266). Why not make prawn cocktail?

1. Get cooked salmon and prawns to room temperature.

2. Arrange avocado and cucumber on plate with greenery.

3. Mix sauce. Dollop onto plate.

YOU CAN

✱ ditch sauce. Use salsa verde (pg 161).

✱ forget salmon. Arrange prawns etc. in a glass/dish for prawn cocktail.

✱ make smoked-fish salad. Mix 1 flaked kipper or smoked mackerel fillet, crisp cooked bacon, cooked new potatoes, green leaves, Honey Mustard Dressing (pg 211).

FEEDS 2 ££ EXPRESS

2 cooked salmon fillets/steaks
Handful cooked prawns
1 avocado, sliced
Cucumber, thinly sliced
Watercress/iceberg lettuce

Cocktail sauce
3 tbsps mayo
1 tbsp plain yogurt
Squirt of ketchup
Shake of Worcestershire sauce
2 tsps vodka
Bit of lemon juice
Crushed garlic clove

171

2kg/4½lb mussels
50g/2oz butter
2 shallots or 1 small onion,
  finely chopped
3 cloves garlic, finely chopped
300ml/½ pint white wine/cider
Parsley (optional)
2 tbsps double cream
  (optional)

Eat with: big chips (pg 178)
and mayo ✱ warm bread to
mop juices

Moules Marinière

Absolutely brilliant. Mussels are so cheap. Get them at the
right season (when there's an r in the month) and fresh from
your local fishmonger. Prepping is key but well easy if you
follow the rules. Great on a date if you like interactive.

1. Always cook mussels on the day of purchase. First check for
cracked ones or any that won't close when tapped. Discard these –
never cook or eat them.
2. Tip the rest into cold water. Scrape/scrub shells clean. If they have
beards (black stringy bits), pull them out. Rinse a couple of times to
get them clean.
3. Melt butter in big pan (or wok). Cook garlic/onion for 2 minutes
without browning.
4. Increase heat. Add wine/cider. Boil for
2 minutes.
5. Add mussels. Cover. Cook over full
heat for 2–4 minutes. Shuffle or uncover
and stir so mussels at the top slip down
and cook up.
6. Remove from heat once shells have
opened completely. Spoon into bowls.
Discard any non-openers – don't try to
open them.
7. Add parsley/cream to wine if using.
Heat very gently. Spoon liquor into
bowls. Slurp from the shell or use shells
as pincers.

YOU CAN
✱ cook mussels tapas style. Boil for 3–4
minutes in a bit of wine to open. Remove top
half-shell. Top base with garlic breadcrumbs
and butter – or with garlic butter. Grill or
bake briefly till bubbling.

Spanish-Style Mussels with Garlic & Chorizo

FEEDS 2 | ££

Another best way with this sexy shellfish. Chorizo plus mussels is indulgent but it's bloody beautiful so when you're wanting to cook impressive you've just got to make this one. Tomatoey. Smoky. Top flavours… Eat with warm bread.

1. Clean and prep mussels – follow the rules opposite.

2. Heat oil gently in big pan. Add garlic, onion. Cook gently 5–10 minutes till soft, not coloured.

3. Add chorizo. Cook 2–3 minutes. Add chilli or flakes, water, passata, purée, sugar. Bring to boil. Simmer 1 min, stirring. Increase heat again.

4. Add mussels. Cover. Boil 3–4 minutes. Shake and stir to cook evenly. Cook a bit longer if you think they need it (don't overcook).

5. Discard any cracked or unopened mussels. Spoon into bowls.

YOU CAN

* cook mussels in tomato sauce (pg 83) with loads of basil
* make Thai-style. Fry 1 chilli with 6 sliced garlic cloves, lemon grass, 2 tbsps fish sauce. Add a bit of coconut cream. Chuck in mussels. Cook as above. Add coriander.

1.2kg/2½lb mussels
1 tbsp oil
4 cloves garlic, finely sliced
2 cloves garlic, crushed
1 onion, finely chopped
110g/4oz cooking chorizo, chopped
A little finely chopped, de-seeded red chilli (or a few dried flakes)
225ml/8fl oz water
125ml/4fl oz tomato passata
1 tbsp tomato purée
Pinch of sugar
Freshly ground black pepper
Finely chopped parsley (optional)

PER PERSON · £ · EXPRESS

1 sea-fresh mackerel
Olive oil
Sea salt and black pepper
Herbs, if you've got any handy
Lemon

Beach-Caught Mackerel

Go fishing with mates. Catch mackerel. Prep on nature's chopping board, rock — you've taken a sharp knife, lemon, oil, herbs along. Cook on a fire. Eat. Drink. Great night out...

1. Prep barbie or fire.

2. With a sharp, short knife or scissors, slit underside of fish from tail to head. Scrape guts out. Run thumb along insides to check all the bits are out. Rinse well in water. Cut gill fins off.

3. Score 2 or 3 diagonal cuts on each side, ½cm into fish.

4. Brush with olive oil. Season inside and out. Tuck herbs inside. Squeeze lemon over.

5. Barbie first side for 5 minutes. Turn once skin is well crispy. Cook other side 5 minutes or a bit longer till fish cooked through and falling off bone.

YOU CAN
* grill or pan-fry at home
* ask fishmonger to gut fish for you
* stew a bit of rhubarb (pg 235) to eat with home-grilled mackerel
* rub wholegrain mustard or Cajun spice into cuts before cooking

FEEDS 1 · £

1 mackerel, filleted (ask fishmonger)
Marinade
2 tbsps soy sauce
2 tbsps rice wine
1 tbsp rice wine vinegar
1 tsp sugar
2 cloves garlic, diced and crushed a bit
1 small red chilli, deseeded, diced

Eat with: noodles or rice
* stir-fry pak choi (pg 116)

Grilled Mackerel Asian-Style

Don't take mackerel for granted. It's stuffed with brain boosters and immune system lifters and cooks well — crisping up when grilled. Oriental flavours cut through it beautifully.

1. Sit mackerel on a plate or dish. Mix marinade. Tip over it. Leave 30 minutes. Prep noodles or rice and pak choi (pg 116).

2. Preheat grill. Place fish flesh side up on grill pan. Brush with marinade. Grill 2 minutes. Turn. Brush again. Grill till skin crisps up.

YOU CAN
* make Indian fish. Rub a little salt into 450g/1lb white fish. Leave 30 minutes. Make paste: juice of 2 limes, crushed garlic, 2 tsps coriander, 2 tsps cumin, ½ tsp chilli powder. Rub into fish. Leave 1 hour. Fry 2 minutes per side.

Fastest Fish in Butter

Do the express thing – cook a fish fillet in a bit of oil and butter. Or get cheffy, clarify your butter. It doesn't take long and means it can withstand higher temperatures.

50g/2oz unsalted butter
1 fillet of really fresh plaice/ lemon sole/other white fish
Bit of plain flour
Salt and pepper
2 tbsps lemon juice
1 tbsp water
1 tbsp fresh herbs, finely chopped

Eat with: baby spuds * beans or peas * avocado and tomato salsa (pg 18)

1. Clarify butter. Melt very gently in pan (don't stir). Scoop froth off. Spoon clear layer into bowl. Discard bottom white sediment.

2. Wash fish. Pat dry. Roll in flour/seasoning mix to coat.

3. Melt half the clarified butter in frying pan. Lay fish in when it froths (skin side up if relevant).

4. Fry 1–2 minutes until just browning. Turn. Remove when done/white/flaky. Don't overcook. Keep warm.

5. Wipe pan. Add rest of butter. Once it starts to colour, add lemon juice, water, herbs. Don't burn it. Shake pan. Pour over fish. Season.

YOU CAN

* cook larger fish, but they take longer. Start in the pan, finish in the oven.

* grill lemon sole or skinned whole dover sole (£££). Brush grill pan and one side of fish with melted butter. Season as above. Grill for 4 minutes (or less/more, depending on size). Turn. Butter and season. Grill another 4 minutes or till cooked through.

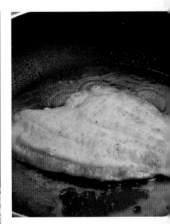

175

FEEDS **2**   £££

2 small salmon fillets

Spread
1 clove garlic, crushed
Small piece fresh ginger, grated
Fresh lemon/lime juice
Little coriander, chopped
Little red chilli, finely chopped
4 drops soy sauce

Parcel
2 tbsps butter
4 sheets filo pastry
Salt and pepper
Sesame or poppy seeds

Crunchy salad
Spinach leaves
Beansprouts
Spring onions
Oriental-style Dressing
   (pg 211)

Crispy Fish Parcels

Filo pastry's perfect for wrapping around soft fish. The crispy, buttery finish does it. It's easy to work, there's no rolling out involved. To keep it flexible, cover with a tea towel.

1. Preheat oven to 190°C/375°F/gas 5.
2. Check fish for bones (tweeze any out). Mix spread. Melt butter.
3. Lay sheet of filo on board, short edge facing. Brush with butter.
4. Cover with another. Sit one fillet across pastry, a quarter-way down from the top.
5. Season lightly. Smear with half of spread. Fold top edge of filo over fish. Roll towards you till parcelled. Trim and seal so fish is covered.
6. Make second parcel. Brush both with butter. Sprinkle with seeds. Bake 15–20 minutes. Make salad. Dress it.

YOU CAN
✱ use puff pastry – keep it thin
✱ top fish with lightly fried mushroom, garlic, parsley
✱ spread up a chicken fillet, wrap it in puff pastry, brush with egg. Bake for 30 minutes at 220°C/425°F/gas 7.

Classic Tuna Niçoise Salad

Use tinned tuna or griddle up a fresh steak for this gorgeous salad. Having a party? Make up a great plate of it.

FEEDS
2   ££

1. Preheat oven to 220°C/425°F/gas 7. Mix dressing ingredients.
2. Hard-boil eggs (pg 59). Cool, peel and halve.
3. Make croûtons: roll bread chunks in oil on baking tray. Bake for 10 minutes or till crisp. Don't burn them!
4. Boil potatoes in water till nearly tender (test with knife). Add beans for final 3 minutes till crisp yet tender. Drain both.
5. Rinse beans in cold water to crisp up and boost colour. Drain again. Chuck potatoes onto serving plate. Drizzle with a bit of dressing.
6. Grill or fry bacon till crisp. Drain on kitchen paper.
7. Either: open can of tuna. Drain. Flake. Or: griddle fresh tuna – rub with oil, garlic clove, season and slap on hot griddle for 1–2 minutes per side. Don't overcook (should be pink in the middle).
8. Chuck torn lettuce, tomatoes, olives, beans in with potatoes. Top with eggs, croûtons, bits of tuna, extra dressing.

Dressing
½ tsp sugar
½ tsp mustard
1 clove garlic, crushed
1½–2 tbsps lemon juice/
   balsamic vinegar
3–4 tbsps olive oil

Salad
2 eggs
2 slices stale bread, cubed
Handful baby potatoes
Handful green beans
3 rashers bacon
1 can tuna or large tuna steak
Bit of crunchy lettuce
   (iceberg/little gem)
Cherry tomatoes
Red onion
Black olives

YOU CAN
✱ fast griddle cubes of salmon marinated in oil, garlic, honey, herbs. Sling on salad.
✱ make a salsa with chopped avacado, tomato, red onion, chilli, coriander, lemon/lime juice. Season. Top with griddled tuna steak.
✱ dress the griddled tuna with Ginger Lime Drizzle (pg 115)
✱ for veggies – skip the tuna/bacon. Combine cheese, avocado, pine nuts.

FEEDS 2 **££**

Cider batter
110g/4oz self-raising flour
Salt and pepper
2 tbsps groundnut oil
125ml/4fl oz cider or good
   beer

Big chips
450g/1lb old potatoes,
   unpeeled
2 tbsps olive oil
Salt

Mushy peas
1 potato
1 small bag frozen peas
Dollop butter
Pinch dried mint
Lemon juice
Salt and pepper

Fish
2 fillets firm white fish
   (pollack, coley, sustainable
   cod, haddock, hake, lemon
   sole, plaice), 175–225g/
   6–8oz each
2 tbsps seasoned flour
Groundnut oil for frying

Cider-Battered Fish & Chips with Mushy Peas

Like most Yorkshire lads I love my fish battered. Doing it this way, in an easy freestyle mix whipped up with cider or beer, gives a crisp boost. Team with big chips, ketchup and God's Own County caviar.

1. Batter: sift flour into bowl. Add seasoning and oil. Slowly beat in cider/beer, using balloon whisk or wooden spoon, to get a lump-free thickish batter – adjust flour/liquid till right. Rest for 30 minutes.

2. Chips: preheat oven to 200°C/400°F/gas 6. Scrub spuds. Dry. Chop into wedges. Dry again. Roll in oil, salt. Bake for 30–40 minutes on tray.

3. Peas: boil potato in pan till just tender. Add peas. Cook 3 minutes. Drain. Mash with butter, mint, lemon, seasoning. Keep warm.

4. Fish: wash and dry. Check for bones – tweeze any out. Slap seasoned flour on plate. Dip fish to coat lightly. Rest on plate.

5. Fry: pour enough oil into deep-sided heavy-based frying pan or wok to shallow-fry (oil to come two-thirds way up fish). Don't overfill or leave. Heat gradually till a dropped breadcrumb crisps instantly.

6. Dip first fillet into batter to coat well. Let excess batter drip off. Carefully lower fillet into hot fat. Fry 3 minutes. Turn. Repeat till crisp outside, cooked and flaky inside.

7. Drain on kitchen paper and keep warm. Repeat with second fillet. Drain. Sprinkle salt and vinegar.

YOU CAN

✱ grill fish fillets/whole fish. Preheat grill. Brush fish with melted butter. Season. Scatter chopped parsley/tarragon/garlic. Cook for a few minutes per side.

✱ make speedy goujons. Cut 350g/12oz white fish in strips. Mix flour, cayenne, salt. Dip strips in mix, then in milk. Fry in hot oil for a few minutes, turning.

Ragu

1–2 tbsps olive oil
225g/8oz onion, thinly sliced
3 cloves garlic, crushed
1 mild chilli, de-seeded, finely chopped
3 rashers bacon, chopped into small bite-size bits
2 red/orange peppers, cored, de-seeded, thinly sliced
1 x 400g/14oz tin chopped tomatoes
1 x 400g/14oz tin butter beans
110–175g/4–6oz piece chorizo cooking sausage, roughly chopped
2–3 tbsps tomato purée
Fresh or dried oregano or thyme
Fresh parsley (optional)
Pinch sugar
Drizzle of sherry (optional)
Salt and black pepper

Fish

4 small fillets any firm white fish
Bit of seasoned flour
Bit of oil/butter

Fish & Chorizo Ragu

A great Spanish style fish and bean combo. PS Make the ragu base to serve with tapas (pg 22), or slap it in a dish, break eggs on the top, season, cover and bake it.

1. Heat oil in large pan. Add onion, pinch of salt. Sweat gently for 5 minutes or till soft, not coloured. Add garlic, chilli and fry for another 5 minutes. Increase heat. Add bacon. Cook till it starts to brown and crisp.

2. Reduce heat. Add peppers. Cook gently till softening.

3. Add tomatoes, beans, chorizo, purée, herbs, sugar, optional sherry, seasoning. Simmer 20–30 minutes, stirring occasionally. Add more purée or cook longer till mix is as thick as you like. Taste and season. Keep warm.

4. Lightly coat fish fillets in seasoned flour. Fry in a little oil/butter or clarified butter (pg 175) till cooked through. Season. Sit on ragu.

YOU CAN

✱ use the ragu to make huevos rancheros. Add kidney beans, more chilli and purée for thicker mix. Eat in warm wraps with fried egg, diced avocado, grated Cheddar, sour cream.

Fish Ready Meal

Set this one up in advance or make it in the moment. Either way, it's a light and healthy alternative to shop-bought ready meals. Great for weight-watching. Customize, depending on who's eating.

1. Cut one piece of foil/greaseproof paper per fish meal. It wants to be of a size to take everything plus extra.

2. Lay on a baking tin/tray. Scrunch edges up slightly. Sit fish in the middle. Season. Cover with garlic, lemon. Arrange cooked potatoes, green beans, olives, cherry tomatoes around. Drizzle a little wine or more lemon juice, olive oil.

3. Pull paper or foil up and over ready meal. Pinch edges firmly to enclose. Chill for later or bake at 200°C/400°F/gas 6 for 10–15 minutes (a bit longer if chilled).

YOU CAN

✱ Chinese it. Drizzle fish with soy and lemon. Arrange beansprouts, spring onions, red chilli on it. Bake as above or put parcel in steamer/sieve over pan of simmering water. Steam for 10–15 minutes.

✱ bake whole trout in foil. Stuff with herb, lemon, sliced garlic. Drizzle wine, cider, apple juice. Season. Add a bit of butter. Close parcel. Bake as above.

✱ bake one big salmon in foil for parties. A 3.5–4kg/8lb salmon needs seasoning, butter, baking at 180°C/350°F/gas 4 for 10 minutes per ½kg/1lb.

FEEDS 1 | ££ | EXPRESS

1 fillet white fish/salmon/
    haddock up to 225g/8oz
Salt and pepper
2 cloves garlic, thinly sliced
Squeeze lemon juice
Few cooked baby potatoes,
    pinched so that they split
Few green beans or spinach
Few black olives
4 cherry tomatoes, skinned
    (see pg 78)
A little white wine (optional)
Olive oil

Not just for
VEGETARIANS

Treat yourself and mates to these delicious vegetarian dishes. Good enough to whet the appetite of the most hardened carnivore. Great for health, looks and budget. Remember, meat's not a daily essential.

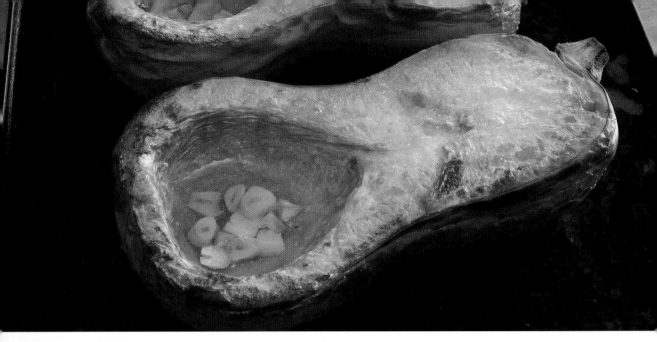

FEEDS
2–4   £   V

1 butternut squash, washed
    and dried
2 cloves garlic, sliced
25–50g/1–2 oz butter
Squeeze lemon juice
Salt and black pepper
Olive oil
175–225g/6–8 oz cheese
    (Cheddar, Gruyère,
    Lancashire, blue cheese)
Bit of grated fresh ginger
    (optional)
Drizzle honey
Mixed herbs

Roast Stuffed Butternut Squash

A bit of a comedy item. Butternut squash melts down from its rock hard former self into an oozing mass of gooey tasty forkfuls. Enjoy vitamins A, C, E and other nutrients in this gorgeous low-fat fit veg.

1. Preheat oven to 200°C/400°F/gas 6. Cut squash in half lengthwise with sharp knife on flat surface (needs muscle).

2. Use a spoon to scoop seeds and fibre out. Leave flesh intact.

3. Scatter garlic, butter, lemon juice in cavities. Season. Brush edges with oil. Bake on tray/tin for 40–60 minutes till tender.

4. Spoon flesh out, leaving a layer in base of skin so it stays upright.

5. Mash flesh in a bowl with ¾ of cheese, ginger, drizzle of honey, herbs. Spoon back in. Top with remaining cheese. Bake 20–25 minutes till scorching hot, cheese melted.

YOU CAN

✳ at step 3, add a few sliced chestnut mushrooms

✳ at step 5, mash in either some wilted baby spinach stirred into crème fraîche, mustard, lemon juice and pinenuts, or some punchy goat's cheese and rocket – or, for non-veggies, a few crumbled rashers of grilled streaky bacon

Roast Ratatouille

Not into neat chopping? Just hack away at the veg then slam them randomly into the pan. Roasting boosts the sugary flavours. Get your five a day in one bowlful. NB You can layer this up in other dishes or eat it cold as a salad.

1 large aubergine
1–2 courgettes
1 red pepper
1 large red onion
1–2 tbsps olive oil
1 tbsp balsamic (or red wine) vinegar
1 x 400g/14oz can tomatoes
4 cloves garlic, sliced
Good pinch sugar
Bit of fresh or dried thyme or oregano
Good pinch cinnamon
Salt and black pepper

1. Preheat oven to 200°C/400°F/gas 6.
2. Cut veg into big bite-size bits.
3. Chuck into tin (approx. 28x23cm/11x9in).
4. Add the oil and half the vinegar. Stir to coat.
5. Roast 15 minutes. Add tomatoes, garlic, sugar, thyme, cinnamon. Roast 30 minutes or till tender/caramelizing.
6. Taste. Season. Add more vinegar if needed. Eat hot, warm, cold.

YOU CAN
* drop in a few half-boiled and squeezed salad potatoes at step 3
* layer the veg with cheese and lasagne sheets, top with cheese sauce, bake for roast veggie lasagne (pg 99)
* chuck into a lunch box with rice, couscous
* throw over hot pasta, mix
* no oven? Heat oil in casserole. Fry onions, garlic. Add aubergines, courgettes, peppers. Add pinch cinnamon, chopped tomatoes, sugar, seasoning, chunk of lemon. Simmer on stovetop till tender.

375g/13oz pack butter puff
   pastry
3–6 tbsps passata
2 cloves garlic, crushed
1 medium aubergine, sliced
1–2 tbsps olive oil
Freshly grated Parmesan/
   Cheddar
Fresh basil/parsley/oregano
Sea salt and black pepper

Cheat's Fast Veg Tart

A proper cheeky little tart. Use all-butter pastry so you're
not getting trans-fats and try it out with different vegetables.
Wants a side salad or two with it…

1. Preheat oven to 200°C/400°F/gas 6. Grease baking tray.
2. Roll pastry into a rectangle about 35x28cm/14x11in.
3. Cut 2 x 1cm/½in-wide strips off the length. Brush with water/milk.
Lay pastry base in tray. Press strips onto base, one each side.
4. Prick base all over with a fork.
5. Mix passata with the garlic. Spread two-thirds over tart base.
6. Griddle or fry aubergine in oil till lightly browned.
7. Lay on base in single layer with slight overlapping.
8. Add rest of passata, cheeses, herbs, seasoning, olive oil. Bake
20 minutes or more till base is crisp, edges browned, pastry risen.

YOU CAN

✳ at step 5, spread base with
tapenade. Layer slices of tomato. Add
bits of Mozzarella and fresh basil if
you like. Top with grated Parmesan or
Cheddar and drizzle with olive oil.
✳ layer up with tomato or aubergine
and dab with goat's cheese
✳ spread with tapenade or seasoned
crème fraîche. Cover with thin slices
of cooked potato. Season well. Add
goat's cheese or grated cheese of
choice, bit of thyme, drizzle of olive
oil.
✳ fry onions in a little oil and sugar
for ages until lightly coloured. Layer
over pastry and top with olives, herb
of choice, Parmesan, dash of olive oil.
✳ spread a bit of mustard over the
pastry. Cover with ham, cheese,
passata.

A Proper Onion Tart

FEEDS 4 · £ · V

A slice a day keeps the doctor away – well, all that onion and garlic must help. A really tasty classic French tart. Useful one to make on a Sunday for leftover eating.

1. For pastry: follow method on pg 238 but add yolk with the water.

2. Grease 23cm/9in tart tin (loose-bottomed is good) or 4–6 tartlets.

3. Roll pastry out very thinly on floured surface to fit base and sides of tin. Lift pastry over on rolling pin. Fit to the tin, repair any tears and finish it. Chill 30–60 minutes.

4. Heat oil and butter in large pan on low heat. Add onions, garlic. Cover. Cook very slowly for 20–30 minutes till soft, uncoloured. Preheat oven to 200°C/400°F/gas 6. Cool onions for 5 minutes. Beat with yogurt, cream, eggs, seasoning.

5. Whack into tart. Bake 30 minutes or till cooked, golden, a bit puffy. Rest for 10 minutes before serving. Great with salad, baked potatoes.

YOU CAN

✱ make cheese and onion tart: add 75g/3oz grated Cheddar/Gruyère

✱ make quiche lorraine: chop 6 rashers bacon, dunk in boiling water 2 minutes, drain, blot dry, slap in base of tart, tip onion/cream filling over

✱ do cheese and asparagus tart: add cheese and crisp boiled asparagus spears

Pastry
175g/6oz plain flour
Pinch salt
75g/3oz butter
1 egg yolk
2 tbsps water

Filling
1 tbsp butter
1 tbsp olive oil
3 large onions (about 700g/1½lb), thinly sliced
2 cloves garlic, crushed
3 large eggs, beaten
1 egg yolk
150ml/5fl oz yogurt
300ml/10fl oz cream
Salt and pepper

Teriyaki Mushroom Burger

Get a full teriyaki hit with this juicy burger. The niacin in Portobello mushrooms helps the body process alcohol by the way. So maybe good for a late breakfast…

2 large Portobello mushrooms
Marinade
4 tbsps soy sauce
1½ tbsps rice or malt vinegar
1 tbsp rice wine
¾ tbsp caster sugar
Small piece fresh ginger, peeled, grated
Little groundnut/sunflower oil
Stack or wrap
2 burger buns, wraps or pittas
Hoisin sauce (optional)
Garlic mayo (pg 211)
Shredded spring onion
Cucumber matchsticks
Spinach, rocket or watercress

1. Mix marinade. Heat 1 minute in small pan. Cool it. Tip over mushrooms. Leave for 5 minutes or up to 1 hour, turning occasionally.
2. Preheat grill. Shake mushrooms. Brush very lightly with oil.
3. Grill 2 minutes per side or till cooked through.
4. Warm, toast or griddle wraps/bread.
5. Stack: spread hoisin and garlic mayo, layer mushroom and choice extras. Close or eat open.

YOU CAN
✳ cheat. Use Kikkoman's teriyaki marinade.
✳ crumble blue/goat's cheese over plain grilled mushrooms. Flash grill to melt.

* bake mushrooms: brush with oil, lemon, seasoning, top with garlic breadcrumbs (pg 88), drizzle with oil, bake at 200°C/400°F/gas 6 for 15 mins. Bake big tomato halves with them and eat on griddled polenta (pg 127).

Bean Burgers with Guacamole & Sour Cream

A Tex-Mex take on this tasty veggie burger. They're habit-forming and stuffed with good cheap ingredients. Don't stint on the extras.

1. Drain beans. Tip onto board. Chop very roughly to break them up a bit (not too much).
2. Blitz bread to crumbs with a handblender.
3. Mix all burger ingredients in bowl with a fork.
4. Shape lightly into 8 burgers. Coat lightly in flour. Chill for flavours to merge or cook now.
5. Heat oil in frying pan. Cook gently 5 minutes per side or till cooked through. Stack or wrap.

Burgers
1 x 400g/14oz can cannellini beans
1 x 400g/14oz can red kidney beans
110g/4oz white bread, crustless
25g/1oz grated Cheddar
1 small carrot, grated
3 cloves garlic, crushed
2 tbsps fresh coriander, finely chopped
½ tsp chilli powder
2 tsps cumin
¼ tsp cinnamon
2 tbsps tomato purée
Salt and pepper

Plain white flour for coating
Olive or sunflower/veg/ groundnut oil for frying

Stack or wrap
Toasted bun/warm tortilla wrap
Guacamole (pg 18)
Sour cream
Salsa
Tomatoes
Grated Cheddar
Red onion
Ketchup
Shredded iceberg lettuce

FEEDS 4   £   V   EXPRESS

Choice Baked Peppers

Look and taste beautiful with two light bright stuffings. Peppers are loaded with antioxidants and vitamins. Sweet.

1. Slice each pepper in half lengthways through the middle. Spoon seeds and core out (leave the stem).
2. Rub a bit of crushed garlic round the inside of each half. Season. Roll the outsides in olive oil or use a brush.
3. Arrange halves side by side in a lightly oiled dish. Stuff with plum or cherry tomatoes. For plum tomatoes: slice in two and sit a half in each pepper. For cherry tomatoes: make a nick in each, cover with boiling water for 1 minute, drain, strip skin and stuff two whole cherry tomatoes into each half-pepper.
4. Top half the stuffed peppers with crumbled feta, sliced garlic, olives. Top the other half with red onion/shallot slices, goat's cheese mashed with crushed garlic, lemon rind. Or go with one filling.
5. Drizzle olive oil. Drop unpeeled garlic cloves, chunk of lemon, basil leaves into the dish. Bake 30 minutes (foil-covered for the first 20 if you like) at 200°C/400°F/gas 6. Eat hot, warm, cold.

YOU CAN
* stuff peppers with cooked couscous (pg 126) mixed with cheese, mushrooms and fried garlic
* fill with diced cooked potatoes, cumin, yogurt, coriander, seasoning, lemon juice
* mix cooked rice (pg 112) with meat ragu (pg 97), stuff into whole peppers, tops removed, and bake as main recipe for 40 minutes in dish with a bit of passata or veg stock
* add anchovies to main recipe at step 4

FEEDS 4   £   V

2 large red peppers
2 large yellow peppers
Bit of crushed garlic
Salt and pepper
4 tbsps olive oil
4–16 baby plum or cherry
   tomatoes
6 cloves garlic, unpeeled
Chunk of lemon
Leaves of fresh basil
Topping 1
50g/2oz feta cheese, crumbled
1 clove garlic, sliced
A few black olives
Topping 2
A few rings of red onion or
   shallot, thinly sliced
50g/2oz goat's cheese
1 clove garlic, crushed
Grated lemon rind

190

Stuffed Tomatoes

Cooking for people with very different palates? One tomato's stuffed with subtle risotto-type tastes, the other's a garlicky bad boy. Quality.

FEEDS
2   £   **V**
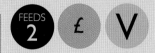

4 large beef tomatoes
Salt
1 clove garlic, crushed

Filling 1
60g/2½oz risotto rice
25g/1oz butter
Grated lemon rind
50g/2oz grated Cheddar/
    Lancashire/Parmesan
Finely chopped parsley/
    basil/tarragon/mint
Salt and pepper
Pinch nutmeg (optional)

Filling 2
10g/½oz butter or 1 tbsp oil
1 small onion, finely chopped
1 clove garlic, crushed
1½ tbsps fresh breadcrumbs
Good pinch dried or finely
    chopped fresh herbs
Salt and pepper

1. Slice off stem ends of tomatoes to make lids and get access.

2. Hollow tomatoes with a small sharp knife and spoon. Don't damage the shell. Roughly chop the scooped out insides to use later.

3. Rub a bit of salt and crushed garlic round the inside of shells. Invert on a plate to drain out excess moisture.

4. Make your filling of choice (or both).

Filling 1: tip rice into pan of lightly salted water. Boil 10 minutes, till half cooked. Drain. Mix with butter, lemon rind, cheese, herbs, seasoning, chopped flesh, nutmeg (if using).

Filling 2: fry onion, garlic gently till soft (5 minutes). Add chopped tomato. Cook 3 minutes. Stir in breadcrumbs, herbs, season to taste.

5. Stuff drained tomatoes with fillings. Sit lid on top. Chill or cook now.

6. Preheat oven to 180°C/350°F/gas 4. Cook on lightly greased baking tray or dish, 25–30 minutes.

YOU CAN
✶ make baked egg-stuffed tomatoes: at step 4 crack a whole egg into each tomato. Top with grated cheese or a mixture of cheese and tomato purée, then a little cream. Bake 15 minutes. Eat on fried bread.

FEEDS 2 · £ · V · EXPRESS

25g/1oz butter
1–2 shallots or 1 small onion,
  finely chopped
2 cloves garlic, crushed/finely
  sliced
1 tsp paprika
350g/12oz chestnut/other
  mushrooms, sliced
1–2 tbsps white wine/veg
  stock/apple juice
150ml/5fl oz sour cream
Pinch of nutmeg
Salt and lots of black pepper
A little fresh parsley or dill,
  finely chopped (optional)

Noodles
175g/6oz tagliatelle
Bit of butter
Sprinkling of caraway seeds
  (optional)

Kicking Mushroom Stroganoff on Seedy Noodles

Wonderful winterful quick mushroom stroganoff. Speedy luxury… Get bread to mop up the juices. Good with a watercress salad (calcium and iron packed).

1. Put pan of lightly salted water on to boil for noodles.
2. For stroganoff, melt butter in frying pan on low heat. Cook onion gently 5–7 minutes. Soften without colouring. Stir occasionally. Add garlic. Cook 1 minute. Add paprika. Cook 1 further minute.
3. Put noodles in to cook.
4. To finish stroganoff, add mushrooms to onion/garlic mix. Stir well. Cook 4 minutes. Increase heat a bit. Pour in wine, stock or juice. Let it bubble till liquid reduces.
5. Decrease heat. Add sour cream, nutmeg, seasoning. Keep stirring. It looks curdly at first but thickens after a gentle 4–5 minutes. Taste. Adjust seasoning. Add any herbs.
6. Drain noodles well. Slap back into pan. Toss with butter, caraway seeds if using. Spoon onto plates. Top with stroganoff.

YOU CAN
✱ serve on stacks of mash or toast
✱ use a pinch of smoked paprika along with the regular stuff
✱ make blow-out beef or pork stroganoff: add thin strips stir-fried pork or beef fillet at step 4

Sexy Tempura Veg & Dipping Sauce

The lovely light crisp Japanese batter transforms vegetables into sexy items. Dip into the sauce for taste explosions. Blooming brilliant … great for impressing…

1. Mix dipping sauce ingredients in a bowl. Prepare vegetables.
2. Make batter: first, tip flour and cornflour onto a plate. Then pour chilled water (or water plus an ice cube) into large bowl with egg.

Whisk together. Slide the flour in. Stir very loosely with a fork/chopstick. It wants to be lumpy. Slide the veg in. Stir to coat in batter.

3. Put 10 cm/4in oil into a deep saucepan or wok. Get the oil really hot – enough to instantly crisp a crumb.

4. To cook veg: slip one at a time into the pan with a slotted or wooden spoon. Don't overcrowd the pan and don't leave it unattended or drip oil outside it.

5. Nudge veg to turn after 1 minute or when golden. Remove when browned all over (different sizes take different times). Drain on kitchen paper. Leave in a warm place until all are done, or serve the queue.

6. Eat off little plates or one big one – with dipping sauce.

YOU CAN

✱ cook small bits of white fish fillet, tofu and prawns in this batter. Dip. Gorgeous…

FEEDS 4 · £ · V · EXPRESS

Dipping sauce
2 tsps grated fresh ginger
2 tbsps caster sugar
2 tbsps soy sauce
2 tbsps rice wine
4 tbsps rice wine vinegar

Batter
175g/6oz plain flour
1 tsp cornflour
2 egg yolks
350ml/12fl oz chilled water
Sunflower oil for frying

Choice vegetables
Button mushrooms (small: leave whole; others: chop)
Courgettes, sliced
Sweet potatoes (peeled, thinnish slices)
Spring onions (trimmed, whole)
White onion (peeled, separate rings)
Aubergine (sliced across)
Tenderstem broccoli

A little oil
2 large onions, finely chopped
3 cloves garlic, crushed
Pinch salt
2 carrots, diced small
Few chestnut mushrooms, diced
Dash of red wine
1 x 400g can chopped tomatoes
1 x 400g can green lentils, drained (or same weight cooked lentils – see pg 120)
1 tbsp tomato ketchup
3 shakes soy sauce
2 shakes Tabasco/pepper sauce (optional)
Black pepper
1–2 tbsps crème fraîche (optional)

Mash
Plain/mustard and lemon/ cheese/coriander and turmeric mash (pg 215), made with 900g–1.35kg/ 2–3lb floury potatoes

Lentil Shepherd's Pie

My veggie sister Polly got herself through two degrees on this one. Lentils bang in useful protein and energy. The pie keeps you going through the week. Get your mash nice and creamy. It's easily adapted for vegans.

1. Heat oil in a pan on low. Add onions, garlic, pinch salt. Cook gently for 10 minutes. Add carrot. Cook for 5 minutes or till onions are very soft, uncoloured. Add mushrooms and cook for a few more minutes. Remove from heat.

2. Tip in dash of red wine if using. Let it bubble. Add tomatoes, lentils, ketchup, soy sauce, optional Tabasco, black pepper. Return to heat and cook through for 2 minutes. Taste. Stir in crème fraîche, if using.

3. Meantime boil up potatoes. Create your favourite mash for a topping (pg 215). Tip lentil mixture into shallowish ovenproof dish or 4 individual ones (great for freezing). Top with mash. Cook in preheated oven at 200°C/400°F/gas 6 for 30–40 minutes.

YOU CAN
✱ use Puy lentils
✱ chilli it up (add chilli powder or flakes)
✱ make lasagne: layer lentil mix with lasagne sheets and cheese sauce (pg 90)
✱ for vegans, use reserved potato water instead of milk in mash, and soy margarine instead of butter
✱ cook different versions in little dishes and mark the vegan ones – e.g. with a tomato on top

Easy Cheese & Potato Comfort Pie

Don't judge it by its looks. Underneath that cheesy exterior lies a whole world of comforting tastes. Re-heats brilliantly. Try baking tomatoes in the oven to eat with it.

FEEDS 3–4 £ V

450g/1lb old potatoes (Maris Piper, King Edward), peeled weight
300ml/10fl oz milk/cream mix
1 medium onion (approx. 50g/2oz), finely chopped
1–3 cloves garlic, chopped
Black pepper
110g/4oz mature/strong-flavoured Cheddar cheese

1. Slice potatoes extremely thinly.

2. Pour milk/cream mix into a large pan. Add potatoes, onion, garlic.

3. Cook very gently on low heat for 10–15 minutes until just softening (test with a knife). Stir occasionally without breaking them up.

4. Preheat oven to 180°C/350°F/gas 4.

5. Spoon half mix into buttered 1-litre/2-pint dish. Season with pepper. Sprinkle with half of cheese. Cover with rest of mix. Top with remaining cheese.

6. Cover with foil. Bake 30 minutes. Remove foil. Bake 20–30 minutes plus till well soft and bubbling.

YOU CAN

✱ use Gruyère, Cheddar/Gruyère mix, Lancashire cheeses

✱ use all cream. Or all milk if skint.

✱ at step 5 layer in fried mushrooms/salmon/sun-dried tomatoes/ham/bacon

✱ make Pan Haggarty: boil 6 big spuds till ¾ cooked. Drain. Slice very thinly. Layer with finely sliced big onion, seasoning, 175g/6oz grated Cheddar. Pour stock/water halfway up dish. Bake as above.

✱ make loads of this for big house parties

Chapattis
225g/8oz wholemeal/chapatti
  flour or mix of wholemeal/
  white flour
½ tsp salt
175ml/6fl oz water
Bombay Aloo
2 tbsps groundnut/
  sunflower oil
1 tsp black mustard seeds
1 very large onion, finely
  chopped
8 fresh/6 dried curry leaves
2.5cm/1in ginger, peeled, grated
1 tsp turmeric
1–2 medium chillies, finely
  chopped
450g/1lb waxy potatoes (e.g.
  Charlotte/salad/new), cut
  into bite-size bits
250–300ml/8–10fl oz water
Handful baby spinach, chopped
3 tsps tamarind paste or juice
  of ½ lemon
Pinch salt

Bombay Aloo & Homestyle Chapattis

A great little side dish or eat as a main. Impress yourself making chapattis. Scoop the aloo – save on the washing up.

1. Make a well in sifted flour and salt. Add water gradually, working together with your fingers for a smooth dough. Add pinch more flour if too sticky. Knead for 7 minutes (pg 11). Leave, covered, in lightly oiled bowl in a warm place.

2. Heat oil in frying pan. Add seeds. Cover pan as they pop. Add onion, leaves, ginger, turmeric, chillies. Cook very gently till soft (10 minutes).

3. Stir in potatoes. Cook 1 minute. Add water and bring to boil. Simmer on gentle heat for 10 mins till potatoes are soft, the spice mix dry. Add spinach, tamarind/lemon, salt. Stir to wilt. Taste. Remove.

4. Cook chapattis. Roll small bits of dough out into very thin circles on floured surface. Heat a dry frying pan. Cook a few seconds per side till done but pliable. Repeat with the rest.

5. Reheat spinachy spuds. Serve with the chapattis for scooping, plus yogurt and mango chutney.

Chickpea, Spinach & Potato Curry

Perfect when you've been freezing your arse off on the sports field. It's full of soft veg, spices and nutritious chickpeas in a creamy curried base. One pot lasts ages... Eat with yogurt, raita, chapattis.

3 large potatoes
1 large sweet potato
2 tbsps sunflower/ groundnut oil
1 large onion, finely chopped
4 cloves garlic, crushed
Pinch salt
2 tbsps korma curry paste
1 x 400g/14oz can chickpeas
500ml/18fl oz water or veg stock
Juice 1 lemon
1 x 200ml/7fl oz carton coconut cream
1 tbsp mango chutney
1 tbsp tomato purée
4 tbsps chopped coriander leaves
1 x 200g/7oz can chopped tomatoes
2 tbsps ground almonds (optional)
Handful spinach

1. Peel potatoes and sweet potato. Cut into bite-size chunks.
2. Heat oil in a large heavy-bottomed saucepan or casserole dish. Add onion, garlic, pinch of salt. Cook till transparent.
3. Stir in curry paste. Cook for 2 minutes. Add potatoes, sweet potato, chickpeas. Stir to coat. Cook for 1 minute.
4. Add water/veg stock, lemon juice, coconut cream, mango chutney, tomato purée, two-thirds of coriander, tomatoes, almonds.
5. Increase heat to boil. Stir. Reduce heat. Cover. Simmer gently for 45 minutes. Check and stir it so it doesn't dry and stick. Stir in spinach and cook till wilted. Taste. Adjust seasoning. Add final coriander.

YOU CAN
* make with butternut squash/pumpkin
* use beans instead of chickpeas

197

FEEDS
4   ££   V

2 large potatoes, peeled
Olive oil
1 large onion, finely chopped
3 cloves garlic, crushed
2 x 400g/14oz cans chopped
  tomatoes
A splash of red wine
1 tsp dried or fresh oregano
Pinch of cinnamon
Pinch of sugar
2 tbsps tomato purée
1 x 400g/14oz can red kidney
  beans
2 aubergines, sliced
2 tbsps fresh parsley, chopped
Salt and pepper
Cheese sauce
20g/³⁄₄oz butter
20g/³⁄₄oz flour
425ml/³⁄₄ pint milk
110g/4oz Cheddar, grated, plus
  extra for topping
½ tsp mustard
1 tbsp lemon juice
Salt and pepper

Vegetable Moussaka

A Greek feast. Layers of soft aubergine and potato in a cinnamon-tinged sauce and creamy topping. Team with meze (pg 14) for skint dinner parties. Freezes well.

1. Boil spuds till just tender. Drain. Slice.

2. Cook onion and garlic gently in a bit of oil for 5 minutes or till soft, not coloured.

3. Add tomatoes, wine, oregano, cinnamon, sugar, tomato purée. Boil. Reduce heat. Simmer gently for 10 minutes. Add beans. Simmer for another 20 minutes. Taste. Season.

4. Fry aubergine slices in 2–3 tbsps olive oil, turning, till just soft. Or griddle them. Drain on kitchen paper.

5. Make cheese sauce (see pg 90). Preheat oven to 190°C/375°F/gas 5.

6. Assemble: use 4 small shallow heatproof dishes or 1 large. Spread tomato/bean mix in the base, then layer aubergine slices, little grated cheese, potato. Repeat till all used, finishing with aubergine. Cover with cheese sauce. Bake 1 hour. Rest 10 minutes before eating.

KR's Japanese-Style Stir-Fry

My vegan sister has to eat the right stuff to get all her nutrients. This fresh-tasting stir-fry's packed with protein (tofu, seeds, seaweed), B vitamins and iron (greens, miso).

1. Mix marinade. Chop tofu and marinate for at least 20 minutes.
2. Prep and cook wild jasmine rice (pg 112).
3. Heat wok. Add bit of oil. Throw tofu in. Cook 2 minutes or till brown.
4. Add seeds, salad leaves and beansprouts. Stir-fry 1 minute.

YOU CAN
* make tofu scramble: use silken tofu instead of eggs to make an omelette – fry with sliced onions, peppers, cherry tomatoes, bit of soy sauce. Eat on toast for breakfast.
* do tofu Italian-style: fry chunks in olive oil with garlic, onions, lemon juice and/or vegan pesto, add tinned tomatoes, simmer 10 minutes. Slap on pasta.

FEEDS 1–2

Marinade
2 tsps miso
Dash sesame oil
2 good squeezes lemon juice
Clove garlic, crushed or chopped fine
½ tsp soy sauce

1 pack tofu (firm) in 2cm chunks
50–110g/2–4oz jasmine rice
Dash sunflower oil

Stir-fry
Mixed seeds (pumpkin, sesame, linseed, sunflower), optional
Green leaves: watercress, rocket, pak choi, etc.
Mixed sea salad (seaweed), optional
Beansprouts

199

SALADS & SIDES

Test your creativity with brilliant fresh salads and pack the good stuff in.
Team veg with main meals for gorgeous tastes and essential nutrition. Best
bought in season when it's tastier and cheaper (why not buy local?).

FEEDS 2 · ££ · EXPRESS

2 cold chicken breasts or
   some cold roast chicken
2–4 slices gammon/ham
110g–175g/4–6oz hard cheese
   (e.g. Cheddar, Gruyère)
1–2 sticks celery
Cos lettuce/white cabbage,
   finely shredded
4 tbsps My Sparky
   Dressing/garlic mayo
   (pg 211)

Crunchy Chicken, Ham & Cheese Salad

A classic French salad packing plenty of useful protein. Get loads of leaves in there to keep yourself balanced…

1. Cut chicken, ham, cheese, celery into shreds/sticks.
2. Spread lettuce/cabbage out on plates/large dish.
3. Top with main mix and dressing. Toss together.

YOU CAN
* throw a few raisins in there for sweetness
* make enough for a salad box, sarnie, wrap, pitta

FEEDS 2 · ££ · EXPRESS

2 chicken fillets, in bite-size bits
Little olive oil
1 clove garlic, crushed
Fresh herbs of choice (optional)
Lemon juice (optional)
4 rashers bacon
2 tbsps pinenuts
Tomatoes (cherry are sweet),
   chopped
Length cucumber, peeled, diced
Any salad leaves
3 tbsps balsamic or Honey
   Mustard Dressing (pg 211)

Hot Wokked Salad Bowl

East meets West (try saying that). Weird I know, but wokking up the leaves really works – just don't overdo it.

1. Heat griddle/pan. Toss chicken in oil, garlic, herbs, lemon.
2. Griddle quickly, turning, till white through, browned outside.
3. Remove. Season. Fry or grill bacon till crispy. Prep salad veg and dressing.
4. Heat wok. Add chicken, bacon, nuts, 2 tbsps dressing. Toss for 2 minutes. Remove from heat.
5. Toss salad in – heat to warm through and wilt a little (add a bit of dressing if it needs it). Eat in bowls.

YOU CAN
* vary combos – mushroom and bacon, tofu and mushroom, salmon and bacon, prawn and avocado
* do it cold. Slap salad bits in bowl. Dress. Top with combo.
* add seeds – sunflower, pumpkin…

Caesar Salad (Chicken Option)

Created by Italian restaurant boss Caesar Cardini in Mexico in 1924 and still world renowned. It's the crunchy cos and the dressing combo that does it. A personal favourite.

1. Preheat oven to 220°C/425°F/gas 7. Mix oil, garlic. Roll bread in mix to coat. Bake on tray 8 minutes or till crisp. It burns fast so watch it.

2. Wash lettuce. Blot dry. Tear. Chuck into a bowl.

3. Tip dressing ingredients into a jar. Shake to mix.

4. Carve up optional cold roast or warm griddled chicken. Cut into bits or shred it.

5. Tip half of dressing over leaves. Turn. Add chicken if using, cheese, bit more dressing. Top with croûtons. Plate it.

YOU CAN

✳ use low-fat mayo for dressing or add crushed roast garlic

✳ top with drained anchovies – whole or mashed

✳ dress with My Sparky Dressing (pg 211)

✳ add crisp grilled bacon and cherry tomatoes

FEEDS 3 · ££ · V OPTION · EXPRESS

Croûtons
2–3 slices white bread/baguette/ciabatta, chopped
Little olive oil
1 garlic clove, cut

Salad
1 large cos/other crisp lettuce
Cold roast or warm griddled chicken (optional)
Parmesan cheese, shaved or curled with potato peeler

Dressing
6 tbsps Hellmann's mayo
1 clove garlic, crushed
1 tbsp water
1½ tbsps lemon juice
Shake Worcestershire sauce
Salt

203

FEEDS **1**   ££   EXPRESS

Cold/warm roast or griddled
  chicken
1 crisp apple, chopped
2 sticks celery, sliced
Walnuts
Few grapes (optional)
2 spring onions/little red onion
  (optional)
Green leaves

Dressing
1 tsp curry paste
2 tsps apricot jam/mango
  chutney
Squeeze lemon juice
2 tbsps plain yogurt
4 tbsps mayonnaise
Crushed garlic

FEEDS **1–2**   £   EXPRESS

110g/4oz soba noodles

Dressing
2 tsps honey/caster sugar
2 tsps fish/soy sauce
2 tsps malt/rice vinegar
1 tsp chilli sauce

Tuna salad
1 can tuna in oil, drained
1–2 spring onions, finely sliced
Red onion, finely chopped
Good grating fresh ginger
1–2 tsps fish sauce
Good squeeze lime juice
1 red chilli, de-seeded, finely
  chopped
Pinch sugar or 1 tsp sweet
  chilli sauce

Coronation Chicken Salad

Dedicated to the Queen (it was made for her 1953 coronation). Tender chicken and choice bits in a creamy curry sauce. Obviously went down well — it's still a headliner.

1. Combine dressing ingredients. Taste. Adjust.
2. Chop or slice chicken. Mix with apple, celery, nuts, grapes, onions.
3. Toss in dressing to coat (save any extra).
4. Sit chicken on leaves.

YOU CAN
* forget the chicken and add more salad
* toss cold roast belly pork or pork loin in this dressing
* make hard-boiled egg (pg 59) salad with this dressing

Spritzy Tuna on Noodles

Tinned tuna can get a bit boring and taste pretty flat but the Thai-style treatment livens it up. Makes a great summer salad even in winter. Try for dolphin-friendly tuna.

1. Cook noodles as pack directs. Drain. Refresh in cold water. Drain.
2. Mix dressing. Add to noodles.
3. Mix all tuna salad ingredients.
4. Plate dressed noodles. Top with salad.

YOU CAN
* box this to go
* use half tuna mix as sandwich filling
* mix tuna with cold rice. Stuff into soft lettuce leaves. Dip in chilli sauce.

Sweet & Salty Duck on Noodles

Duck breast works well with noodles but feel free to mix and match it with other carbs (rice, rosti, crushed or sautéed potatoes). The sugar, spice, salt rub boosts flavour.

FEEDS
2

££

1–2 duck breasts
1 tsp sugar
½ tsp salt
½ tsp five spice powder

Noodle salad
110g/4oz soba noodles
1 x noodle dressing
  (see opposite)
1–2 spring onions, finely sliced
Little lime/lemon juice

1. Duck: slash fat diagonally 5 times. Mix sugar, salt, five-spice on plate. Press duck into mix, fat side down. Put weighted plate on top, 15 minutes plus.
2. Preheat oven to 220°C/425°F/gas 7. Heat griddle pan. Griddle duck 2–3 minutes per side. Finish in oven 10–15 minutes (depending on size) till done but still pink. Relax for 5 minutes.
3. Cook noodles as pack directs. Drain. Swish in cold water. Drain again.
4. Mix dressing. Tip noodles into bowl with dressing, spring onions, and lime/lemon juice. Cut duck in diagonal slices. Pile onto noodles.

YOU CAN
* team noodle salad with veg/prawn/tofu tempura (pg 192), griddled tuna/salmon/steak, Garlic Prawns (pg 170)
* use wholewheat spaghetti/somen/udon noodles or rice vermicelli
* add sliced radish, cucumber moons (pg 117), carrot matchsticks
* serve duck on Rosti (pg 214) with green salad (pg 210)

1–2 steaks, such as ribeye,
   sirloin (if using rump,
   marinate overnight in
   lemon/garlic/ginger to
   tenderize)
1 clove garlic
Few drops olive oil
1 small red onion, finely sliced
Length cucumber/courgette,
   cut into matchsticks or thin
   ribbons
1–2 red chillies, de-seeded,
   finely chopped
Fresh coriander
Juice of 1 lime
1 tbsp fish sauce
2 drops sesame oil

FEEDS
1–2   £   V

Salad
1 can cannellini beans
Bit of red onion, finely chopped
Bit of red pepper, finely
   chopped
1 tbsp fresh parsley/
   coriander/basil, chopped
2 tomatoes, very finely chopped
2 tsps olive oil
1 tsp balsamic vinegar

Garlic bread
1 baguette
Soft butter
Cloves garlic, crushed

Easy Thai Steak Salad

A sparky eat when there's cash about. You'll be getting sharp and refreshing tastes and a bit of a chilli hit plus lean protein and iron. Helps with general health, sport and mental focus.

1. Heat griddle pan. Rub garlic/oil into steak.
2. Cook till rare (pg 143) or as you like. Rest for 2 minutes.
3. Prepare onion, cucumber/courgette (cut ribbons with potato peeler), chillies. Tip into bowl with coriander.
4. Cut meat on diagonal into very thin slices. Add to bowl. Toss in mix of lime juice, fish sauce, sesame oil.

YOU CAN
* eat with cold noodle salad (pg 205)
* cook and slice beef. Slap on bed of rocket/spinach, cherry tomatoes and drizzle with balsamic dressing (see right). Top with sliced Parmesan.

White-Bean Salad & Garlic Bread

A great store-cupboard salad – it's what beans are for. Get your windowsill herbs in and boost the flavour (cheap, grown from seeds). Garlic bread? Get it in your repertoire.

1. Rinse beans very well. Tip into bowl.
2. Add other salad bits. Mix well. Let flavours develop.
3. Heat oven to 200°C/400°F/gas 6.
4. Slash baguette across diagonally at roughly 2–3cm/1in intervals.
5. Spread cuts with mix of soft butter and garlic. Wrap in foil. Bake 25 minutes.

YOU CAN
* add drained tuna
* add egg, diced gammon
* stir in mix of yogurt/Dijon mustard
* use any other bean, or mix of beans, or chickpeas

All-Day Bacon & Egg Salad

Healthier version of a fry-up. Reduces the guilt factor…

1. Make croûtons. Wash and dry leaves. Stick them in a bowl.
2. Fry bacon or pancetta in a drop of oil on low heat.
3. Heat water in small pan. Poach eggs till set, yolks still soft.
4. Tip croûtons and bacon into salad bowl. Add a little dressing. Toss. Top with egg.

YOU CAN
* at step 1, fry cold or fresh cooked potatoes as base to salad
* add cherry tomatoes, sliced red onion, fried black pudding, mushrooms, sliced cooked sausage
* use fried or hard-boiled eggs. Throw in fresh green beans, boiled till just softening.

FEEDS 2 · ££ · EXPRESS

Croûtons (pg 203)
Good handful salad leaves
4–6 rashers bacon or pancetta, chopped
2 poached eggs (pg 60)
My Sparky Dressing (pg 211)

Mozzarella & Tomato Salad

Only worth making with ripe and fruity tomatoes (summer's the season) and soft Mozzarella from a ball (the bar is for pizza toppings). Brilliant…

FEEDS 1 · ££ · V · EXPRESS

4 slices Mozzarella (from a ball)
2–3 good tomatoes (beef, vine) or handful of cherry tomatoes
A few fresh basil leaves

Balsamic Dressing
Olive oil
Salt and pepper
Balsamic vinegar

Or
My Sparky Dressing (pg 211)

1. Slice or tear Mozzarella. Slice tomatoes.
2. Pile onto plate or arrange in neat overlaps.
3. Drizzle with a bit of oil, vinegar, seasoning or toss in my dressing.
4. Toss torn basil over. Eat immediately.

YOU CAN
* add sliced avocado just before eating (not too early – it oxidizes)
* top with thinly sliced red onion

FEEDS
2
££
V
EXPRESS

1–2 heads chicory, chopped
Bunch watercress
2 pears, peeled, sliced
  lengthways
Lemon juice
Honey Mustard Dressing
  (pg 211)
Diced/crumbled cheeses
  (blue, smoked/unsmoked
  Cheddar, Wensleydale,
  Lancashire, goat's)

Autumn Crunch

Autumn wonder. A classic combination of soft sweet pear, dark leaves, and bitter crunch of chicory. Seasonal and easy.

1. Tip chicory into bowl with watercress.
2. Brush pear slices with lemon juice and add them to bowl.
3. Turn in dressing. Toss cheese in.

YOU CAN

* add beetroot: roast in foil till tender. Peel. Chop while warm. Arrange on plate alongside salad.
* add chopped orange and walnuts, or croûtons (pg 203)
* seal leaves in bag in fridge to keep sweet for longer

FEEDS
1–2
££
V
EXPRESS

4–6 slices French bread/ciabatta
Lettuce/spinach/rocket/herbs
1 orange
My Sparky Dressing (pg 211)
4–6 slices goat's cheese

Goat's Cheese Toast

A sophisticated starter or an anyday snack. This works both ways. I'm loving the mix of textures and the balance of flavours.

1. Toast bread lightly on both sides.
2. Wash, rinse, dry leaves.
3. Peel and roughly chop orange, saving juice.
4. Tip leaves and orange into bowl. Make dressing (pg 211), adding the saved juice. Toss salad with dressing.
5. Cover toast completely with layer of cheese.

6. Grill on low heat till soft, lightly browned.

7. Plate salads. Top with hot toasts.

YOU CAN
* throw on some walnuts
* make with untoasted cheese and add croûtons
* grill or bake bigger slices of cheese on foil till soft. Slap on salad.
* spread chilli jam on toast before adding goat's cheese

Raw Energy Dipping Plate

Healthiest recipe in the book? No vitamins lost here. Perfect for dipping and chatting when mates are round. Raw power-food… Note: limp veg makes perfect speedy soup.

1. Either: chop veg into sticks for dipping. **Or:** slice or grate veg and toss in dressing of choice. Eat with great bread.

YOU CAN
* add olives, hard-boiled egg to make a meal
* dip broccoli, green beans, broad beans (steamed for 4 minutes)

Butternut Squash Salad

A bit of a still-life when it's on the plate. Be arty and make it look stunning. Tastewise, the squash hits a good bass note.

1. Preheat oven to 200°C/400°F/gas 6. Make croûtons (pg 203).

2. Lay squash flat. Slice ends off. Cut in two lengthways. Spoon seeds out. Cut into large bite-size chunks, skin on.

3. Slap onto roasting tray. Drizzle with olive oil. Turn to coat. Scatter with garlic, cumin, chilli. Roast till soft – check after 20 minutes.

4. Scatter over plates. Add other ingredients of choice. Drizzle chosen dressing.

YOU CAN
* make soup with roast squash. Cook onion in butter till soft. Add ginger and garlic. Cook 5 minutes. Add squash, lime juice, 600ml/1 pint veg stock, seasoning, coriander, Tabasco, bit of creamed coconut. Simmer 15 minutes. Blitz. Taste. Adjust.

PER PERSON · ££ · V · EXPRESS

Choice of veg
Carrots
Cucumber
Courgette
Tomatoes
Radishes
Mushrooms
Celery
Spring onions
Caulifower florets
Peppers, sliced
Choice of dips
Garlic mayo (pg 211)
Guacamole (pg 18)
Hummus (pg 14)
Choice of dressings
Olive oil
Sparky (pg 211)
Blue Cheese (pg 211)

FEEDS 3–4 · £ · V OPTION

Croûtons (pg 203)
1 butternut squash
Olive oil
3–4 cloves garlic
½ tsp cumin
Spinkle chilli flakes
Salad choices
Cherry or good tomatoes
Red onion, peeled, thinly sliced
Cucumber, diced
Spinach/watercress/rocket
Olives
Cheese, cubed (feta, smoked, Cheddar, Edam, Gouda, Wensleydale, Stilton, goat's)
Crispy bacon or pancetta bits
Parma or other good thin ham
Salami/chorizo
Dressing of choice

SIDE SALADS

Mix-&-Match Green Salad
Any green leaves (e.g. rocket, little gem, English salad lettuce, watercress, lamb's lettuce, baby spinach, cos, chopped chicory)

1. Mix any of these.
2. Toss in a simple olive oil dressing or something creamy.

Fruity Coleslaw
110g/4oz white or red cabbage, shredded
1 large carrot, grated
1 apple, grated/diced small
2 sticks celery, thinly sliced
2 heaped tbsps mayo (you may need more)
1 tsp mustard
Drizzle of honey
Little lemon juice (optional)
Handful raisins/chopped dates (optional)
Salt and black pepper

1. Prep cabbage, carrot, apple, celery. Throw into bowl.
2. Mix mayo, mustard, honey, lemon, seasoning.
3. Toss together with raisins/dates.

YOU CAN
* add chopped cheese or orange, walnuts, pecans, cashews, sesame seeds, sunflower seeds
* toss in olive oil and balsamic

Classic Tomato Salad
Good ripe tomatoes (cherry vine, beef – try a variety)
Salt and pepper
Pinch caster sugar

Dressing
1 tbsp red/white/balsamic vinegar
3 tbsps extra virgin olive oil
Clove garlic, crushed (optional)
Basil, oregano, thyme, chives, parsley

1. Prep tomatoes: slice neatly or chop roughly, or cut in half-moons, or in half. Tip into bowl.
2. Season with bit of sugar, salt. Leave.
3. Mix dressing. Slap tomatoes onto serving plate (leave water behind). Toss in dressing. Add herbs.

YOU CAN
* make my top tomato and onion salad: cover neat tomato slices with sliced red onion

Roasted Pepper Salad
4 red/orange peppers
3 tbsps olive oil
Salt and pepper

1. Preheat oven to 230°C/450°F/ gas 8.
2. Sit peppers on baking tray. Cook 30 minutes till blistered. Turn once.
3. Put in a freezer bag for 15 minutes. Strip skin away. De-seed with spoon. Cut into strips.
4. Drizzle with olive oil. Season.

Vitamin-Boost Citrus Salad
2 oranges, peeled, sliced, chopped
2 carrots, peeled, grated
Few fresh/dried dates, chopped
Green leaves: spinach/watercress/ rocket/chopped chicory
Nuts and seeds (optional)
Honey Mustard Dressing (see right)

1. Prepare fruit and carrots. Make dressing.
2. Mix salad ingredients together.
3. Toss with dressing. Serve.

YOU CAN
* use satsumas, grapefruit, clementines
* scatter pomegranate seeds (cut fruit in two, knock seeds out by hitting skin with a spoon)
* drizzle pomegranate molasses – it fizzes…

Courgette & Carrot Ribbon Salad
1 carrot, peeled
1 courgette, unpeeled
Little lemon juice
1 tbsp Oriental-Style/Honey Mustard Dressing (see right)

1. Make carrot and courgette ribbons using potato peeler.
2. Sprinkle with lemon juice. Dress them.

YOU CAN
* griddle slightly thicker courgette ribbons. Dress with lemon, salt, fresh red chilli.
* boil carrot ribbons 2 minutes. Drain. Stir-fry in a little butter, sugar, dried thyme. Season.

DRESSINGS

Honey Mustard Dressing

2 tsps Dijon/wholegrain mustard
1 tsp runny honey/caster sugar
1 clove garlic, crushed, or a little
  shallot (optional)
2 tbsps lemon juice/white
  wine/cider/tarragon vinegar
6 tbsps extra virgin olive oil
Salt and black pepper

Mix everything together in a jar. Or
whisk all except oil in a bowl, and
when integrated, add oil.

YOU CAN
✱ use balsamic vinegar for a darker
flavour

My Sparky Dressing

1 tsp Dijon/English mustard
1 tsp caster sugar
1 clove garlic (optional)
1½–2 tbsps vinegar (red wine/
  white white/sherry/cider)
6 tbsps olive oil
½ shallot (optional)
Chopped parsley (optional)

Salt and black pepper

Shake everything together in a jar.
Or mix everything except oil, and
whisk that in at the finish.

YOU CAN
✱ go freestyle. Pour oil, vinegar
onto salad at the table.

Hard Cheese Option

4 tbsps olive oil
Juice 1 lemon
2 tbsps freshly grated Parmesan
Salt and black pepper

Chuck in a bowl. Whisk together.

Blue Cheese Option

4 tbsps olive oil
½ tsp runny honey
½ tsp Dijon mustard
Juice ½ lemon
Up to 50g/2oz blue cheese
  (Roquefort/other sharp blue)

Mix oil, honey, mustard, lemon
juice. Smash cheese in.

Oriental-Style Dressing

75ml/3fl oz sunflower oil
1 tsp sesame oil
4½ tsps white wine vinegar
1 tbsp soy sauce
1 small shallot, chopped
1 small clove garlic, chopped
  (optional)

Whisk the lot together.

Homestyle Mayo

2 egg yolks
½ tsp each salt, dry mustard,
  caster sugar
250ml/8fl oz sunflower/
  groundnut oil
50ml/2fl oz olive oil
2 tbsps white wine/cider
  vinegar/lemon juice
1 tbsp hot water

1. Sit bowl on teatowel. Slap in
yolks, salt, mustard, sugar. Beat with
balloon whisk/wooden spoon.
2. Mix oils in jug. Drip by drip, add
to eggs, beating continuously. Don't
go too fast or mix will curdle.
3. When half oil added and mix
thickening, add 1 tbsp vinegar/juice.
Add rest of oil in slow, steady
stream, beating.
4. Add rest of vinegar/juice and
hot water. Taste. Adjust seasoning.

YOU CAN
✱ add 2 crushed cloves garlic for
garlic mayo
✱ add chopped, dill and 2 tbsps
Dijon mustard for mayo to go with
salmon/prawns

211

VEGETABLE SIDES

(recipe cross-references: pg 90, pg 83)

Edgy Cumin Cauliflower for 3–4

1 cauliflower, in small florets
3 cloves garlic, peeled, sliced
Olive oil
Ground cumin
Sea salt

1. Preheat oven 220°C/425°F/gas 7.
2. Tip cauli, garlic onto baking tray.
3. Drizzle a bit of oil, sprinkle cumin, salt. Turn to coat. Roast till tender (about 20 minutes).

Cauliflower Cheese for 4

1 cauliflower, in small florets
1 x cheese sauce (pg 90)

1. Boil or steam cauli 10 minutes or till just softening. Drain. Tip into dish. Meantime, make cheese sauce.
2. Preheat oven to 200°C/400°F/gas 6. Tip sauce over cauli. Bake 30 minutes. Or slap under grill, cook till bubbling. Classic. Love it.

Stir-Fried Broccoli for 1–2

2 tsps sesame oil
1 tbsp sunflower oil
2 cloves garlic, sliced
A little fresh ginger, grated (optional)
200g/7oz tenderstem or other broccoli
4 tbsps water/stock
2 splashes soy sauce
2 tbsps oyster sauce

1. Heat wok or pan. Add oils. Heat.
2. Add garlic, ginger. Stir-fry a few seconds. Add broccoli. Toss and turn for 2–3 minutes.
3. Add water. Reduce heat. Cover and fry 2–3 minutes till softening but crisp. Add sauces.

YOU CAN

✱ stir-fry thinly shredded cabbage, pak choi and spinach with garlic and ginger
✱ stir-fry green beans in garlic and sesame oil. Add optional cashews for last 2 minutes.

DIY Steamer Pak Choi for 2

2–4 heads pak choi
Dressing
1 tsp sunflower oil
Few drops sesame oil
2 tsps soy sauce
2 tbsps oyster sauce

1. Bring water to boil in pan. Sit sieve in it over water. Put lid on.
2. Cut each pak choi in 2 or 4 lengthways. Sit in sieve.
3. Replace lid. Steam till tender (3–4 minutes). Mix dressing.
4. Warm dressing in a pan. Tip over drained pak choi.

Bubbling Baked Veg for 2

Olive oil
Garlic clove, crushed
1 large aubergine
2 courgettes
1 x tomato sauce (pg 83) or bought passata
Fresh basil leaves
110g/4oz grated Cheddar/ Parmesan, or fresh breadcrumbs with garlic

1. Preheat oven to 220°C/425°F/gas 7.
2. Slice aubergine and courgettes in 5mm/¼in circles. Turn in a little garlicky oil. Top with basil. Bake 10 minutes on tray or griddle them.

3. Smear tomato sauce/garlicky passata in shallow dish. Layer with aubergine, courgette, little cheese, more sauce.
4. Repeat till finished. Top with cheese or breadcrumbs. Bake 10 minutes till hot, bubbling.

YOU CAN
✱ use all courgettes or aubergines
✱ make more. Serve as main dish.

Herb Roasted Root Vegetables for 3–4
Choice of
2 carrots
2 sweet potatoes
2 old potatoes, peeled, or handful new/salad potatoes
2 parsnips
3 red onions
2 cloves garlic, crushed
4 tbsps olive oil
Sprigs rosemary/thyme or sprinkle of dried herbs
Salt and pepper

1. Preheat oven to 200°C/400°F/ gas 6.

2. Peel all veg. Cut into chunks/ wedges.
3. Mix oil, crushed garlic, herbs (bash in pestle and mortar if you like).
4. Toss veg in herby oil. Season. Roast 30–40 minutes.

YOU CAN
✱ roast aubergines, corn, courgettes, shallots, mushrooms, peppers, asparagus. Eat hot, warm or cold with salad
✱ drizzle with balsamic vinegar

Squeaky Beans & Tomato for 2
200g/7oz fine green beans
2 cloves garlic, crushed
1 large tomato, chopped
Little olive oil
Salt and pepper

1. Boil beans in water for 3–4 mins or till softening. Drain.
2. Heat oil in pan/wok. Add garlic. Toss for a few seconds.
3. Add tomato, beans. Turn till well heated.

Fruity Red Cabbage for 4
1 red cabbage, finely shredded
1 onion, roughly chopped
1 large apple, roughly chopped
1–2 cloves garlic, sliced
Few pinches mixed spice/ cinnamon
1 tbsp brown sugar
1–2 tbsps wine vinegar
Few dabs butter
Salt and pepper

1. Preheat oven to 180°C/350°F/ gas 4.
2. Make layers of cabbage, onion, apple in dish/casserole, sprinkling garlic, spice, sugar between.
3. Pour vinegar in. Dot with butter. Cover. Bake 20 minutes. Stir. Cook another 20 minutes or till done as you like it. Taste. Adjust seasoning.

PROPER POTATOES

Using the right spud ensures success. Get floury: Maris Piper, Estima, Désirée, King Edwards for mash, roast, rosti, chips, baked. Get waxy: Charlotte, Salad, Jersey Royals for hash, omelettes, salads. Boil either spud in a load of water with a pinch of salt until tender.

Swiss-style Rosti with Cheese & Bacon for 3–4

900g/2lb floury potatoes, unpeeled
75g/3oz Gruyère/Cheddar, grated
110g/4oz good streaky or back bacon
2–3 tbsps butter/olive oil
Salt and black pepper

1. Boil spuds whole for 10 minutes. Remove. Drain. Cool.
2. When ready, fry bacon in 1 tbsp oil till crisp.
3. Peel and grate cool spuds into a bowl. Add cheese, bacon, pepper, scant salt.
4. Heat rest of oil/butter in shallow frying/crêpe pan. Cover base with rosti mix pancake-style. Cook till lightly browned. Cover with plate larger than pan. Invert so rosti slips out. Slide back into pan. Cook second side till crisply finished.

YOU CAN
* make plain rosti – cut out cheese and bacon
* add spring onions, herbs, grated lemon rind
* make small rostis by shaping with your hands or frying in cooking rings or cutters
* top plain rostis with fried eggs, sausages, bacon
* serve plain rostis with steaks, meat, griddled fresh tuna

Garlic & Herb Potato Nibbles for 3

4 large floury potatoes
Olive or vegetable oil
6–8 cloves garlic, chopped
3–4 sprigs fresh rosemary/thyme/sage
Bit of sea salt

1. Preheat oven to 220°C/425°F/gas 7. Cut potatoes into very small cubes. Turn in a bowl with oil, garlic, herbs, salt.
2. Bake on roasting tin/baking tray in single layer for 40 minutes or till crunchy.

Popcorn Potatoes for 4

900g/2lb small waxy potatoes
25g/1oz caster sugar
50g/2oz butter
Sesame seeds (optional)
Salt and black pepper

1. Cook spuds till just tender. Drain.
2. Strip skins off when cool enough.
3. Put sugar into frying pan on very low heat. Stir with wooden spoon. Add butter, spuds.
4. Turn to brown slowly.
5. Sprinkle with sesame seeds. Cook 1–2 minutes.

YOU CAN
* sprinkle with poppy seeds
* add grated lemon rind

Frying Pan Crunchy Potatoes for 2

4 large floury potatoes, or left-over boiled potatoes, chopped bite-size
Olive/sunflower/veg oil or duck fat
Sea salt
Lemon juice

1. If cooking from scratch, boil spuds till just tender. Drain well.
2. Heat oil in frying pan. Add cold or freshly cooked potatoes. Fry over medium/low heat for 20 minutes, turning, till well crispy.
3. Sprinkle with seasoning, juice.

YOU CAN

* add a few sliced shallots and garlic
* make oven-free roasties. Cover base of heaviest sauce/fry pan with olive oil. Add 450g/1lb waxy spuds in 2.5cm/1in cubes, diced garlic, herbs. Shake to coat. Cover. Cook on low heat for ages (shake sometimes) till golden outside, soft inside.

Creamy Mash for 2

450g/1lb floury potatoes peeled, quartered
50g/2oz butter
75 ml/3fl oz warm milk
Salt and black pepper
Optional flavourers
Garlic
Dijon/English mustard
Lemon juice
Grated nutmeg
Fresh dill, coriander, parsley, basil

1. Boil spuds until tender. Drain. Slap back in warm pan. Shuffle on heat for 1 minute to dry.
2. Mash with fork or masher till lump-free.
3. Beat in milk, butter, flavourings with wooden spoon or balloon whisk.

YOU CAN

* mix with olive oil instead of milk and butter
* for light mash, get a potato ricer (large press) and cook spuds whole, unpeeled. Press through ricer. Quality.

French Cheese & Onion Mash for 2

450g/1lb floury potatoes
2 cloves garlic, peeled

25g/1oz butter
2 tbsps milk
110g/4oz Gruyère cheese
2 spring onions, finely chopped
Salt and black pepper

1. Boil potatoes with garlic. Drain. Shuffle dry. Mash.
2. Slap in butter, milk, cheese. Beat till creamy with wooden spoon/ balloon whisk.
3. Season well. Add spring onion.

YOU CAN

* add a splash of white wine

Sweet Potato Mash for 2

450g/1lb sweet potato, peeled, cut into large chunks
Few gratings fresh ginger
Butter
1 tsp honey
Squeeze lemon/lime
Salt and black pepper

1. Boil chunks of potato in lightly salted water.
2. Add ginger. Drain when soft.
3. Slap back into pan to dry for a few seconds.
4. Bash with a masher or fork. Add butter, honey, lemon, seasoning.

Bubble & Squeak for 1–2

1 bowl left-over or fresh cold mash
½ bowl left-over or fresh cooked cabbage, chopped small
A bit of beaten egg
Salt and pepper
White flour
Salt and pepper

1. Mix mash, cabbage, seasoning, egg. Shape into burger-style cakes.

2. Mix flour and seasoning on a plate. Coat cakes in flour.
3. Heat oil in a pan. Fry cakes till golden each side, hot right through.

YOU CAN

* eat with cold roasts, eggs, bacon, beans, gammon, salad
* leave out cabbage for plain potato cakes
* add a bit of grated cheese, spring onion, mustard, Worcestershire sauce, cold roast or ham at step 1

Potato Salad

450g/1lb potatoes (old: peeled, cut into large chunks; new: unpeeled, whole/chopped)
2–4 garlic cloves, unpeeled (optional)
2–3 tbsps plain yogurt
2–3 tbsps good mayo
Salt and pepper
Squeeze lemon
Parsley/dill/coriander/chives/ basil (optional)

1. Boil spuds and garlic till just soft.
2. Drain. Separate spuds from garlic.
3. Spread spuds on a plate to cool a bit. Remove garlic from skins. Mix with yogurt, mayo, seasoning, herb. Toss spuds in dressing.

YOU CAN

* add crisp bacon and cooked broad beans
* add sliced sausage/chorizo and dill pickle
* throw in chopped ham, sliced cucumber and radish, cress
* try cherry tomatoes, red onion/ shallot, any herbs you fancy

PUDDINGS

Exceptionally impressive puddings. Treat yourself and friends to these little beauties. Buying fruit for the healthy options? Try to get local and beware perfect-looking fruit – it may taste of nothing.

1 nectarine or peach
2 plums
4–6 strawberries
1 banana, peeled
Lemon juice
2 tbsps rum/apple or orange
  juice
Caster sugar
Ground cinnamon

Hot Sugar Fruit Kebabs

Gorgeously soft and juicy fruit starts to caramelize in the cinnamon heat. Grill at home or barbie.

1. If using wooden skewers, soak them in water for 20 minutes.
2. Prep fruit. Halve and stone nectarine/peach and plums.
3. Cut banana in 5cm/2½in lengths. Brush with lemon juice.
4. Slap fruit in bowl with rum/fruit juice for 20 minutes.
5. Preheat grill or barbie. Line pan with foil. Thread fruit on skewers.
6. Sprinkle sugar and cinnamon on plate. Roll fruit in it or sprinkle. Grill for 3–4 minutes. Turn. Cook till soft, holding shape, just browning. Transfer carefully. Good with yogurt (pg 46), nuts and honey.

YOU CAN

✳ cut larger fruit into 4 to help pieces stay on skewers
✳ cook on barbie for beach party etc. Take sugar and cinnamon mixed in bag. Cut fruit in advance. Let it soak in rum in a plastic box or prep on beach.
✳ chill out. Skewer any fresh fruit. Enjoy as is.
✳ thread chunks of watermelon, Galia, cantaloup on skewers for low-fat energy
✳ thread berries on small skewers, drizzle with Choc Sauce (pg 243)

Baked Bananas

It's all about the tastes with these scrumptious Jamaican-style bananas. A great winter warmer when there's not much fresh fruit. (Store bananas separately – their gases age other fruit.)

4 bananas
200ml/7fl oz orange juice
1 tbsp brown sugar
Splash rum (optional)
25g/1oz butter

1. Heat oven to 180°C/350°F/gas 4. Peel bananas. Cut each one lengthways then across, to give 4 pieces.

2. Slap into buttered dish. Add juice, sugar, rum if using. Dot with butter. Bake for 20 minutes or till tender. Great with yogurt or ice-cream.

YOU CAN
✳ add scooped insides of a passion fruit
✳ barbecue unpeeled in foil, or grill 4–6 minutes, turning. Or boil 4 minutes. Eat with warm jam (pg 247) or Choc Sauce (pg 243).

Turkish Delight Plums & Sugared Hot Bread

Contrasting textures work here. Think soft sharp fruit with crunchy sugary French toast. Looks and tastes beautiful. PS Multi-tasks – works for simple/posh dinners, even breakfast. Use leftover plums in crumble (pg 235).

Plums
240ml/8fl oz water
110g/4oz caster sugar
450g/1lb plums
1 tsp rosewater (optional)
1 vanilla pod, slit, or 1 tsp
  natural vanilla extract
1 small sprig rosemary

Hot bread
3 slices bread (stale or fresh),
  crusts removed
1 large egg
1½ tsps sugar
75ml/3fl oz milk
Pinch cinnamon
Glug sherry (optional)
Butter

1. Heat water, caster sugar in pan till dissolved.

2. Add plums, optional rosewater, vanilla pod/extract, rosemary.

3. Simmer gently 10–15 minutes till the skins split and fruit's soft. Turn heat off.

4. Cut bread into fingers. Beat egg with sugar. Heat milk until it almost boils. Cool 1 minute. Beat into egg mix with cinnamon, optional sherry. Soak bread fingers in the mix.

5. Melt butter. Fry fingers briefly till crisp. Sprinkle with sugar, cinnamon. Enjoy with the plums and maybe yogurt or custard.

YOU CAN
✳ make easy cinnamon toast: mix 50g/2oz soft butter, 35g/1½oz caster sugar, 1 tsp cinnamon. Toast bread on one side. Spread mix on other side and toast that. Or cinnamon a muffin.

FEEDS 4 · £ · V

4 Bramley/other apples
1 level tbsp golden syrup (or
    runny honey)
Grated lemon rind
Squeeze lemon/orange juice
25–50g/1–2oz butter
4–6 tbsps cider/fruit juice

Brilliant Baked Apples

Perfect after a roast dinner. Bake them as you're cooking your meat (saves cash and energy). Enjoy with a table full of mates … simple to do and best in season (August–March).

1. Preheat oven to 180°C/350°F/gas 4.
2. Prep apples. Wash. Dry. Remove top two-thirds of core with a corer/knife to make cavities.
3. Score a line round apples, one-third down, to preserve their shape.
4. Stuff cavities with mix of syrup, lemon rind and juice. Top with bits of butter.
5. Sit fruit in dish. Surround with cider/juice (use more if needed).
6. Bake for 45–60 minutes or till browned, puffy.

YOU CAN

* stuff with dates, orange, dried figs, rum, cinnamon, allspice, brown sugar
* peel the top bit of skin off. Cover with basic meringue (pg 234). Cook for an extra 15–20 minutes or till brown, crispy.
* bake peaches. Cut in half. Stone. Stuff with a little brown sugar, butter, lemon rind. Sit in dish with a bit of fresh orange juice. Bake 20 minutes at 200°C/400°F/gas 6. Also good stuffed with butter, lemon, crushed amaretti.
* do it with soy margarine in a separate dish for a vegan

Battered Apple Pudding

Yorkshire pud stuffed with lovely sweet apple, basically. If you're a batter fan give it a go. Well filling – dead easy... Drizzle with golden maple syrup.

FEEDS 4 £ V

1 x batter (pg 132)
50g/2oz butter
450g/1lb apples (peeled, cored weight), thickly sliced
3 tbsps caster sugar
Cinnamon

1. Preheat oven to 220°C/425°F/gas 7.

2. Make batter (see pg 132).

3. Heat tin for 5 minutes. Add butter. After 3 minutes add apples. Sprinkle with sugar, cinnamon.

4. Pour in batter. Cook for 20–30 minutes, till high and golden.

YOU CAN
* make with plums, rhubarb

Crunchy Apple Charlotte

Got a few apples lying about ... bit of stale bread ... sugar in the jar ... then bang this one together. It's gorgeous and just what your granny would've made.

FEEDS 2–3 £ V

450g/1lb apples (peeled, cored weight), sliced thinly
110g/4oz caster sugar
110g/4oz breadcrumbs (pg 88) from stale loaf
Grated lemon rind
Pinch cinnamon/mixed spice
75g/3oz butter, melted

1. Prep apples. Mix sugar, breadcrumbs, lemon rind, cinnamon/mixed spice. Preheat oven to 190°C/375°F/gas 5.

2. Butter 2-pint/1-litre dish. Stack alternate breadcrumbs, butter, apples. Finish with crumbs. Bake 30–40 minutes or till apples soft, top crispy. Eat with ice-cream, cream, yogurt, custard.

1–2 bananas, peeled, chopped
1–2 apples, peeled, chopped

Batter
50g/2oz plain white flour
Pinch fine salt
1 tsp icing sugar
2 tsps butter, melted
4 tbsps warm water
1 egg white
Sunflower oil for frying

Sprinkle
Caster sugar
Ground cinnamon

Apple & Banana Hot Sugared Doughnuts

Turn out a batch of innocent doughnuts. Dunk bits of healthy fruit in batter then roll in cinnamon sugar. Makes a great snack or finger-food pudding.

1. For batter: sift flour, salt, icing sugar into a bowl.
2. Melt butter. Add water. Mix liquid gradually into the flour, beating constantly with a balloon whisk/wooden spoon till smooth and thick.
3. Whisk egg white till stiff. Fold gently into the batter with a metal spoon. Add bits of prepared fruit. Turn to coat them for doughnuts.
4. Heat approx 9cm/3½in of oil in a deep frying pan/saucepan till a breadcrumb crisps instantly.
5. Fry doughnuts in hot oil, a few at a time, turning once, for 2–3 minutes or till golden, crisp. Drain on kitchen paper.
6. Roll in mix of sugar and cinnamon. Eat immediately.

Boozy Crêpes

A French classic. Thin crêpes soaked in a citrus sauce. If you're not confident, make the sauce in a separate pan. Drizzle it over your hot cooked pancakes.

1. Make batter mix (pg 64) with addition of sugar and lemon rind. Fry very thin crêpes in 15–18cm/6–7in pan using 1½ tbsps batter for each one. Stack between bits of greaseproof paper till needed.
2. Make sauce: mix juice and rinds of fruit with booze (if using) and sugar. Set aside.
3. To cook: melt butter in the frying pan. Add the sauce (don't overheat).
4. Add first crêpe. Heat through. Fold it in half, then again. Add next crêpe and repeat till all are hot.

YOU CAN
✱ heat a spoon. Fill with extra booze. Ignite. Pour over crêpes on plate.

MAKES 8–10   ££   V

1 x pancake batter (pg 64)
  plus ½ tsp caster sugar plus
  a little lemon rind
50g/2oz butter for frying

Sauce
2 oranges
2 lemons
3 tbsps rum/brandy/Cointreau
25g/1oz caster sugar

223

Base
225g/8oz ginger or digestive
　biscuits
75g/3oz butter

Cake
675g/1½lb curd or cream
　cheese
175g/6oz caster sugar
3 small eggs
Bit of lemon rind
Squeeze lemon juice
1 tsp natural vanilla extract

Topping
Berries/cape gooseberries/
　chocolate flake/whipped
　cream

Big Baked Cheesecake

This big cheesecake feeds loads and makes a great party
piece if you pile on a fruity topping, though I like it plain
sometimes – depends on my mood and what's in season.

1. Preheat oven to 150°C/300°F/gas 2. Grease a 23cm/9in loose-based
cake tin.

2. Make biscuit base: melt butter gently in a pan. Stick biscuits into
freezer bag/plastic jug. Bash into crumbs. Stir into butter. Press into tin.
Chill for 15 minutes.

3. Blitz cheese, sugar, eggs, lemon rind, juice, vanilla with handblender
or beat with wooden spoon.

4. Pour mix over base. Bake 35–40 minutes. Turn oven off. Leave to
cool and firm up. Chill 2 hours minimum. Decorate or not.

Hot Chocolate Fudge Pudding

The prepared mix looks disastrous – but don't panic…
Once cooked you've got a delicious chocolate sponge with
a self-made fudge sauce. PS Reheats well.

1. Preheat oven to 180°C/350°F/gas 4. Grease 850ml/1½ pint dish.
2. Dissolve coffee in boiling water.
3. Cream butter and sugar with a wooden spoon (pg 10) till light, creamy (3–4 minutes). Beat eggs into mix gradually, adding pinches of flour if it starts to curdle.
4. Sift flour and cocoa onto mix. Add vanilla, coffee. Fold lightly together with a metal spoon, using large scooping movements, till it just falls off the spoon. Scoop into dish and level top.
5. Make sauce: mix cocoa, brown sugar, boiling water. Pour over sponge. Sit in roasting tin with boiling water to reach halfway up.
6. Bake 45 minutes or till toothpick comes out clean. Dust with sugar. Enjoy with vanilla ice-cream.

1 tsp instant coffee
1½ tbsps boiling water
110g/4oz soft butter
110g/4oz caster sugar
2 medium eggs, beaten
110g/4oz self-raising flour
25g/1oz cocoa powder
½–1 tsp vanilla bean paste or
   vanilla extract
Icing sugar for topping

Sauce
1 level tbsp cocoa powder
110g/4oz soft brown sugar
150ml/¼ pint hot water

MAKES
12 £ V

1x135g/5 oz packet of lime
  jelly, cubed
100ml/3½fl oz boiling water
150ml/5fl oz vodka
Juice of 1 lime

Vodka Jelly

Don't be tempted to add extra vodka – your jelly won't set.
All flavours work – but lime's tasty.

1. Slap jelly cubes in jug. Add boiling water. Stir to dissolve. Add vodka,
lime juice.

2. Pour into shot glasses. Sit in fridge till set.

FEEDS
2–3 £ V

200g/7oz pudding or risotto
  rice
2–3 big strips of lemon rind
2 tbsps caster sugar (a bit less
  for chocolate option)
Few drops natural vanilla
  extract or vanilla pod
1.2 litres/2 pints milk (I use
  semi-skimmed)
2 squares milk chocolate
  (optional)

Lemon Vanilla Rice
(with Chocolate Option)

Old-school rice pudding with a twist. Try it with chocolate.

1. Tip rice, lemon rind, sugar, vanilla, milk into a pan.

2. Heat without boiling. Simmer very gently on very low heat for
20–30 minutes, stirring occasionally till thick and creamy, adding more
milk if needed.

3. Chocolate option? Chuck it in at the finish. Stir to melt. Lovely.

YOU CAN

✱ stir warm jam in to serve

✱ add strong coffee to rice

✱ use honey instead of sugar.
Add a few drops of rosewater
in place of vanilla. Chuck some
pistachios on there.

✱ stir in some poached fruit
such as plums, peaches, rhubarb

✱ bake it. Stick 50g/2oz rice and
25g/1oz caster sugar in a dish
with 600ml/1 pint boiling milk.
Bake at 180°C/350°F/gas 4
dotted with butter, sprinkled
with nutmeg, for 1–2 hours.

Proper Fruit Jelly (with Berries)

Get your chef skills sorted with gelatine (Vege-Gel or agar agar for vegetarians). Once you're down with it experiment with other tasty fruit juice and berry combos.

MAKES **4** £ **V** OPTION

1. Sit gelatine leaves in shallow dish. Cover with cold water. Soak for 5 minutes. Set aside.
2. Heat sugar and water very gently till sugar's dissolved.
3. Add to orange and lemon juice to get liquid to 500ml/18fl oz.
4. Squeeze water out of gelatine leaves. Slap them into a pan with 3–4 tbsps of the juice mix. Heat very gently till dissolved. Add to rest of juice immediately.
5. Pour into ramekins/glasses. Drop berries in. Chill till jellied.

5 leaves gelatine
Some cold water
50g/2oz caster sugar
150ml/5fl oz water
300ml/10fl oz fresh orange juice
Juice of 1 lemon
Some raspberries, strawberries, blueberries

££ V EXPRESS

Peach Melba Sundae
Peaches, ice-cream, meringue, raspberry sauce. Gorgeous.

2 fresh peaches (cut in half,
  stones removed)
1 tbsp sugar
200ml/7fl oz water or water/
  white wine mix
Raspberry Sauce (pg 243)
1–2 meringues (pg 234)
Vanilla ice-cream

1. Put peaches, sugar, water or water/wine mix in pan. Simmer very gently for 5–10 minutes till fruit is tender but keeping its shape. Remove. Tip into a dish. Cool it.

2. Make Raspberry Sauce (pg 243). Slice peaches.

3. Assemble: drizzle a bit of sauce into tall glasses. Randomly add crumbled meringue, sliced peach, ice-cream, sauce. Delicious.

YOU CAN
* serve neatly on a plate as Peach Melba
* use unpoached peaches
* use chocolate sauce and fresh raspberries
* butter both sides of 2 slices crustless bread or brioche. Cover with a layer of sliced poached or skinless fresh peach. Dust with sugar/cinnamon, drizzle with melted butter. Bake at 220°C/425°F/gas 7 till soft and crispy.

Hot Choc Profiteroles

Ridiculously cheap given their expensive reputation. Choux pastry is well easy. My sister Poll made these every week at uni. Pile 'em up to treat friends/impress family when they come to visit. Save extra sauce for ice-cream.

1. Preheat oven to 220°C/425°F/gas 7.
2. Sift flour and salt onto a bit of greaseproof/baking paper.
3. Heat butter and water in pan. Boil. Lower heat. Shoot flour in.
4. Beat like mad with a wooden spoon (1–2 minutes) to get a smooth paste ball. Cool choux for 5 minutes.
5. Beat eggs. Beat into dough, very gradually, for a shiny mix.
6. Spoon 15 blobs well apart on greased tray.
7. Bake 25 minutes till golden/puffy. Nick a slit in each.
8. Turn oven off. Put puffs back to crisp for 5 minutes. Cool on rack.
9. Whip cream with sugar, vanilla (don't overbeat).
10. Spoon/pipe into puffs up to 1 hour before eating. Drizzle with Choc Sauce.

YOU CAN
* fill with ice-cream/drizzle with Butterscotch Sauce (pg 243)

MAKES
15   £   V

Choux pastry
75g/3oz plain flour
Pinch salt
50g/2oz butter
150ml/5fl oz water
2 medium eggs, beaten

Filling
Double or whipping cream
Caster sugar to taste
3 drops vanilla extract

Choc Sauce (pg 243)

225g/8oz raspberries or
   blackberries
50g/2oz sugar
1 tbsp apple/blackcurrant
   juice/white wine
300ml/10fl oz double cream
1 tbsp white wine
1 tbsp lemon juice
2 egg whites

175g/6oz good white
   chocolate, in chunks
2 sheets gelatine (agar agar or
   Vege-gel for vegetarians)
3 tbsps cold water
2 large eggs
250ml/9fl oz double cream

Fruity Mousse

Does what it says on the tin – all the flavour of a fruit smoothie with a lovely light moussey texture. Don't overbeat the cream though. Out of season? Use frozen berries.

1. Tip berries into a pan with sugar and juice or wine. Heat briefly till the berries soften, their juices running.

2. Blitz with a handblender, or mash. Sieve into a bowl.

3. Beat cream with a balloon/handwhisk till soft and holding shape. Stir in wine, sieved fruit smush, lemon juice. Whisk the egg whites till stiff (see pg 11).

4. Fold beaten whites into the mousse. Spoon or pour into mugs/glasses. Chill 1–2 hours.

White Chocolate Mousse

White, smooth, mellow, gorgeous.

1. Sit heatproof bowl over pan of barely simmering water.

2. Put chocolate in the bowl and leave to melt very slowly – no stirring.

3. Submerse gelatine sheets in a bowl of cold water. Leave 5 minutes.

4. Separate eggs (see pg 11). Whisk cream into thick folds. Don't overbeat it.

5. Squeeze water out of gelatine. Put leaves into pan with 3 tbsps cold water. Dissolve for a few seconds over low heat.

6. Stir gelatine and melted chocolate into egg yolks, then fold the cream in with a large metal spoon.

7. Whisk egg whites till stiff (not dry). Fold lightly into mousse. Pour into ramekins/glasses and chill for 1–2 hours.

YOU CAN
* add lime juice and rind to mix at step 5
* cover base of ramekins/glasses first with crushed Ginger Chilli Hits (pg 257)

Chocolate Mousse

I haven't come across a better one. Just be patient when you're melting the chocolate and don't get any water or steam in the mix. Use fair-trade chocolate if possible.

1. Sit heatproof bowl over a pan of barely simmering water.
2. Add chocolate, sugar, water. Leave to melt slowly, no stirring. Remove bowl. Stir in butter, rum, egg yolks. Cool.
3. Whisk egg whites till stiff, not grainy, using electric/hand/balloon whisk. Fold lightly into choc mix with a metal spoon and using large scooping movements. Don't overmix.
4. Spoon or pour into cups/glasses/ramekins. Chill for 1–2 hours.

MAKES 4 · £ · V

175g/6oz good dark chocolate, in chunks
1 level tbsp caster sugar
5 tbsps water
35g/½oz soft butter
1½ tbsps rum
3 eggs, separated (see pg 11)

75g/3oz caster sugar
150ml/5fl oz water
Juice and rind of 3 lemons or
  lemon/lime mix
85ml/3fl oz semi-skimmed milk
1 egg white

Sherbet Lemon Shots

Taste exactly like sherbet lemons. Pretty sharp and blooming tangy. Drizzle with vodka if feeling extravagant. Excellent for party cool-downs.

1. Heat sugar and water in a small pan till the sugar dissolves. Boil on increased heat for 5 minutes. Remove.
2. Stir in lemon rind, juice, milk. Tip into a freezer-proof container.
3. Stick into freezer. Remove 2–3 times during setting and stir up crystals with a fork.
4. Just before set, stir in a whisked egg white. Freeze.
5. To serve: scrape into shot glasses.

Strawberry Sorbet & Orange Lollies

Perfect for summer days or for sucking virtuously on the sofa … no dodgy ingredients, just natural fruit flavours.

40ml/1½fl oz water
30g/1¼oz caster sugar
160g/6oz fresh strawberries, chopped
Juice of 3 large fresh oranges, or equivalent bought unsweetened juice

1. Heat water and sugar in pan till sugar dissolves. Tip into blender or jug (to use with handblender).

2. Add strawberries. Blitz till puréed. Sieve to remove pips.

3. Pour into bottoms of lolly moulds. Add stick. Freeze for 30 minutes.

4. Remove. Fill moulds to the top with orange juice. Freeze properly.

YOU CAN
* use other juices/fruits
* make frozen strawberry smoothie lollies. Follow smoothie method (pg 54). Pour into moulds. Freeze. Easy.

233

Meringue
Whites of 5 large eggs (to
 separate, see pg 11)
275g/10oz caster sugar

Topping
A load of raspberries
300ml/½ pint double cream

Pavlova (with Meringue Options)

One giant meringue, basically. Don't be intimidated – it's so easy.

1. Put egg whites in a very clean big bowl. Whisk till stiff (not dry) using grease-free implements. Add sugar, 1 tbsp at a time, whisking constantly. Keep whisking till the mix is very, very thick. It stays put, held upside down.

2. Preheat oven to 140°C/275°F/gas 1. Line baking tray with greaseproof/baking paper/silicone sheet.

3. Tip mix onto paper. Tease into a circle. Cook 1½ hours. Turn oven off. Let meringue dry out. Sit on rack. (Can store in a tin for 1 week.)

4. Whip cream. Slather over meringue. Top with fruit.

YOU CAN

✱ make 2 or 3 thinner layers. Sandwich with cream/fruit. Make a mountain.

✱ shape into big blobs for individual meringues. Cook 1 hour, then dry out.

✱ whisk 1 tsp coffee granules in with sugar for cappuccino meringues

✱ for chocolate meringues sift 1 tbsp cocoa in at step 1 or dip white meringues into melted chocolate

✱ use meringues for Eton Mess. Crumble meringue into whipped cream. Mix with mashed raspberries, strawberries, blueberries.

✱ make loads of mini-meringues for picnics/parties

Rhubarb (& Strawberry) Crumble

Classic. Use seasonal fruit (see what's about). Handle your topping lightly. Lovely…

1. Cook rhubarb in a pan with ginger beer/water, sugar for 3–4 mins or till just soft, releasing juices but holding shape. Add lemon juice.

2. Sift flour, salt into a bowl. Cut butter in. Rub in (pg 10) till it looks like fine breadcrumbs. Mix in sugar. Preheat oven to 180°C/350°F/gas 4.

3. Tip strawberries into dish. Add rhubarb plus gingery juice to come halfway up the dish.

4. Sprinkle crumble evenly over top to cover. Don't press it down. Cook 30 minutes till pale gold, juices bubbling. Serve with custard, ice-cream, yogurt.

YOU CAN

* use all rhubarb – skip the strawberries and make up the weight
* add sliced banana, blueberries, raspberries
* make old-style apple crumble. Poach the apples as above till just soft, then slap in the dish and top. May take 30–40 minutes to cook.
* add blackberries to the apple
* make gorgeous plum crumble: poach plums (pg 219). Slap into dish. Substitute some of crumble flour with ground almonds.
* add a bit of cinnamon, mixed spice, grated lemon to the crumble

FEEDS 4–6   £   V

500g/18oz rhubarb, in
  2.5cm/1in chunks
200g/7oz strawberries
4 tbsps ginger beer/water
1 tbsp caster sugar
Good squeeze lemon juice

Crumble
110g/4oz white flour
Pinch salt
50g/2oz butter
50g/2oz caster sugar

FEEDS 4–6 ££ V

Pastry
110g/4oz plain white flour
50g/2oz butter
Pinch salt
1–2 tbsps very cold water

Filling
1½ tbsps breadcrumbs
1 tbsp caster sugar

Lemon curd
Juice and rind of 2 large
  lemons
3 large eggs, beaten
175g/6oz caster sugar
225g/8oz butter

Meringue
Whites of 2 large eggs
110g/4oz caster sugar

Lemon Meringue Pie

Sumptuous. You've got crisp pastry, gooey lemon curd, crisp light meringue. One to make an impression.

1. Make speedy pastry (pg 238). Chill for 20 minutes.
2. Preheat oven to 190°C/375°F/gas 5. Grease 20.5cm/8in round tart tin 3cm/1¼ in deep (loose-bottomed is good). Line with pastry. Save any extra.
3. Prick base with a fork. Line with baking paper. Fill with dry or baking beans or pasta to weigh it down. Bake 20 minutes.
4. Meantime mix breadcrumbs, sugar on a plate.
5. Make lemon curd. Slap lemon rind, juice, eggs, sugar into heavy pan. Stir well with wooden spoon on low heat. Add butter, stirring. Don't boil. Stir patiently till it starts to thicken.
6. Remove baking beans, paper from tart. If pastry case has cracked/shrunk, mould bits of spare pastry into spaces to mend. Reduce heat to 150°C/300°F/gas 2.
7. Sprinkle breadcrumb/sugar mix over base. Pour curd in. Return to oven for 10 minutes while you make meringue (pg 234).
8. Remove tart. Spoon or pipe meringue over entire tart. Bake 40 minutes. Eat warm or cold.

YOU CAN
✱ make treacle tart. At step 2 prick pastry with fork. Mix 9 tbsps breadcrumbs, 9 tbsps golden syrup, 1 tbsp lemon juice, grated rind, 3 tbsps cream. Tip into case. Bake 25–30 mins till golden.

FEEDS 6 **£** **V**

Speedy shortcrust pastry
350g/12oz plain flour
175g/6oz butter
Pinch salt
3 tbsps cold water

Pie filling
900g/2lb good eating or
  cooking apples
  (e.g. Bramleys)
2 tbsps caster sugar
Pinch cinnamon/all spice
Little grated lemon rind

Finish
A little beaten egg or milk
Sprinkle of sugar

Yorkshire Apple Pie

Bake this up in a brownie-style tin. Cut a slice out whenever you fancy or share with your housemates. Vary the filling using other fruit, spice, maybe get a little bit of cheese in there for authentic Yorkshire...

1. Grease 30.5x18x3cm/11x7x1¼ in tin.

2. Pastry: sift flour, salt into bowl. Add butter, cut very small. Rub mix together lightly between fingers to amalgamate (see pg 10).

3. Add two-thirds of the water. Mix with a fork. Add last one-third for a soft smooth pastry. It mustn't be dry or overly sticky.

4. Line tin: sit dough on floured board. Cut in two, one bit slightly bigger. Roll this out till it will cover the base and sides of the tin plus a bit. Lift into tin on a rolling pin or drape over hands. Mould into place, filling any cracks or holes.

5. Fill: fill to very top with thinly sliced apples, sugar, spice, lemon rind.

6. Top: roll pastry out in rectangle just bigger than tin. Lift over pie. Press/pinch the edges together firmly. Trim with sharp knife if needed.

7. Brush pie with milk/egg. Rest it for 1 hour. Poke 2 or 3 holes in top.

8. Heat oven 230°C/450°F/gas 8. Cook 10 minutes. Reduce and cook at 180°C/350°F/gas 4 for 20–35 minutes till pastry's golden, filling bubbly.

YOU CAN

✳ cut shapes (leaves etc) from any extra pastry and use to decorate top – stick on using milk

✳ add 50g/2oz thinly sliced Cheddar/Lancashire cheese at step 5

✳ add berries/pear/banana

✳ slice up for pack-up or take whole to beach/picnic

✳ fill with meat ragu (pg 180) for savoury pie – great with mash and gravy

Tutti-Frutti Flapover Pie

Think seasonal with this open-topped pie. Here's the summer soft-fruit version. Flapping the pastry over means you don't need to be too careful with the rolling out…

FEEDS 4–6   ££   V

1. Make pastry: sift flour, salt, sugar into bowl. Add butter, lemon rind. Rub in (pg 10). Fork in beaten yolk, water. Pull into smooth ball. Chill 30 minutes in clingfilm. Preheat oven to 200°C/400°F/gas 6.

2. Toss fruit in a bowl with cinnamon, sugar, flour, lemon juice.

3. Roll pastry into a rough circle on lightly floured board, pizza-style, 30–35cm/12–14in. Transfer to a large greased baking tray. Heap fruit up in the centre, leaving the edges free. Brush borders with beaten egg/milk, then fold up over and onto fruit, leaving centre open.

4. Pinch and roughly crimp the border to repair holes/cracks, create pattern, hold juices. Brush lightly with egg/milk. Sprinkle sugar. Bake 30–40 minutes. Eat hot or cold.

YOU CAN

* make a winter pie with thinly sliced apples and pears/apples and blackberries
* slide baking paper over top of pie if it's browning too fast

Pastry
225g/8oz plain white flour
Pinch fine salt
2½ tbsps caster sugar
120g/4½oz butter
Grated rind of ½ a lemon
1 egg yolk, beaten
2 tbsps cold water

Tutti frutti filling
2–3 nectarines, stoned, chopped
Blueberries
Blackberries
1 banana, sliced
1 apple, peeled, sliced
Pinch cinnamon
2 tbsps caster sugar
Sprinkling plain flour
Lemon juice

Glaze
Bit of beaten egg/milk
Sprinkle sugar

FEEDS 6 · £ · V

175g/6oz dates (fresh or dried), chopped
300ml/10fl oz water
1 teabag
1 tsp bicarbonate of soda
50g/2oz butter
175g/6oz sugar
2 eggs, beaten
175g/6oz self-raising flour
1 tsp vanilla extract

Sauce
25g/1oz butter
2 tbsps golden syrup
175g/6oz soft brown sugar
4 tsps single cream

MAKES 4 · £ · V

1 very large or 2 smaller lemons (juice and rind, grated)
250ml/9fl oz double cream
50g/2oz caster sugar
50g/2oz Quark, own cream cheese (pg 47) or other
3 drops vanilla extract (optional)

Base
6–8 Ginger Chilli Hits (pg 257) or ginger biscuits

Sticky Toffee Pudding

You can't really beat this one when it comes to hot puds. Quintessentially English. Hot toffee sauce on scrumptious pudding. Personal favourite…

1. Preheat oven to 180°C/375°F/gas 4. Grease baking tin 28x18x2.5cm/ 11x7x1in.
2. Simmer dates in pan with water and teabag for 5 minutes. Remove teabag. Add bicarb.
3. Beat butter, sugar vigorously in bowl with a wooden spoon for 3–4 minutes till white, light (pg 10).
4. Beat eggs in a very small bit at a time. If mix curdles, add a little flour.
5. Stir in the flour, date mix, vanilla extract. Spoon into tin. Cook 30 minutes till risen, springy. Cut into squares.
6. Make sauce: melt butter, syrup, sugar in pan over low heat. Boil 1 minute. Stir in cream. Pour over pudding.

YOU CAN
✱ stop mix curdling. Start with everything at room temperature. Add pinch of flour if it kicks off.

Little Lemon Ginger Cheesecakes

Perfect dinner-party pud modelled on one made by M&S that we all fell in love with. Think ginger biscuit base and lemon cream topping. Note: really good with Ginger Chilli Hits (pg 257) if you've got any.

1. Whisk lemon rind, cream, sugar till just thick. Add lemon juice. Whisk again, taking care to leave it quite soft.
2. Gently fold in mashed Quark/cream cheese, vanilla until soft and smooth.
3. Bash biscuits to crumbs in a freezer bag/plastic jug.
4. Sprinkle crumbs into 3–4 ramekins/cups. Top with lemon cream. Leave plain or top with berries or choc flake. Chill for 2 hours.

Little Hot Chocolate Puds

Like chocolate fondant. But you've got to get your timing right or the chocolate centre won't be melty…

FEEDS 4 £ V

60g/2¼oz good dark chocolate, broken into squares
60g/2¼oz soft butter
½ tsp orange rind
2 tsps black coffee
2 medium eggs plus 2 extra yolks
50g/2oz caster sugar
50g/2oz plain flour, sifted (see pg 10)

1. Preheat oven to 180°C/350°F/gas 4. Grease four 150ml/5fl oz ramekins/dishes.

2. Put choc squares, butter, orange rind, coffee into bowl over pan of gently simmering water (pg 11). Let it melt before stirring. Remove.

3. Chuck eggs, sugar into medium bowl. Whisk for 3–4 minutes with balloon/hand/electric whisk till double volume, pale. Add melted chocolate mix and sifted flour.

4. Fold together very lightly with large spoon. Pour into dishes.

5. Cook on baking tray 12 minutes (don't open oven door) till risen, firm outside, saucy inside (test with a skewer). Eat from dish or loosen with a knife. Place a plate over. Invert. Turn it out.

No-Wait Smoothie Ice-Cream

Frozen berries plus yogurt equals instant ice-cream.
Nice one.

1. Stick cold yogurt and frozen berries in blender or in bowl to use with handblender. Mush up. Eat immediately.

YOU CAN
* blitz chunks of frozen banana for instant banana ice-cream

175g/6oz favourite berries, frozen
250ml/9fl oz plain yogurt (pg 46), or use bought plain or vanilla

Hot-and-Cold Coffee Ice-Cream

Fastest hot and cold Italian-style pudding. Speedy but sophisticated.

1. Make coffee (pg 53).
2. Sit ice-cream in a cup (or mug).
3. Pour coffee over it.
4. Serve with a spoon. Eat immediately.

FEEDS 1

1 cup very strong black coffee
1 ball of best vanilla ice-cream

Tangy Lemon Yogurt Ice-Cream

Slapping yogurt into ice-cream gives it real sharpness and makes it a bit healthier.

1. Mix lemon juice and grated rind in a bowl. Stir in sifted icing sugar gradually. Leave 30 minutes.
2. Whip yogurt, cream, water together till softly thick. Add the lemon/sugar mix. Freeze in box/freezer bag.
3. Remove yog-ice 10 minutes before serving.

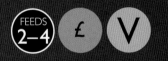

FEEDS 2–4

3–4 lemons (unwaxed's best)
175g/6oz icing sugar
250ml/9fl oz Greek yogurt
200ml/7fl oz double cream
3 tbsps very cold water

Fresh Raspberry Sauce

Simple. Pour it over ice-cream, yogurt, for a sweet and sour contrast.

225g/8oz raspberries
1 tbsp icing or caster sugar

1. Heat berries and sugar in a pan till soft and releasing juices.
2. Press mix through a sieve over a bowl. Eat immediately or chill.

Best Chocolate Sauce

Smooth and chocolatey. Beats all the bought ones…

110g/4oz dark chocolate, in chunks
15g/½oz butter
2 tbsps golden syrup
2 tbsps water
1 tsp natural vanilla extract

1. Tip choc chunks into bowl over pan of simmering water (pg 11).
2. Add butter, syrup, water. Let it all melt together.
3. Stir till smooth. Add vanilla.
4. Pour hot over cold ice-cream or profiteroles.
YOU CAN
✱ store in fridge for 1 week

Butterscotch Sauce

Multi-disciplinary sauce – bang it on appropriate puddings, crêpes, ice-cream. Sticky.

25g/1oz butter
2 tbsps golden syrup
175g/6oz soft brown sugar
4 tbsps single cream

1. Melt butter, syrup, sugar in pan.
2. Bring to the boil briefly. Stir

cream in.
3. Pour over ice-cream, sliced bananas, pancakes.
YOU CAN
✱ store in fridge for 1 week

Mars Bar Sauce

Our doctor's favourite chocolate sauce – seriously.

1 Mars bar, chopped into chunks
3 tbsps milk

1. Chuck Mars into a pan with milk.
2. Stir with wooden spoon till almost melted (leave bits of caramel).
3. Pour immediately over ice-cream.

CAKES & BREADS

Celebrate your independence with excellent cakes, breads, muffins, jams, biscuits. Just like home – and the way to my heart. Get mates round now for plates of great baked stuff.

225g/8oz self-raising flour
1 tsp baking powder
Pinch salt
50g/2oz butter
25g/1oz caster sugar
About 150ml/5fl oz milk
Beaten egg, to brush
Granulated sugar, to sprinkle

Fillings
Jam
Double cream, whipped
Fresh fruit

Scone & Jam Cream Tea

The ultimate afternoon tea, Teacake Tuesday style (my mates and I set aside Tuesday afternoons to meet in an old-school teashop for this sort of eating). The key to a light scone is to handle your dough gently. Serve with tea from a pot.

1. Preheat oven to 220°C/425°F/gas 7. Grease baking tray.

2. Sift flour, baking powder, salt into bowl.

3. Cut butter into bits and add to bowl. Rub fat/flour between fingers (pg 10), holding your hands over the bowl, to amalgamate.

4. Stir in sugar. Add milk gradually, mixing with fork till you get a soft sticky dough. Pull into a ball, handling very lightly now.

5. Roll out very lightly on floured surface approx 2.5cm/1in thick. Cut in 5cm/2in rounds with floured cutter/wine glass. Don't twist. Or cut into triangles. Re-roll the remaining dough and repeat. Brush with egg. Sprinkle sugar.

6. Place well apart on baking tray and bake for 12–15 minutes till risen, golden. Cool on rack. Fill with butter, jam, whipped cream.

YOU CAN
✳ whack in chopped dates, grated lemon or orange rind, sultanas, cinnamon at step 4

Simple Raspberry Jam

Every scone needs this fruity jam or whack it into a cake. Cheat's method. Frozen raspberries are fine in winter.

250g/9oz raspberries (fresh or frozen and defrosted)
250g/9oz caster sugar

1. Preheat oven to 180°C/350°F/gas 4. Wash jar. Dry out in oven a few minutes to sterilize it.
2. Lay fruit out in shallow dish. Bake 20 minutes.
3. Stir sugar in. Spoon into a clean jar. Seal. Cool.
4. Store in fridge (keeps for up to a week).

YOU CAN
* stir into yogurt, rice pudding
* fill sponge cakes/Swiss roll
* make jam semolina. Add 20g/¾oz semolina to 300ml/½ pint warm milk. Stir, cooking slowly, till it begins to thicken. Add 25g/1oz caster sugar, dollop butter. Cook 5 minutes. Stir jam in.

Cheese Scone Tea

Sort some of these out to go with soup or get them for tea if you don't have a sweet tooth. Good in a lunch box with celery, fruit, etc. Spread with butter or cream cheese (pg 47).

225g/8oz plain white flour
4 level tsps baking powder
Good pinch salt
Pinch dry mustard and/or cayenne pepper
50g/2oz finely grated tasty Cheddar
50g/2oz butter
1 large egg, beaten
4 tbsps cold water

1. Preheat oven to 220°C/425°F/gas 7. Sift flour, baking powder, salt, mustard, cayenne into bowl. Add cheese. Rub butter into mix (see pg 10).
2. Add beaten egg and water. Mix lightly with a fork.
3. Pull dough into soft (not sticky) ball. Add a drop of water if dry.
4. Roll and cut out as for sweet scones (see left), handling very gently.
5. Cook on greased baking trays for 10 minutes or till high.

YOU CAN
* make these while a soup cooks – eat them together
* at step 2, stir in chopped olive, fried onion. Sandwich with cream cheese.
* make cobbler. Fry chopped onion and garlic in oil for 5 mins. Add 2 chopped carrots, 1 chopped courgette, some mushrooms, 1 tin chopped tomatoes, 1 tin butter beans, herbs, seasoning. Stew till veg soften. Tip in dish. Top with scones. Scatter grated cheese. Bake at 230°C/450°F/gas 6 for 20 mins.

225g/8oz self-raising flour
Pinch salt
1 tbsp caster sugar
2 eggs
300ml/½ pint milk

25–50g/1–2oz butter, melted,
  for frying

Drop Scones

Slap a batch of these together for your housemates anytime. Trick is to turn them when they're just right – that's when the base starts to colour and the top bubbles.

1. Sift flour, salt, sugar into bowl. Tip eggs and a bit of milk into a well in the centre. Beat together gradually with wooden spoon/balloon whisk for smooth batter.
2. Brush a little melted butter over crêpe pan/frying pan on medium heat. Using 1 tbsp batter per scone, drop 4–5 tbsps, well apart, onto hot pan.
3. Cook 1–2 minutes till bases brown, tops bubbling. Flip over. Cook 1–2 minutes till browned. Keep warm in teatowel. Cook rest of batter. Eat with butter, jam, syrup, lemon curd or savoury bits (cheese etc).

Lemon Curd

It's sweet and smooth, lemony and sharp – and faster to make than a trip to the corner shop. Watch the mix doesn't boil or the whole thing could curdle. (Slowly does it.)

MAKES 1 JAR · £ · V · EXPRESS

Juice and grated rind of 2 big
   (or 3 small) unwaxed lemons
110g/4oz caster sugar
50g/2oz butter
2 large eggs, beaten

1. Tip everything except eggs into bowl.

2. Sit bowl over a pan of simmering water (base not touching). Melt ingredients slowly. Stir with a wooden spoon and watch it.

3. Add the beaten eggs. Stir constantly till the curd thickens, coating the back of spoon. Be patient.

4. Cool. Store in a clean jar. Or cover and chill it.

YOU CAN
* eat on toast, muffins, crumpets. Fill sponge cakes, Swiss roll.
* stir equal quantity of curd into yogurt. Chill. Or freeze to make ice-cream.
* use 4–5 limes or 2 oranges for lime/orange curd

Cinnamon Jam Buns

If you haven't had experience of making cakes this could be a tasty start (and it's a good one if you don't have bun cases).

MAKES 8–10 · £ · V · EXPRESS

225g/8oz self-raising flour
Pinch salt
2 pinches ground cinnamon
50g/2oz butter
50g/2oz caster sugar
1 egg, beaten
2 tbsps milk
Some good fruity jam
Granulated sugar, for sprinkling

1. Preheat the oven to 220°C/425°F/gas 7. Grease baking tray.

2. Sift flour, salt, cinnamon into bowl. Cut the butter in.

3. Rub everything together between your fingers till amalgamated.

4. Mix in caster sugar and beaten egg, using a fork. Mix milk in very gradually. Knead the stiff dough very lightly on a board to get it smooth.

5. Roll into 12 balls. Make a hole in each with finger/teaspoon.

6. Whack a bit of jam in. Seal over hole and pinch so it stays firmly shut. Sit buns seam side down on tray. Spinkle with granulated sugar.

7. Cook for 10 minutes or till lightly browned. Cool. Split and eat with more jam if you like.

YOU CAN
* fill with choc spread instead of jam
* add lemon rind instead of cinnamon and fill with lemon curd

150g/5oz self-raising flour
1 tsp baking powder
110g/4oz soft butter
110g/4oz caster sugar
2 eggs
Grated rind of 1 large lemon
    or mix of orange and lemon

Icing
110g/4oz soft butter
1 egg yolk
225g/8oz icing sugar
3–4 tsps lemon juice
Few drops pink/blue/green
    food colouring

275g/10oz plain white flour
1 tbsp baking powder
½ tsp cinnamon
½ tsp salt
175g/6oz polenta/cornmeal
150g/5oz caster sugar
Grated rind 1 lemon/orange
350ml/12fl oz milk
175ml/6oz sunflower oil
4 eggs, beaten
½ tsp almond/vanilla extract
1 large eating apple, skin on,
    cut into small dice
Demerara or crushed sugar
    lumps/pumpkin seeds

Fairy Cakes with Colourful Icing

Not really a student essential but who cares. There's nothing like a fairy cake to remind you of your birthday. Bang out loads of these beauties for parties or treat a houseful.

1. Cakes: preheat oven to 200°C/400°F/gas 6. Sit bun cases on baking tray or thoroughly grease a bun tin.

2. Slap all cake ingredients in a bowl. Beat furiously with a wooden spoon for 3 minutes till very soft and creamy.

3. Put 1 heaped tsp of mix into cases or hollows in tin.

4. Cook for 15 minutes or till browned and springy. Cool on rack.

5. Icing: beat butter till creamy. Add egg. Beat sugar in a little at a time. Add lemon juice and a few drops pink/blue/green colouring. Pipe or blob it onto cakes.

YOU CAN

✱ use the same mix to make a speedy jam sponge cake. At step 1 preheat oven to 170°C/325°F/gas 3. At step 3 omit lemon/orange rind. At step 4 divide mix between two 18cm/7in sandwich tins, greased or lined with lightly oiled greaseproof paper. At step 5 cook for 20–25 minutes. At end fill with jam or whipped cream, jam and fresh fruit.

Cinnamon Apple Muffins

Grab and go breakfast or enjoy anytime. Chunks of soft apple burst through light cake making this one a fruity option. Keep the muffin batter lumpy.

1. Preheat oven to 200°C/400°F/gas 6. Grease the holes in muffin trays or line with muffin cases.

2. Sift flour, baking powder, cinnamon, salt into large bowl. Add polenta, sugar, lemon/orange rind. Make a well in the centre.

3. Beat milk, oil together with a fork. Add beaten eggs and almond/vanilla extract.

4. Tip into flour well with diced apple. Stir quickly but roughly so the flour's in but batter's still lumpy. Fill almost to top of holes/cases.

5. Sprinkle optional sugar/seeds. Bake for 20–25 minutes.

YOU CAN

* add fresh blackberries, blueberries or raspberries, bits of date or dried apricot, bit of muesli. Or spoon a bit of marmalade/jam/syrup into centre. Or add a bit of powdered ginger. Or top with a bit of lemon icing (pg 255), or cream cheese (pg 47) mixed with a little lemon juice.

Blueberry Crumble Muffins

Blueberries bang in the vitamin C and dominate this US–style muffin. And you can always have a go at the chocolate ones … they taste awesome. Drizzle with lemon icing.

1. Preheat oven to 200°C/400°F/gas 6. Grease holes in muffin trays or line with muffin cases.

2. Crumble: tip crumble ingredients into bowl. Rub together between fingers (pg 10).

3. Muffins: sift flour, baking powder, bicarb into a bowl.

4. Beat eggs, sugar, oil, lemon rind, milk, poppy seeds together. Tip into flour. Mix with a fork for a lumpy batter.

5. Stir in lemon juice, blueberries. Spoon into tray holes/muffin cases.

6. Sprinkle crumble on top. Bake 15–20 minutes till risen high, cooked through.

YOU CAN

* make Choc Crumble Muffins. Swap 25g/1oz of flour for cocoa. Use orange instead of lemon. Substitute bits of roughly chopped dark chocolate for blueberries.

* make lemon icing (pg 255)

Crumble
40g/1½oz plain white flour
20g/¾oz brown/demerara/
    granulated sugar
25g/1oz butter

Muffins
250g/8oz plain white flour
2 tsps baking powder
½ tsp bicarbonate of soda
2 eggs
75g/3oz caster sugar
2 tbsps sunflower oil
Grated rind 1 lemon
150ml/5fl oz milk
2–3 tbsps poppy seeds
1 tbsp lemon juice
110g/4oz blueberries

MAKES 1 **££** **V**

110g/4oz soft butter
110g/4oz caster sugar
2 eggs
110g/4oz self-raising flour, sifted
1 tsp baking powder
2 level tbsps drinking chocolate powder
1 level tbsp cocoa powder
2 tbsps milk
½ tsp vanilla extract

Icing
50g/2oz chocolate, melted
110g/4oz soft butter
225g/8oz icing sugar, sifted
2 tsps milk

Chocolate Cloud Cake

It's all about the air so get a good beating action into your mix for this easy all-in-one job. Get everything at room temp before you get started. Chocolatey, light. Most impressive.

1. Preheat oven to 180°C/350°F/gas 4. Grease or line the base of two 18cm/7in sandwich tins – loose-based are best.

2. Beat cake ingredients with electric mixer. Or by hand: beat butter, sugar for 3 minutes till light and creamy, then beat eggs in gradually (add pinch flour if curdling), finally beat in dry ingredients, milk and vanilla extract.

3. Spoon mixture evenly into tins. Bake 20–25 minutes till springy. Cool in tin for 3 minutes then turn out onto rack.

4. Make icing: melt chocolate (pg 11). Beat butter till creamy. Beat in sugar gradually. Stir in melted chocolate, and milk if needed. Use to sandwich the sponge layers and spread on top. Decorate.

Amazing Chocolate Cake & Fudge Icing

Run out of eggs or just fancy an amazing cake? It's all chocolate. You won't taste the mayo bit. PS The fudge icing's special. Try it on the Cloud Cake and muffins.

1. Preheat oven to 180°C/350°F/gas 4. Grease or line 20.5cm/8in tin.
2. Sift flour, baking powder, sugar into bowl. Beat in mayo with wooden spoon for lumpy mix.
3. Pour boiling water over cocoa and vanilla extract. Stir to dissolve.
4. Beat into main mix till soft and creamy.
5. Tip into tin. Bake 40 mins till cake starts to shrink from edges, skewer comes out clean. Cool in tin 10 mins, then turn out on rack.
6. Make icing: sift sugar, cocoa. Gently heat butter and water without boiling. Beat gradually into sugar (you may not need all the liquid) till smooth, not too runny. Pour over cake, letting it drip over sides.

YOU CAN
∗ make extra icing with sugar and water. Pipe a message.

275g/10oz white self-raising flour
1½ tsps baking powder
225g/8oz sugar
200g/7oz Hellmann's mayo
225ml/8fl oz boiling water
4 tbsps cocoa powder
1 tsp vanilla extract
Icing
275g/10oz icing sugar
25g/1oz cocoa powder
110g/4oz butter
3–4 tbsps water

Brownie Basics

Your standard brownie. Well simple. Don't like nuts? Leave them out then.

1. Preheat oven to 180°C/350°F/gas 4. Grease or line base of 20.5cm/8in square tin or similar.
2. Beat butter, sugar together with wooden spoon till very light, creamy. Beat egg in. Sift flour, baking powder in. Beat well.
3. Let chocolate, milk/cold coffee melt in bowl over pan of simmering water. Add vanilla and stir into mix with nuts, if using. Pour into tin.
4. Bake 25 minutes or till skewer comes out clean. Cool in tin 5 minutes, then turn out onto rack. Cut into 12.

75g/3oz soft butter
75g/3oz caster sugar
1 large egg, beaten
100g/4oz plain white flour
¼ tsp baking powder
75g/3oz plain chocolate
1 tbsp milk or cold black coffee
4 drops vanilla extract
75g/3oz pecans, walnuts or hazelnuts roughly chopped (optional)

MAKES 1 · £ · V

175g/6oz soft butter
175g/6oz caster sugar
2 eggs, beaten
175g/6oz self-raising flour
Grated rind of 1 lemon
4 tbsps milk
1 tbsp lemon juice

Glaze
2–3 tbsps icing sugar, sifted
Juice of 1 lemon

Lemon Drizzle Cake

Pricking the top and pouring syrup over is the secret with this one. It's moist and lemony with a slightly crunchy top. You can't beat a slice or two with a cuppa … and if it sinks a bit in the making don't worry.

1. Preheat oven to 160°C/325°F/gas 3. Grease a 900g/2lb loaf tin. Line base with baking paper.

2. Beat butter, sugar in bowl with wooden spoon for 2–3 minutes till light and creamy. Dribble egg in gradually while beating. If mix starts curdling, beat some flour in.

3. Sift flour over mix. Grate rind. Fold in with large metal spoon using light movements (pg 10). Fold in milk, lemon juice.

4. Spoon into tin. Bake 55 minutes or till skewer comes out clean.

5. Mix sugar and juice for glaze. Prick cake 12 times with a fork. Pour glaze over. Take out of tin after 15 minutes. Cool on rack.

MAKES 12 · £ · V

225g/8oz dates, stoned and
   chopped small
1 tbsp runny honey
3 tbsps water
1 tbsp lemon juice
½ tsp ground cinnamon
175g/6oz self-raising flour
175g/6oz semolina
175g/6oz butter
50g/2oz brown or demerara
   sugar

Honey Date Crumbles

Enjoy the sandwich effect of these neat sweet squares. You've got crunchy buttery layers for the top and base, with a spicy honeyed date paste filling. Good for a lunch box.

1. Grease a 20.5cmx20.5cm/8x8in tin.

2. Heat and stir dates, honey, water, lemon juice, cinnamon very gently in a pan to make a thick paste. Cool a bit.

3. Preheat oven to 180°C/350°F/gas 4. Sift flour into a bowl.

4. Add semolina, butter. Rub mix between your fingers till it looks like breadcrumbs. Add sugar.

5. Tip half the crumble into tin. Spread and press to cover.

6. Spread date paste evenly over the top. Sprinkle the rest of the crumble evenly over that. Cook for 25 minutes or till light brown.

7. Cool in tin. Cut into 12. Remove with spatula.

YOU CAN
✱ replace dates with dried apricots

Ginger Apple Tealoaf

Best cake here if you're a ginger fan, packing punches on different levels. Think moist dark cake, sweet dates, fruity apple and tangy lemon icing. Proper good cooking.

1. Preheat oven to 180°C/350°F/gas 4. Grease a 900g/2lb loaf tin.

2. Sift flour, spice, ginger into bowl. Add sugar.

3. Cut butter in. Rub between your fingers till mixed in (pg 10).

4. Beat in eggs and treacle to make a smooth batter. Add $^2/_3$ of apple.

5. Heat milk till boiling. Stir into mix. Add bicarb. Beat well.

6. Pour evenly into tin. Drop dates over top. Finish with rest of apple slices. Bake 40 minutes–1 hour or till skewer comes out clean. Cool in tin. Turn out. Mix icing ingredients. Cover evenly. Keeps well.

175g/6oz self-raising flour
½–1 tsp mixed spice
2 tsps ground ginger
50g/2oz brown/demerara sugar
50g/2oz soft butter
2 eggs
2 tbsps black treacle
1 apple, thinly sliced
150ml/5fl oz milk
1 tsp bicarbonate of soda
A few dates, stoned and
  chopped

Lemon icing
110g/4oz icing sugar, sifted
10g/½oz butter, melted
1 tbsp lemon and a bit of rind
1 tbsp milk or single cream

MAKES
20 £ V

225g/8oz self-raising flour
Pinch salt
150g/5oz butter
110g/4oz caster or sifted icing
   sugar or a mix
1 egg, beaten
Choice of flavourings
50g/2oz currants, chopped
50g/2oz desiccated coconut
50g/2oz glacé cherries,
   chopped
Few squares chocolate, grated
Orange/lemon rind, grated
1–2 tsps cinnamon

A Big Tin of Mixed Biscuits

If you can think of a flavour you want, make it – it should work with this basic dough. Earn brownie points with flatmates.

1. Sift flour, salt into a bowl. Cut in the butter.

2. Rub between your fingers (pg 10) till the butter disappears.

3. Add sugar. Mix in enough beaten egg with a fork to make a stiff dough. Divide it up. Add different flavourings to each bit.

4. Chill in clingfilm/foil for 30 minutes. Preheat oven to 180°C/350°F/ gas 4.

5. Roll out dough on floured board till it's thin. Cut into 5cm/2in rounds using a floured cutter or wine glass.

256

6. Cook till pale brown (12 minutes or longer). Cool on tray for 3–4 minutes. Transfer to a rack.

YOU CAN
✳ top with lemon icing (pg 255) or melted chocolate (pg 11)
✳ brush with egg white and sprinkle with sugar before baking
✳ sandwich together with red jam

Ginger Chilli Hits

Eating just one of these cleared my mate's sinuses more effectively than his prescription. Leave out the chilli if you can't hack it for a simply gorgeous ginger biscuit.

MAKES 14 | £ | V

100g/4oz self-raising flour
1 tsp bicarbonate of soda
2 tsps ground ginger
A very few chilli flakes
50g/2oz butter, in bits
40g/1½oz demerara sugar
2 tbsps golden syrup
A few gratings of orange peel (optional)

1. Preheat oven to 190°C/375°F/gas 5. Grease 2 baking trays.
2. Sift flour, bicarbonate, ginger into bowl. Add chilli and butter.
3. Rub lightly together between fingers till it resembles fine breadcrumbs.
4. Stir in sugar, syrup, orange peel. Mix to a soft dough with a fork.
5. Roll into 14 balls. Sit well apart on trays (they spread). Flatten lightly with your fingers.
6. Bake 15–20 minutes till golden brown. (Watch – they can burn.)
7. Cool on trays. Remove with spatula.

YOU CAN
✳ make in 2 batches if you've only got one tray
✳ use caster sugar for a softer finish
✳ top cooled biscuits with melted dark chocolate

MAKES
12 £ V

110g/4oz butter
2½ tbsps golden syrup
½ tbsp peanut butter
75g/3oz brown sugar
275g/10oz organic oats
   (not jumbo)
100g bar milk chocolate

Chocolate Peanut Butter Flapjacks

Just a bit of peanut butter gives these an addictive quality or leave it out for a traditional bar. Don't overheat your initial syrup mix or give them too long in the oven, as there's nothing worse than a rock-hard flapjack.

1. Preheat oven to 190°C/375°F/gas 5. Grease a 18x30.5x4cm/7x11x1½in tin. Line with baking paper or silicone paper.

2. Melt butter, syrup, peanut butter, sugar in a pan.

3. Stir oats in. Tip into tin. Press down well.

4. Bake for 15–25 minutes till mix is just firming up and golden. If it boils during cooking, reduce heat a bit.

5. Cool in tin. After 15 minutes, mark into 12.

6. When cold, cut and remove flapjacks. Sit them on a rack. Melt chocolate if using (pg 11). Spread over tops. Set.

YOU CAN
✳ use all syrup, no peanut butter
✳ add seeds, dried fruit

Fridge-Bake Tiffin

Don't have an oven or saving on the bills? Make this one…

1. Bash biscuits into varied-size crumbs/bits. Add raisins, cherries.
2. Melt butter, sugar, syrup, cocoa over a low heat.
3. Stir into biscuit/fruit mix. Tip into 18x30.5cm/7x11in tin. Press mix down as evenly as you can.
4. Set in fridge. Mark into 12. Prise out with spatula.

YOU CAN
* add seeds, nuts etc.

MAKES 12   ££   V

200g/7oz chocolate digestive
 biscuits
50g/2oz digestive biscuits
110g/4oz raisins
110g/4oz glacé cherries
110g/4oz butter
10g/½oz sugar
4 tbsps golden syrup
3 tbsps cocoa powder

Birdies Perch Malteser Slice

A big shout-out for Julie who runs Birdies Perch – the Teacake Tuesday teashop. She invented this cheeky little number (her top seller). Hint: let your chocolate melt slowly and never overheat it.

MAKES 12   ££   V

100g/3½oz margarine/butter
100g/3½oz golden syrup
150g/5oz milk chocolate
225g/8oz digestive biscuits
175g/6oz bag Maltesers

Topping
2 x 150g/5oz bars white
 chocolate
Grating of milk chocolate

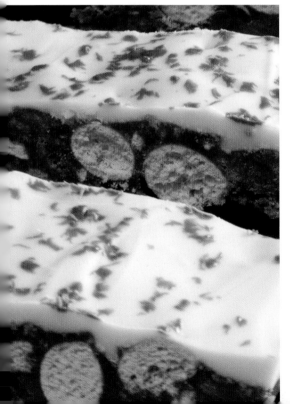

1. Melt butter, syrup, milk choc in pan over very low heat. Stir constantly (don't boil). Remove from heat.
2. Bash biscuits to fine crumbs in freezer bag. And bash Malteser bag, unopened, 3 times. Stir both lots of crumbs into chocolate.
4. Spread mix in shallow tin 19x29cm/7½x10½in.
5. Melt white choc (pg 11). Stir. Spread over slightly cooled base. Sprinkle grated choc. Chill in fridge. Slice.

MAKES 12 · ££ · V

175g/6oz plain white flour
50g/2oz caster sugar
110g/4oz soft butter, in bits
Few drops natural vanilla
  extract

Filling
200ml/7fl oz double or
  whipping cream
Icing sugar (to taste)
Few drops natural vanilla
  extract
Fresh strawberries/
  raspberries/blackberries
Icing sugar for sprinkling

Valentine Fruit & Cream Shortbreads

A sexy little stack that should win over anyone. Get the shortbread nice and thin and watch the clock – don't burn your biscuits… NB Eat unstacked or ice if you like.

1. Preheat oven to 180°C/350°F/gas 4. Grease trays or line with baking/silicone paper.
2. Sift flour, sugar into bowl. Add butter, vanilla extract.
3. Rub lightly together between fingers (pg 10).
4. Pull dough into a ball – the heat of your hand helps.
5. Roll out to 5mm/¼ in thick on lightly floured/sugared board. Cut in heart shapes or 5cm/2in rounds.

6. Bake for 10–15 minutes till pale brown. Cool on trays for 5 minutes, then move to rack.
7. To fill: whip cream, icing sugar, vanilla extract till softly stiff. Sandwich with cream, berries. Anchor another berry on top with cream. Sprinkle with icing sugar.

YOU CAN
* make crunchy hearts – substitute 25g/1oz of the flour with semolina
* make ginger hearts – substitute the vanilla extract with a little ground ginger
* make icing – mix water/ lemon juice and icing sugar

Millionaire Shortbread

Definitely an occasional treat. These are rich, moreish and make for a sophisticated toffee and chocolate bar (on a shortbread biscuit).

1. Preheat oven to 180°C/350°F/gas 4. Lightly grease a 28x18x3cm/11x7x1in tin. Make shortbread dough (see left).

2. Sprinkle board with caster sugar. Roll out dough to fit tin.

3. Use rolling pin to lift dough up and into tin. Press, mend and mould any cracks or breaks till base is covered.

4. Bake for 20 minutes or till pale brown. Cool in tin. Set aside.

5. Tip toffee ingredients (not vanilla) into a thick-bottomed pan. Stir over low heat to melt sugar. Boil. Cook for 6–7 minutes, stirring to prevent burning, till a thick golden-brown fudgy mix. Stir in vanilla. Pour over base in tin. Cool.

6. Melt chocolate in bowl over pan of water (pg 11). Stir once melted. Spread over toffee. Set. Mark into 12 bars. Remove.

YOU CAN

＊ make banoffee pie. At step 1 use a circular tin. At end of step 5, layer 4–6 sliced bananas over toffee. Top with whipped cream, grated chocolate.

MAKES **12**   ££   V

Shortbread
175g/6oz plain white flour
50g/2oz caster sugar
110g/4oz soft butter
Toffee
175ml/6fl oz low-fat
  condensed milk
4oz/110g butter
4oz/110g brown sugar
2 level tbsps golden syrup
½ tsp vanilla extract
Chocolate topping
150–175g/5–6oz milk
  chocolate

MAKES
1   ££   V

175g/6oz caster sugar
2 tbsps honey
250ml/8fl oz sunflower oil
3 large eggs
175g/6oz self-raising
  wholemeal flour
1 tsp ground cinnamon
½ tsp salt
Grated rind of ½–1 lemon
Squeeze lemon juice
300g/10oz carrot, grated
150g/4–5oz pecans/walnuts,
  chopped
Topping
175g/6oz cream cheese
110–175g/4–6oz icing sugar,
  sifted
Juice of ½–1 lemon
Or
Lemon icing (pg 255)

Carrot Cake with Citrus Cheese Topping

As cakes go this is pretty nutritious. Wholemeal flour packs fibre (slows sugar release into the body) and energy. Carrots add beta-carotene (helps vision). Nuts have good oils. This cake tastes gorgeous.

1. Preheat oven to 180°C/350°F/gas 4. Grease and line base and sides of 20cm/8in circular tin.

2. Tip sugar, honey, oil into bowl. Beat well with wooden spoon/balloon whisk. Add eggs, one at a time, beating between additions.

3. Add sifted flour, cinnamon, salt, lemon rind, juice, carrots, nuts. Fold lightly together. Tip mix into tin.

4. Bake for 1 hour (skewer should come out clean). Cool in tin for 15 minutes. Turn out onto rack. Cool.

5. Make topping: beat cream cheese to soften. Add icing sugar and lemon juice gradually. Spread over cooled cake. Or make lemon icing.

YOU CAN
* use lime or orange juice instead of lemon in the topping
* use grated peeled courgettes instead of carrots

Old Style Jam & Cream Swiss Roll

This is beautifully light and airy. Whisking the sponge instead of beating does it. Sophisticated enough for a dinner party but cheap and easy enough to eat anytime… Eat fresh (use extra for trifle).

110g/4oz caster sugar
4 eggs
½ tsp vanilla extract
2 tbsps warm water
110g/4oz plain flour

Filling
Raspberry jam
Whipping cream
Smushed fruit

1. Preheat oven to 190°C/375°F/gas 5. Grease a 33x23cm/13x9in Swiss roll tin. Line and grease base. Sprinkle with extra sugar.

2. Tip sugar, eggs into a bowl. Whisk for a few minutes with electric handwhisk till moussey, thick. Or sit bowl over pan of simmering water and whisk till moussey with balloon or handwhisk.

3. Very gently, using a large metal spoon and a few scooping movements, fold in vanilla, water and one-third of sifted flour (pg 10).

4. Sift and fold in another third, followed by the final third.

5. Bake for 12–15 minutes until pale gold and just firm in the centre.

6. Meantime sprinkle sugar over a bit of baking paper just bigger than your tin. Remove cake from oven. Loosen edges with a knife. Invert onto paper. Remove tin. Peel off lining.

7. For just jam: spread jam over sponge. Roll it up. Hold for 1 minute. Cool on rack.

8. For jam, cream and fruit: roll up with paper inside. Hold for 1 minute. Cover with teatowel till cool. Unroll. Remove paper. Spread with cream, fruit, jam. Roll up again.

YOU CAN
✱ soak left-overs with sherry, then top with fruit, custard and whipped cream – it's a trifle… Give other cakes the same treatment.
✱ vary fillings – try lemon curd or apricot jam
✱ substitute cocoa for bit of the flour to make choc Swiss roll

MAKES 1 | £ | V

450g/1lb strong white bread flour
2 tsps fine salt
½ tsp caster sugar
1 x 7g pack easy-blend yeast
50g/2oz butter
1 large egg
250ml/8fl oz warm milk

To finish
1 egg yolk mixed with a little water
poppy seeds (optional)

Classic Split Tin Loaf

Making your own bread defines you as a cook. And it doesn't take much to get the hang of it. There's egg in this one, which makes the finished result a bit sweet like brioche. Not in a loaf mood? Roll it… (Vegans – make Classic White Loaf, below.)

1. Sift flour, salt, sugar into bowl. Add yeast, butter.
2. Rub butter into flour till it's invisible.
3. Crack egg into hollow in flour. Pour in warm milk. Mix with hands (or wooden spoon) till incorporated. Dough should be soft, warm, not sticky. Add more flour/warm milk if needed. Roll dough into ball.
4. Knead on floured board for 8–10 minutes (pg 11) or use dough hook on mixer till dough is elastic.
5. Put in lightly oiled bowl covered with teatowel. Leave to rise in warm place till doubled in size (about 1 hour).
6. Knead for 2 minutes. Grease a 900g/2lb loaf tin. Shape dough into rectangle as long as tin. Roll sides under so it fits neatly into tin, seam side down. Cover. Leave for 20 minutes or till well risen.
7. Cut deep lengthwise gash centrally to create split. Leave for 10 minutes.
8. Preheat oven to 230°C/450°F/gas 6. Sprinkle loaf with flour or brush with egg and poppy seeds (if using). Cook 20–30 minutes. Turn out. Bread is done if bottom sounds hollow when tapped.

YOU CAN
✱ make rolls: at step 6 divide into 10; or knots: roll into sausage, then tie in knot; or plaits: roll into 3 thin sausages, plait, then press ends together; or cottage rolls: sit one small ball on top of large one, stick thumb through middle. Brush with egg/milk, sprinkle with seeds, bake 10–15 minutes.
✱ make Classic White Loaf. At step 1 use 700g/1½ lb flour. At step 3 add 425ml/15fl oz water (no milk or egg). At step 5 fit loaf into tin. Rise till higher than tin top. Bake 30 minutes.

Speedy Energy Seed Bread

A chuck it in and stir recipe packed with good slow-release nutrients, which makes this a great breakfast bread.

1. Preheat oven to 200°C/400°F/gas 6. Grease 900g/2lb loaf tin.
2. Sift flour, baking powder, salt into bowl. Mix in bran left in the sieve, apricots, dates, seeds, apple juice, honey.
3. Spoon into tin. Brush top with extra juice. Sprinkle with seeds. Bake for 25–30 minutes.

275g/10oz plain wholemeal flour
1 tbsp baking powder
Pinch salt
100g/3½oz dried apricots (diced)
50g/2oz stoned dates (diced)
75g/3oz mix of pumpkin/ poppy/sunflower seeds
175ml/6fl oz apple/apple and elderflower juice
4 tbsps runny honey

2 generous tbsps black treacle
Up to 850ml/1½ pints warm
    water
2 x 7g sachets dried yeast
450g/1lb strong wholemeal
    bread flour
450b/1lb strong white bread
    flour
1 tsp salt

225g/8oz plain flour
1 tsp salt
25g/1oz white vegetable
    fat/lard
125ml/4fl oz warm water

Best-Ever Treacle Bread

My mum's famous loaf. It's fully flavoured and a bit sweet and I haven't found anyone who doesn't like it (or try to skank the recipe). It needs one short rising, lasts days, goes with pretty much everything (try it with Vegemite and butter or with my chicken-liver pâté). Makes perfect toast – it caramelizes a bit. Makes two loaves – so have one, freeze one.

1. Grease insides and rims of two 900g/2lb loaf tins.
2. Stir treacle into 150ml/5oz warm water. Add yeast. Stir. Cover. Leave for 5–10 mins till frothy. Meantime, sift flours, salt into large bowl.
3. Add frothy yeast mix to remaining 700ml/1½ pints warm water. Tip into flour, mixing with wooden spoon for a soft dough (it's a bit stickier than regular dough).
4. Spoon into tins. Cover with cloth. Leave to rise for 10–15 minutes or till risen higher than tin tops (not spilling over).
5. Preheat oven to 200°C/400°F/gas 6. Bake 30–40 minutes till cooked. Turn out to test. Tap the base. It should sound hollow.

YOU CAN
✱ use 50g/2oz fresh yeast. Or fast action dried yeast – add to flour, no frothing.
✱ make with honey instead of treacle, adding a handful of muesli or granola

Tortillas

It's a right laugh making these … do it.

1. Sift four, salt into bowl.
2. Rub fat into flour between your fingers.
3. Add water bit by bit, mixing with fork.
4. Knead into ball. Rest, covered, in bowl for 15 minutes.
5. Divide dough into 10 equal bits. Cover.
6. Roll each bit into a 15cm/5in circle on floured surface and cover.
7. Cook tortillas 1–2 minutes per side in dry frying pan. For pliable tortillas, don't overcook.
8. Keep warm in cloth. Freeze extras.

Yorkshire Croissants

Make the batter the night before then chuck these in the oven while you take a shower. Or make in the moment ... sweet.

MAKES
8   £   **V**

2 large eggs
220ml/7fl oz milk (I use semi-skimmed)
110g/4oz plain white flour
Pinch salt
1 tbsp sunflower oil
Butter for greasing

1. Beat eggs and milk together in a jug. Sift flour, salt into a bowl.
2. Tip egg/milk mix bit by bit into a well in centre of flour, beating continuously with wooden spoon/balloon whisk to get smooth batter.
3. Let mix rest for 30 minutes (for lighter result) or cook now. Meanwhile, preheat oven to 220°C/425°F/gas 7.
4. Grease a deep 8-hole muffin tin very generously. Preheat in oven for 5 minutes.
5. Whisk oil into batter. Pour into scorching hot tins (two-thirds fill holes). Cook for 35–40 minutes or till high, brown, crisp. Eat with butter, jam, lemon curd (pg 249), marmalade.

YOU CAN
* drop 1 tsp of jam/marmalade/lemon curd into each portion of uncooked batter in tray. Cook for 10 minutes. Reduce heat to 180°C/350°F/gas 4 and cook for further 25 minutes or till ready.
* store extras in tin or freeze and reheat

Thanks to my brilliant mates for helping out with the photography for this book: to Vez, Joe and Henry. Also: Jamie, Sophie, Popeye, Andy, Dom, Yuley. Special thanks to Julie, Bev and Jo of Birdies Perch, York (home of Teacake Tuesday).

For letting us take photographs: Rafi's Spicebox, Barnitt's of York, Neal's Yard Dairy, Flour Power City, Elsey & Bent, Borough Market, Patisserie Lila, King's College London, Dotan of Camden Market, The Ginger Pig, Fish Works, Alligator Wholefoods.

Special thanks to Denise, Louise and Barry for their patience and support. And Louise Rooke – for food testing.

Finally, love and thanks to Dad (great photographs), Polly, Rob, Tom, KR, Alice, Mickey and Shelley

First published 2008 by Walker Books Ltd
87 Vauxhall Walk, London SE11 5HJ

10 9 8 7 6 5 4 3 2 1

© 2008 Sam and Susan Stern

Photography by Peter Goulding
Additional photographs by Lorne Campbell (front cover, pages 5, 9, 18, 23, 47br, 81tl, 85, 93, 95br, 97, 101, 126, 131, 138, 149, 151, 161, 166, 187, 198, 201l, 212, 225, 235br, 241), Richard Cannon (front flap, pages 1, 2, 4, 6, 8, 31, 37br, 41, 43, 48tl, 53, 55br, 66, 75bl, 77bl, 92, 104r, 119, 129br, 137, 154, 162, 163, 165tl, 175bc, 259br, 261, back cover l, back cover tr), Trish Gant (pages 10c, 57bl, 143, 168, 172, 177, 197, 224, 246tr, 248bl, 262bl) and Jeffrey Stern (pages 10tc, 10tr, 12, 13tl, 13bl, 24, 32, 33tr, 39tr, 45, 48br, 49, 50, 51, 52, 54, 55tl, 56, 57tr, 57br, 59, 60tl, 61tr, 64bl, 67tl, 69, 71, 75tr, 75br, 77br, 81bl, 81br, 87, 88, 89, 91, 104tl, 107, 108, 110, 115, 118, 121, 123, 125, 127, 129bl, 129cr, 134, 136, 139, 141br, 144, 153, 164, 165tr, 173, 174, 176, 180, 183tb, 183bl, 189, 193br, 194, 195, 199, 204, 207, 213, 214, 216, 217l, 218, 242l, 243, 245tr, 247, 248br, 249, 250, 251, 253, 254cl, 260, 262tr, 263, 264, 266, 267, back flap, back cover br).

The right of Sam Stern and Susan Stern to be identified as authors of this work has been asserted by them in accordance with the Copyright, Designs and Patents Act 1988

This book has been typeset in GillSans Printed in Italy

British Library Cataloguing in Publication Data: a catalogue record for this book is available from the British Library
ISBN 978-1-4063-0818-1
www.walker.co.uk   www.samstern.co.uk